MODERN APPLIED LINGUISTICS

An Introduction

N. KRISHNASWAMY, S.K. VERMA
CIEFL, Hyderabad

and

M. NAGARAJAN
National College, Trichy

TRINITY
PRESS
(An Imprint of Laxmi Publications Pvt. Ltd.)
An ISO 9001:2008 Company

BENGALURU • CHENNAI • COCHIN • GUWAHATI • HYDERABAD
JALANDHAR • KOLKATA • LUCKNOW • MUMBAI • RANCHI • NEW DELHI
BOSTON (USA) • ACCRA (GHANA) • NAIROBI (KENYA)

MODERN APPLIED LINGUISTICS

Printed and bound in India

First Published : 1992, *Reprinted* : 2000-2011 *(seven times)*
2012, 2013, 2014, 2015, 2016

ISBN : 978-93-5138-124-2

PUBLISHED IN INDIA BY

TRINITY
PRESS

(An Imprint of Laxmi Publications Pvt. Ltd.)
An ISO 9001:2008 Company
113, GOLDEN HOUSE, DARYAGANJ, NEW DELHI-110002, INDIA
Telephone : 91-11-4353 2500, 4353 2501
Fax : 91-11-2325 2572, 4353 2528
www.laxmipublications.com info@laxmipublications.com

Branches

© **Bengaluru**	080-26 75 69 30
© **Chennai**	044-24 34 47 26
© **Cochin**	0484-237 70 04, 405 13 03
© **Guwahati**	0361-254 36 69, 251 38 81
© **Hyderabad**	040-27 55 53 83, 27 55 53 93
© **Jalandhar**	0181-222 12 72
© **Kolkata**	033-22 27 43 84
© **Lucknow**	0522-220 99 16
© **Mumbai**	022-24 91 54 15, 24 92 78 69
© **Ranchi**	0651-220 44 64

C—10659/015/08

Printed at : Mittal Print-N-Pack, Delhi.

Contents

Preface

Modern Applied Linguistics is designed to explain what applied linguistics means in the present context and how it has come to mean what it does. Applied linguistics is multidimensional and polyparametric. A short precise definition cannot bring out even its essential features.

The thinking underlying *Modern Applied Linguistics* is that applied linguistics covers all those branches of knowledge which are related to language, literature, and linguistics.

Words. Words. Words. We live in a world of words. God might have created the world, instantaneously, without toil and pains: but we toil in language, till our feelings and emotions, and express our pains and pleasures in words; we meet people and interact with them in language; we contemplate and communicate in language and in that process create/recreate it. We read—newspapers, stories, novels, plays, poems ...; we refer to dictionaries and some of us write them; we learn and teach languages as well as sectors of knowledge through language; we translate our thoughts into words, from language to language, and from language into action; we interpret, misinterpret, understand and misunderstand languages. In all these activities, and many more, we not only use language but also produce it, cultivate it, and enrich it. In other words, it is in its use that language lives and not somewhere out there. It is our firm conviction that applied linguistics is a useful discipline since it studies the use of language; that is why it is not only interesting and challenging, but also bewildering; like some rivers, it has many sources and several outlets.

Selectivity — some might call it bias — is unavoidable in a modest volume like this. We have included some of the important sectors in which a lot of research has been done. Pit Corder's (1973) *Introducing Applied Linguistics* and the *Edinburgh Course in Applied Linguistics* (1973-77 in four volumes) reflect the thinking and understanding of the seventies. Much water has rolled down the rivers in India and abroad since then but no one has yet come out with a problem-centred book on Applied Linguistics. An attempt has been made in this book to make teachers and learners familiar with new ideas and then wrestle with problems.

This book brings together in one volume several interrelated areas like sociolinguistics, psycholinguistics, discourse analysis, stylistics, language learning and teaching, translation and lexicology; and some developing areas like Artificial Intelligence. The ideas expressed and concepts explained are those of well-known scholars in the field and we make no claim to originality. Based on our long experience of English language teaching (ELT), applied linguistics and doing research in some of the areas, we have made an attempt to make the subject comprehensible to people who have little or no prior knowledge of applied linguistics. It can be regarded as a companion volume to *Modern Linguistics* by S.K. Verma and N. Krishnaswamy.

After pointing out that applied linguistics is not just the application of theoretical linguistics to other areas like language teaching, the Introduction outlines the scope of applied linguistics, which is now considered a feeder discipline to a number of disciplines like linguistics, sociology, psychology, translation theory etc.

The first chapter on language and society shows how language, society, culture, and thought are interrelated and the usefulness of understanding such relationships in studying social problems like language planning, social inequality, language variations and attitudes to variations, etc.

The second chapter points out the significant advances in language acquisition, language production, second language learning, and their implications.

The third chapter presents the recent developments in discourse analysis and textology, and their importance.

The fourth chapter outlines the various developments and their usefulness in the study of the language of literature, from structuralist poetics to emerging areas like post-structuralism.

The fifth chapter traces the history of the connection between linguistics and language teaching, the impact of linguistics on language teaching, particularly on second language teaching with special reference to India.

The sixth chapter discusses the theory of translation, the important models in the field, and the processes of transcreation. A closely related sector, lexicography (monolingual, bilingual, and multilingual dictionaries), is discussed and the problems in lexicology, a fast developing area, are outlined.

The last chapter keeps the door open for bringing in problems like the battle of the sexes and the language weapon, Artificial Intelligence, etc.

Each chapter is divided into convenient units followed by *questions* and *topics for discussion.* The section labelled *focal points* presents the salient features and theoretical positions; *questions* and *topics for discussion* are to be used primarily as learning devices to get additional insights into the issues raised in each unit; they are meant to provoke further thinking and not intended to be testing tasks. Ideally, after the first reading, one can work through the questions and topics for discussion and try to locate the issues raised in the units in the second reading; this will facilitate a better understanding of the problems involved.

Suggestions for further reading, with brief comments, are given at the end of each chapter, apart from a list of references at the end.

It is hoped that teachers, students, and researchers in the field of linguistics and language teaching will find the book useful and interesting.

We are grateful to Dr. T. Sriraman, CIEFL, Hyderabad, who read the book in typescript and made valuable suggestions. We record our appreciation of the very valuable assistance of Mrs. Lalitha Krishnaswamy, who has helped us with the correction of proofs.

AUTHORS

INTRODUCTION

The Scope of Applied Linguistics

'We are like mariners who must rebuild their ship according to a new plan on the open sea, ever unable to dock it and construct it anew from the best parts.'

— *Otto Neurath*

Focal points

I. What is applied linguistics? Who is an applied linguist? What do applied linguists do? what is the scope of applied linguistics? How does applied linguistics differ from theoretical linguistics? How does applied linguistics relate to other disciplines like sociology, psychology, philosophy, literary theory and such other disciplines?

As Kaplan (1978) points out, the term *applied linguistics* is tautological because the two words reinforce the same seminal notion: 'linguistics in action and interaction'. Applied linguistics is not merely an application of linguistics (that is, of linguistic theory) to something; if it were just that, applied linguistics would have been an appendix, but it has a philosophy of its own and is a discipline in its own right with an independent theory— a theory independent of other disciplines to the extent that any theoretical formulation can be independent of the total body of human knowledge.

What is known as modern linguistics derived its ideas and methodology from the works of Saussure, Bloomfield, Sapir, Trubetzkoy, Jakobson, Louis Hjelmslev, Chomsky, Firth, Halliday, Pike, to mention only some of the important names.

In the early days of linguistics, some linguists made a distinction between *microlinguistics* and *macrolinguistics;* the former refers to a narrower and the latter to a much broader view of the scope of linguistics. According to the microlinguistic view, languages should be analysed for their own sake without any reference to their social function, to the human mind and the manner in which languages are acquired by human beings, and to the literary or communicative function of language. Microlinguistics was considered *pure* or *theo-*

retical linguistics not contaminated by social, psychological, pragmatic, and other mundane considerations. Macrolinguistics was the field that was supposed to cover all other aspects of language not included in microlinguistics. Since linguistics was considered a scientific study of the system/principles underlying human language and languages, it was supposed to follow the general methodology of science (controlled observation, hypothesis-formation, analysis, generalization, prediction, testing by further observation and confirmation, modification, or rejection of the hypothesis); the impression that linguistics is scientific gave the discipline respectability and a privileged status. The application of the concepts and methods used in the scientific study of language (that is, theoretical linguistics) to other areas like language teaching and testing, translation and the language of literature was called *applied linguistics*. Emerging disciplines in the late 1960s and early 1970s like sociolinguistics and psycholinguistics were regarded as related disciplines.

Chart 1 shows the thinking of the 1950s and 1960s and the visualization of the area of linguistics, its applications, and the related disciplines.

The overall goal of the linguistic sciences is to understand how human languages work. We must therefore find out whether the arbitrary decisions and actions of linguists in the 1950s and 1960s led to the specified goal and to what consequences. Theory building is a continuous exercise; if a theory provides a general, systematic and explicit reconstruction of the preliminary understanding or knowledge of a specified area, it should also allow the reconstruction of cognitive operations within the field after a study of the relations among the components within the field; such a thing has happened in all areas of knowledge and theory building. The shift towards user-oriented approaches to the study of language (like reader-response theories in literary criticism, learner-centred pedagogy in education, etc.), the formation of the International Association of Applied linguists (AILA - Association Internationale de Linguistique Appliquee) in 1973, the formation of the American Association of Applied Linguists (AAAL) in 1977, (BAAL: The British Association of Applied Linguists was formed in 1967), the work done in the areas of sociolinguistics, psycholinguistics, discourse analysis, etc., the weakening of structuralism, the emergence of post-structuralism and such other factors contributed to a definite reformulation of the difference between 'pure' and 'applied' linguistics.

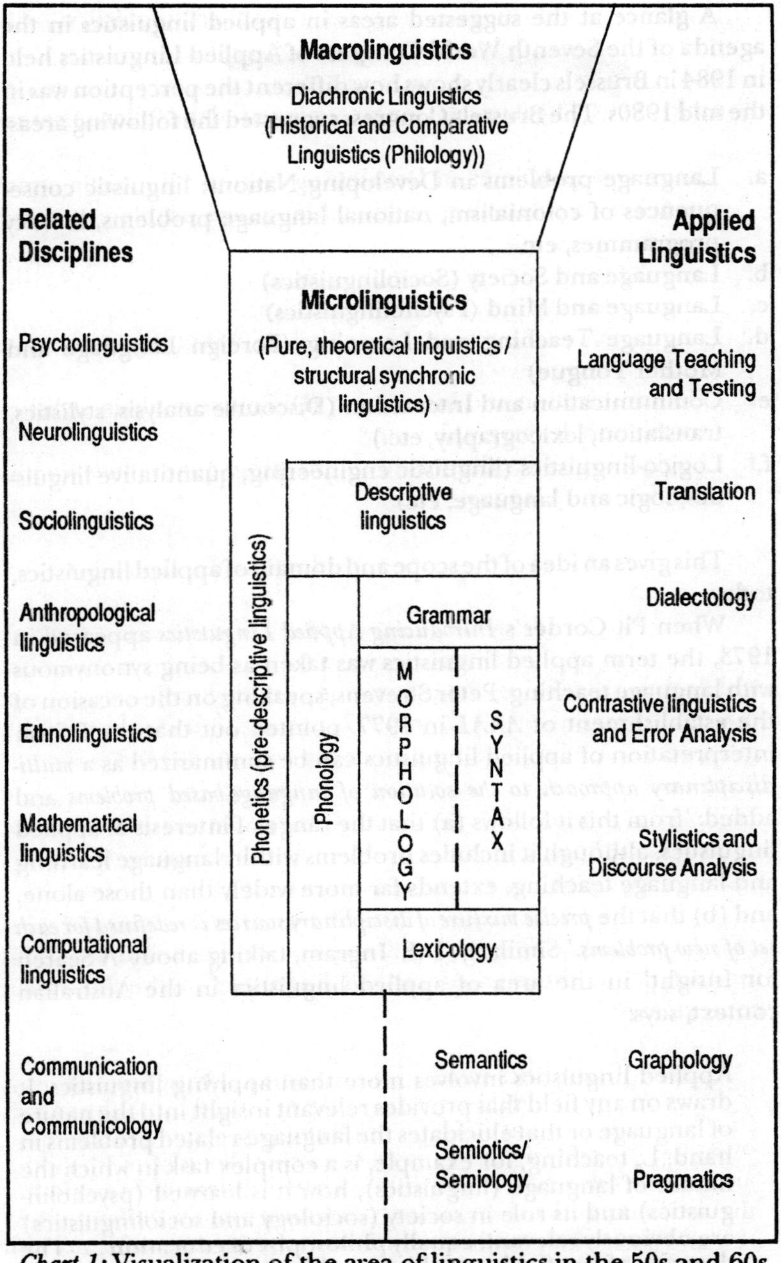

Chart 1: **Visualization of the area of linguistics in the 50s and 60s**

A glance at the suggested areas in applied linguistics in the agenda of the Seventh World Congress of Applied Linguistics held in 1984 in Brussels clearly shows how different the perception was in the mid 1980s. The Brussels Congress suggested the following areas:

a. Language problems in Developing Nations: linguistic consequences of colonialism, national language problems, literacy programmes, etc.
b. Language and Society (Sociolinguistics)
c. Language and Mind (Psycholinguistics)
d. Language Teaching and Learning (Foreign Language and Mother Tongue)
e. Communication and Interaction (Discourse analysis, stylistics, translation, lexicography, etc.)
f. Logico-linguistics (linguistic engineering, quantitative linguistics, logic and language, etc)

This gives an idea of the scope and domain of applied linguistics, today.

When Pit Corder's *Introducing Applied Linguistics* appeared in 1973, the term applied linguistics was taken as being synonymous with language teaching. Peter Strevens, speaking on the occasion of the establishment of *AAAL* in 1977, pointed out that the British interpretation of applied linguistics can be summarized as a *multi-disciplinary approach to the solution of language-based problems* and added: 'from this it follows (a) that the range of interests of applied linguistics, although it includes problems within language learning and language teaching, extends far more widely than those alone, and (b) that the *precise mixture of disciplinary sources is redefined for each set of new problems.*' Similarly, D.E. Ingram, talking about 'A Search for Insight' in the area of applied linguistics in the Australian context, says:

> Applied linguistics involves more than applying linguistics; it draws on any field that provides relevant insight into the nature of language or that elucidates the language-related problems in hand. L_2 teaching, for example, is a complex task in which the nature of language (linguistics), how it is learned (psycholinguistics) and its role in society (sociology and sociolinguistics) are obviously relevant; equally philosophy of education . . . The diversity of the fields on which applied linguistics draws is the

inevitable result of the complex nature of language as the instrument of man in society, the functional tool he uses to get things done, the mediator between himself and society and the means by which he establishes his own identity and that of others (cf. Halliday 1974). Language is a distinctively human characteristic and distinctively determines man's nature and personality. Consequently, a science that aims at elucidating language-related problems will often require an understanding of the non-language factors that *impinge* on language and the applied linguist will then seek his insights in those nonlinguistic sciences that describe those factors. Clearly, applied linguistics is not just the application of linguistics but is, rather, the search for insight in a variety of language-informative disciplines. It is interdisciplinary, multidisciplinary and integrative.

Kaplan has argued that 'applied linguists are the most humanistic of the breed of linguistics' since they are the most directly concerned with the solution of *human* problems stemming from various uses of language. He adds:

> Linguists, on the other hand, are specialists, who solve language problems related to some of the sub-systems of the body language. Because their study is scientific, they are limited to those subsystems which can be made static and which can be isolated from the complex range of variables that affect human behaviour. What they find is of the greatest use to applied linguists; and the problems that applied linguists discover in their attempts to deal with *human* problems ought to be the central concern of theoretical linguistics. That has not, unfortunately, been the case; on the contrary, applied linguists have convulsed themselves trying to apply to something every new notion of the theoretical linguist whether that notion has been demonstrated valid or useful, or not.'

It is clear that in the 1980s applied linguistics was perceived differently. Applied linguistics is seen as *dynamic* as compared to the static theoretical linguistics since applied linguistics is concerned with *human* problems; furthermore, applied linguistics is interdisciplinary and multidisciplinary and, thereby, is highly interactive whereas 'pure' linguistics is isolated since it tries to study the phenomena in isolation; applied linguistics interacts even with theoretical linguistics. Applied linguistics, being a human as well as an interactive discipline, gets redefined for each problem and is not a discipline that is defined 'well in advance'.

Applied linguistics, thus, is a constantly changing colligation of subjects and in the process of interaction several inter-disciplines have come to stay. This can be represented as in Chart 2 (only some inter-disciplines that have clearly emerged are shown). Though inter-disciplines or hybrid-disciplines are 'created', applied linguistics is not to be equated with anyone of them; in other words, applied linguistics is not just educational linguistics or sociolinguistics or psycholinguistics; it is not an antonym of theoretical linguistics. As J.D. Palmer points out in his 'Linguistics in *Medias Res*,' that the name applied linguistics is a tautology and that recent attempts to define applied linguistics have become formal and abstract to the point of airy-fairiness. This is because of the shades of thesis, antithesis, and synthesis. It can be pointed out negatively that if all human contexts are removed from applied linguistics (social, psychological, textual, situational, cultural, political, technological, etc.) then applied linguistics will get 'purified' and become 'pure' theoretical linguistics; but this is a negative way of looking at modern integrative phenomena. Applied linguistics invites us to evolve a new kind of synthesis of disciplines that have been taken as clearly demarcated and well defined. The art of cooking, for instance, involves several things; can we call this applied chemistry? First of all cooking is an art as well as a science; secondly, it gets redefined according to the human situation in which it is practised. Similarly, applied linguistics is a new synthesis that should not be viewed in the light of a traditional notion of 'discipline'.

The interactive nature of applied linguistics can be represented as in Chart 3.

II. The kind of interactive approach suggested to the conception of applied linguistics will have to examine several dualities that have been accepted in the field.

First of all, is it possible to maintain a clear cut dichotomy between theory and practice? This dichotomy is not acceptable and the claim that theory is objective and practice is only its application has been questioned. Lucien Goldmann (1971— translated into English from French 1976:91) says in his *Cultural Creation:* 'Insofar as science is a knowledge of the world which not only permits its transformation but also, in the domain of the human sciences, transforms society by its mere development (society is no longer the same if collective thought changes), it is not a matter of affirming a

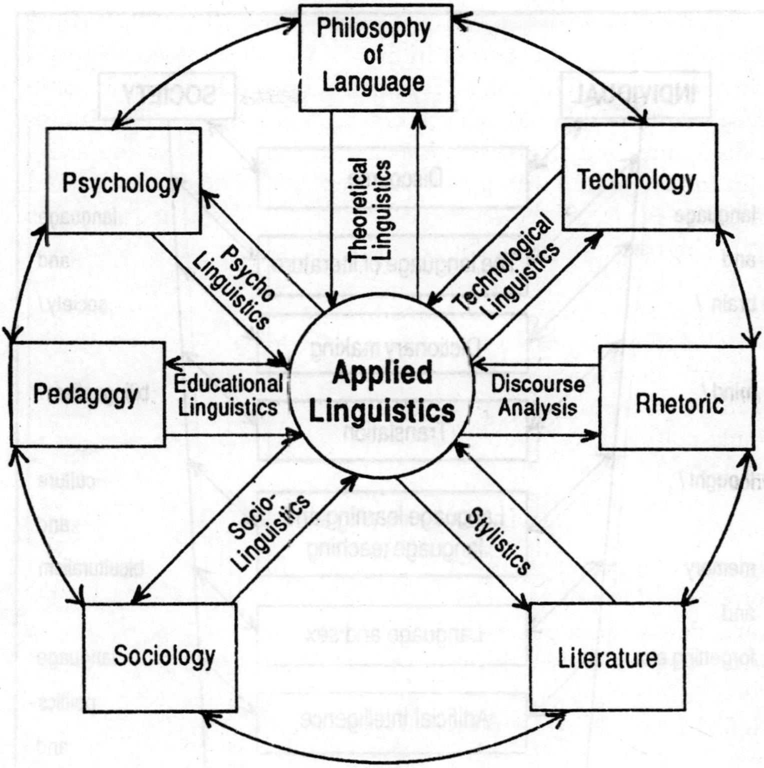

Chart 2: Representation of the process of interaction and the growth of inter-disciplines

radical separation of theory and praxis ...clearly every development of a theoretical claim has a practical character and transforms social reality in one direction or another, to a more or less developed degree.'

Similarly, the dichotomy between the individual subject and the society that is maintained in the contemporary human sciences is a fuzzy one; we try to maintain that there are individuals, groups, and 'facts'. *Facts are constructed by somebody with a conceptual apparatus* which *that somebody has not created;* every individual constructs facts first within the thought processes and perception and later going outside the immediate perception, upto the most elaborate theories; but

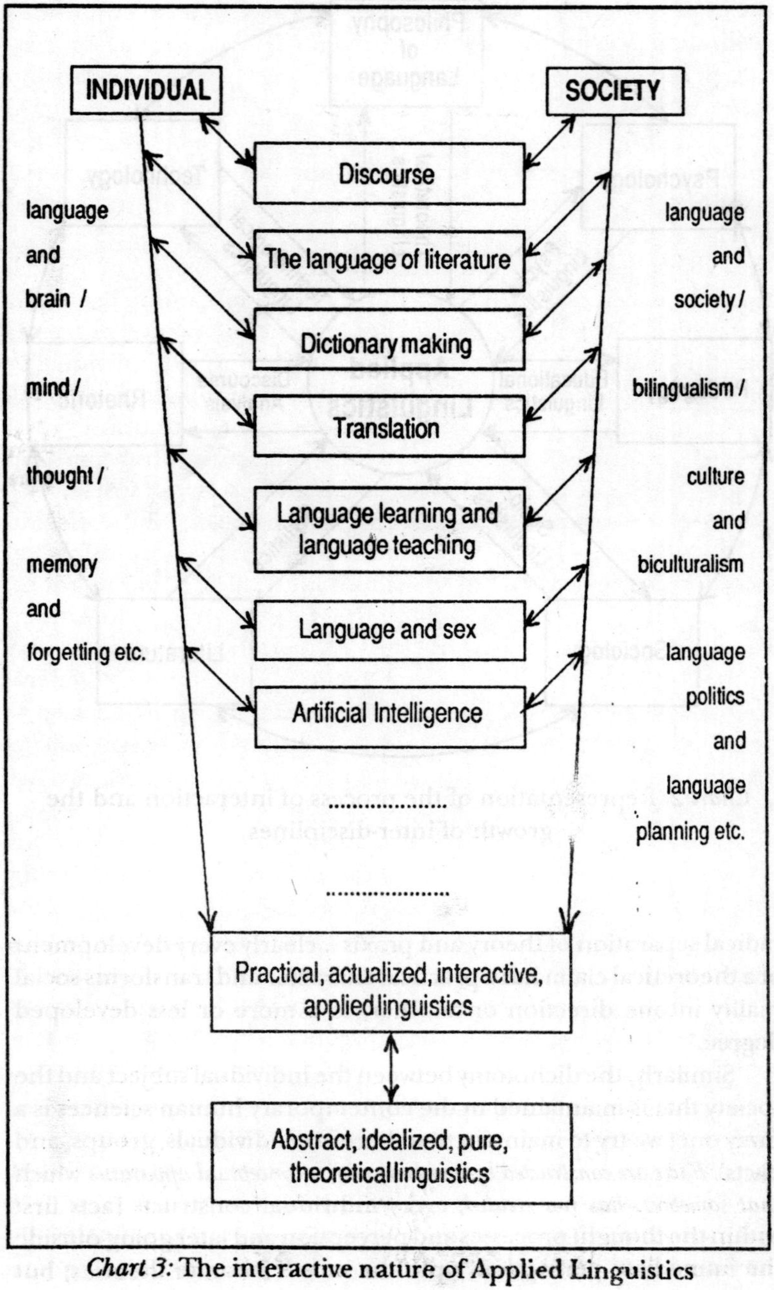

Chart 3: The interactive nature of Applied Linguistics

the individual subject perceives and constructs subjectively within a civilization, within the logicality of mental structures, categories, values, judgements and criteria which (s)he has not created but those that are given by the world/group which (s)he wants to comprehend. This means we cannot negate the subjectivity of the subject (a neutral term for the 'individual') who perceives; at the same time, we cannot negate the objectivity, (if that is the right term) of what is given ('given' in the sense of not only what is external to the subject but also internal to the subject that makes an individual think in a certain way). This shows that one cannot be totally 'subjective' or totally 'objective' because the interactive processes blur this distinction; similarly, we cannot take only the individual or only the group for our study because such distinctions are artificial. There is an individual subject and there is also a transindividual subject, something beyond a particular subject (but not transcendental/metaphysical) — may be social groups or the world. The paradox is that every individual participates in creating the world and in that process finds the world before him/her; the transindividual has already created the world-institutions, values, social relations, etc. with which a particular subject tries to create the world. Understanding of this interactive process (a dialectical process) is very crucial for understanding several dualities in philosophy, general linguistics, as well as applied linguistics, whether it is idealism vs materialism or Saussurian 'langue' and 'parole' and 'synchronic' vs 'diachronic' or even the popular language-literature dichotomy. Are they 'real' or 'illusionary'?

For example, Saussure says *la langue* is 'the social side of language, outside the individual who can never create or modify it by himself; it exists only by virtue of a sort of contract signed by the members of a community' and *la parole* is 'always individual and the individual is always its master' (*Course pp.13-14*). Is it possible to separate *langue* from *parole* even for purposes of analysis? How can we detach the linguistic sign from discourse, the discourse from the subject and the subject from the transindividual subject? Following Yeats we can ask, "How can we know the dancer from the dance?"; either we give up or try to understand the integrative process without totally rejecting the dualities but at the same time questioning, problematizing and looking at them from different perspectives. This constitutes the notion of 'application' and, in the context of this book, applied linguistics.

This view of applied linguistics, that it has to be multidisciplinary, represents one of the most important concerns of modern academic thinking; no phenomenon, be it linguistics or literature, can be studied and understood in isolation. For example, students of literature consider sociological factors as mere external conditioning and sociologists always miss the literary fact that literature is a reflection of collective consciousness. The relations among sociology and psychology, education and sociology, sociology and literature, linguistics and psychology, linguistics and sociology, and ultimately all sectors of the human sciences can become truly interdisciplinary only by redefining the creative and interactive aspects of applied sciences. For administrative purposes we may think of different disciplines and even academically each discipline may formulate its own perspective; each branch of knowledge can wear a single hat but it will remain always partial.

This book, *Modern Applied Linguistics,* is divided into chapters for the sake of convenience, for the sake of organizational compulsions. Sociolinguistics, psycholinguistics, discourse analysis, stylistics, language teaching, translation, and other sectors are discussed from the point of view of applied linguistics, from the point of view of interdisciplinarity. Often, the interactive processes are emphasized to bring out the dynamic nature of language. For example, speech communities are not taken as static entities that exist but as dynamic organisms that are created in which discourse is constructed and discourse includes literary discourse. This line of interdisciplinary thinking, which highlights dependency and non-deterministic, interactive processes may appear to be rather confusing and even puzzling to begin with; but, in any applied branch—from architecture to cookery—the unfolding of the configurations, the constant tension among established categories and the creativity involved in the conflicts are the most important principles. The subversive nature of any applied branch should not be misconstrued; it checks the tendency to overrate the degree of achievement in any theoretical area and points out the *failure* of pure theory to perceive the other forces that are 'always already there'; applied sectors try to show how pure areas are caught up in their own forms of blindness and how insights can be drawn from blindness by showing that blindness is not a defect to be remedied but a condition that makes insight possible.

Before doing applied linguistics, it is good to understand that it is unnecessary and even futile to define the scope of applied linguistics. The study of the relevance of language in all human activities and the problems arising out of such relevance is the pursuit of applied linguistics and such a pursuit must necessarily be a cooperative venture.

Questions and topics for discussion

1. 'The theatre is the point at which all of the arts come together and are actualized.' - American theatre critic George Jean Nathan
   Can you use the statement given above to explain the scope of applied linguistics? Give reasons for your answer.
2. 'Applied linguistics may contribute to theoretical linguistics in this way: Models of second language performance need to be consistent with good teaching and efficient acquisition. Ultimately, the best theory will be consistent with the best materials and methods, even thoiugh the theory may have been developed in the 'laboratory' and not in the classroom.' — Stephen Krashen
   Explain and illustrate. Can you extend the same argument to other areas of applied linguistics like sociolinguistics or psycholinguistics?
3. Do you think that in trying to encompass within applied linguistics all of the disciplines in which language use is relevant we are faced with the risk of destroying the meaning of the term applied linguistics? (Because it is everything, it is nothing). Give reasons.
4. 'Applied linguistics is a problem-solving enterprise'
   - Russel N. Campbell
   Do you agree? Give reasons for your answer.
5. What is abstract is theoretical linguistics and what is practical is applied linguistics. - Do you agree? Give reasons for your answer.
6. 'It is possible - even likely - that principles of psychology and linguistics and research in these disciplines, may supply insights useful to the language teacher. But this must be demonstrated, and cannot be presumed. It is the language teacher himself who must validate or refute any specific proposal. There is very little in psychology or linguistics that he can accept on faith.' - Noam Chomsky
   Can you extend this argument to applied linguistics in general and place the responsibility on the applied linguist?
7. '. . . an abstraction
   Remaining a perpetual possibility,
   Only in the world of speculation.' - T.S. Eliot
   In the light of the above quotation, do you think empirical validation can be a frustrating business? Illustrate your answer with reference to applied linguistics.
8. 'Life contains death within itself'. If opposites are not mutually exclu-

sive, there is a lot of theory in practice. Explain this with reference to applied linguistics and its relation to other disciplines.

Suggested reading

Allen, J.P.B., and S. Pit Corder. (eds.) 1973. *The Edinburgh Course in Applied Linguistics. Volume 1. Readings for Applied Linguistics.* London : Oxford University Press.

This is the first of a series of four volumes and it contains seminal articles on functions of language, varieties of language, the scope and methodology of linguistic study of language. There is also a section on linguistics and language teaching.

Allen, J.P.B., and S. Pit Corder (eds.) . 1974. *The Edinburgh Course in Applied Linguistics. Volume 3. Techniques in Applied Linguistics.* London: OUP.

This, third of a series of four volumes, has seminal papers on specific questions of 'educational linguistics' like course design and programmed instruction, as well as on issues of pedagogic interest like phonetics, phonology, grammar, language laboratory materials and stylistics. There are also papers on Error Analysis, Contrastive Analysis, Reading and Writing and Language Testing.

Allen, J.P.B., and S. Pit Corder (eds.). 1975. *The Edinburgh Course in Applied Linguistics. Volume 2. Papers in Applied Linguistics.* London: OUP

This, second of a series of four volumes, has its focus on language teaching. Papers on the relevance of linguistic theories on grammar, phonology, semantics, sociolinguistics psychology and so on to language teaching are presented as a projection of the theme paper on Applied Linguistics and Language Teaching by Pit Corder.

Allen, J.P.B., and A. Davies. (eds.) 1977. *The Edinburgh Course in Applied Linguistics. Volume 4. Testing and Experimental Methods.* London: OUP

This, fourth of a series of four volumes, has its focus on language testing and experimentational methods in applied linguistics.

Corder, S.P. 1973 *Introducting Applied Linguistics.* London : Penguin.

In this book the focus is on language teaching and the book is intended primarily for practising language teachers and teachers in training.

Kaplan, Robert, B. (ed.). 1980. *On the Scope of Applied Linguistics.* Rowley, Mass. : Newbury House, Inc.

This is a useful collection of papers on the history and scope of applied linguistics. It attempts to redefine applied linguistics according to the changing perceptions.

CHAPTER ONE
Language and Society

'Language and society are so intertwined that it is impossible to understand one without the other. There is no human society that does not depend upon, is not shaped by, and does not itself shape language.'

1 LANGUAGE AS A SOCIO-CULTURAL SYSTEM

No matter how eloquently a dog may bark, he cannot tell you that his parents were poor but honest.

— *Bertrand Russell*

Focal points

I. It is very obvious that language is essentially a *social phenomenon* since language lives in the minds and tongues of its users; philosophers like Locke have explained linguistic forms with reference to their functions in social settings. However, it is one thing to hold such a view, and quite another to attempt to construct a theory in which language is examined in terms of its socio-cultural functions.

Sociolinguistics is the study of language in relation to society; in other words, sociolinguistics studies the interactions between language as a network of relations and society as a network of relations.

Though much of the work in sociolinguistics was done in the late 1960s and early 1970s, there is a long tradition in the general study of word-meanings and their relation to culture and in the study of dialects; both these aspects are now subsumed under sociolinguistics.

There is a growing awareness that sociolinguistics can provide a richer empirical basis for linguistic theory itself, since what language is cannot be separated from what it does: how and why it is used and how considerations of use are often treated as prerequisites for the understanding of linguistic form. There is also a growing feeling that sociolinguistic insights can be used in finding solutions to some of the important problems in the field of education, language planning, bilingualism and biculturalism, multilingualism, multiculturalism and national integration, etc.

II. Is there a difference between *sociolinguistics* and *sociology of language*? Hudson (1980) defines sociolinguistics as 'the study of language in relation to society' and sociology of language as 'the study of society in relation to language'. He, however, admits that there is a great deal of overlap between the two. Earlier, Fishman (1972) pointed out that 'sociology of language examines the interaction between... the use of language and the social organization of behaviour.' He uses the label *sociolinguistics* to refer to the same concerns. It is possible to make a distinction between the two, depending upon the focus of interest—*the study with a focus on society being sociology of language* and *the one that focuses on language being sociolinguistics.*

III. Is there a difference between *linguistics* and *sociolinguistics*? Again, it depends on how we define the terms. Some point out that linguistics is a discipline that studies a network of relations at various levels like phonology, morphology, syntax, semantics, etc. and formulates the 'rules' of language X; only then, sociolinguistics enters the scene to study the rules as used by a variety of people in a variety of contexts. But there are others who hold the view that language is essentially a network of socio-culturally determined relations and hence the so-called formal rules cannot and should not be studied in isolation, that is, without any reference to the social functions of the language being studied; according to this view even the notion of 'language' is a social notion and there are no languages without social groups. One can well argue that all linguistics is sociolinguistics but such an extreme position will tend to ignore the individual and his/her desire for self-expression. The processes of 'conformity' and 'individualism' make language such a complex and creative activity.

Ferdinand de Saussure made a distinction between *langue* (as a set of abstract rules and conventions that are impersonal, 'a self-contained whole and a principle of classification', which determines the nature of each manifestation) and *parole* (as the concrete manifestation in the actual performance of the individual). In order to study *langue*—the dimension of language shared by all its speakers—one has to study *parole*, since *parole* and *langue* *always interact with each other*. It is not possible to take an extreme asocial position and claim that linguistics can study the structure of a language without studying how it is used.

IV. In linguistics the primary concern is the description of the structure of human language in general, and the descriptions of natural languages used by human beings in particular. Most linguists agree that human language has the following features:

1. Language is a means of communication and self-expression; it is a form of *social* behaviour that enables the *individual* to cooperate with others in a group.
2. Language is *arbitrary* and *vocal*.
3. It is *non-instinctive, conventional, symbolic,* and *systematic*.
4. It is *human, open-ended, extendable* and *modifiable*.
5. It is *multilayered* and *structurally complex*.

The features mentioned above clearly show that language is a human phenomenon, which is as complex as human relationships in a society.

Language is not a monolithic system. What we refer to as language X (i.e., English, Hindi, Tamil, etc.) is just a label, an abstraction. Underlying it we have a network of varieties—varieties of English, varieties of Hindi, varieties of Tamil, etc: dialectal, sociolectal, diglossic, registral, and stylistic varieties.

In sociolinguistics language is viewed as a system of communication, as an interactive process, as a tool by human beings in a variety of contexts, and as an interpersonal and socio-cultural activity. Since language is looked at not just as a set of sentences but as a system of forms, interacting with socio-cultural systems, there is a tendency to use only those terms that are relevant to the study of language functioning in the context of the culture of society.

V. Sociolinguistics is partly practical and partly theoretical. A sociolinguist tries to capture the use of language in actual as well as potential contexts; a sociolinguist studies not only the context-bound use of language (i.e., in specified contexts) but also its context-free potentials and possible realizations. This implies that a sociolinguist must *decontextualize, regularize,* and *standardize* in order to *generalize;* in other words, this means that generalizations and abstractions will have to be made and we cannot stop only with descriptions of what appears to be a highly confusing, quite often even contradictory, forces and relationships operating in the phenomenon being observed. Any theory-building exercise involves the narrowing down of variations, discarding certain irregularities in order to regularize the process or processes.

The theory formation process in sociolinguistics can be described as shown in Chart 4. The two terms that are used, *language* and *society,* cannot be clearly defined.

We can set up an imaginary society and an imaginary language where there is complete uniformity so that we can establish a neat network of relations between the two. Chomsky's theory is concerned with *ideal speaker-hearers,* in a *completely homogeneous* speech community, who know its language *perfectly* and are *unaffected* by such grammatically irrelevant conditions as memory hesitations, distractions, shifts of attention and interest in applying their knowledge of the language in actual performance. Such a society does not exist and speakers of such a language do not exist; they are *imaginary, unreal, fictitious.* If we postulate imaginary speech-communities and languages in order to study the relationships, the very purpose of the study is defeated because they do not exist.

What we actually have is a real world that is exotic, a real community that is full of variations, a real society that defies any kind of classification because it is always in a state of flux; what we have is a real language that is used to express the feelings and experiences of people living in a real world, a language user is constantly affected by distractions, shifts of attention, interest, in interactive situations. We cannot assume that there are no connections between language and culture and establish connections; culture is one of the most important features of language as well as society.

Only a careful study of the real society and the real language can reveal how much conformity and how much individualism are there in both, how much is familiar and how much unfamiliar and exotic, how much is stable, how much unstable, how much is predictable and how much unpredictable. So idealized communities and idealized language-speakers are not only non-existent but also uninteresting, in the sense, a study of these fictitious entities may not reveal anything. The study of language is the study of the relational networks that exist among its components such as phonemes, morphemes, words, sentences, paragraphs, etc. These components themselves are abstractions based on their actual occurrence in various contexts.

Similarly, the study of society is the study of relational networks that exist among its components such as individuals, groups, communities, classes, castes, nations, etc. These components too are abstractions based on their actual manifestations in real life.

Linguists try to find answers to the following questions:

a) What are the main components of language?
b) How are they organized in generating larger units?
c) How does the organisation of the various components help human beings use language as a system of communication?

Sociologists try to find answers to the following questions:

a) What are the main components of society?
b) How are they organized in the formation of larger units?
c) How does the organization of various components help human beings cooperate and coordinate their activities?

Sociolinguists try to find answers to the following questions:

a) How do formal and socio-cultural organizations interweave?
b) How do social relations and patterns shape language patterns?
c) How do language patterns shape social relations and patterns?

As stated earlier on, language and society are so inextricably intertwined that we cannot and should not study language divorced from society and society divorced from language. Language and society in interaction form the main field of sociolinguistics.

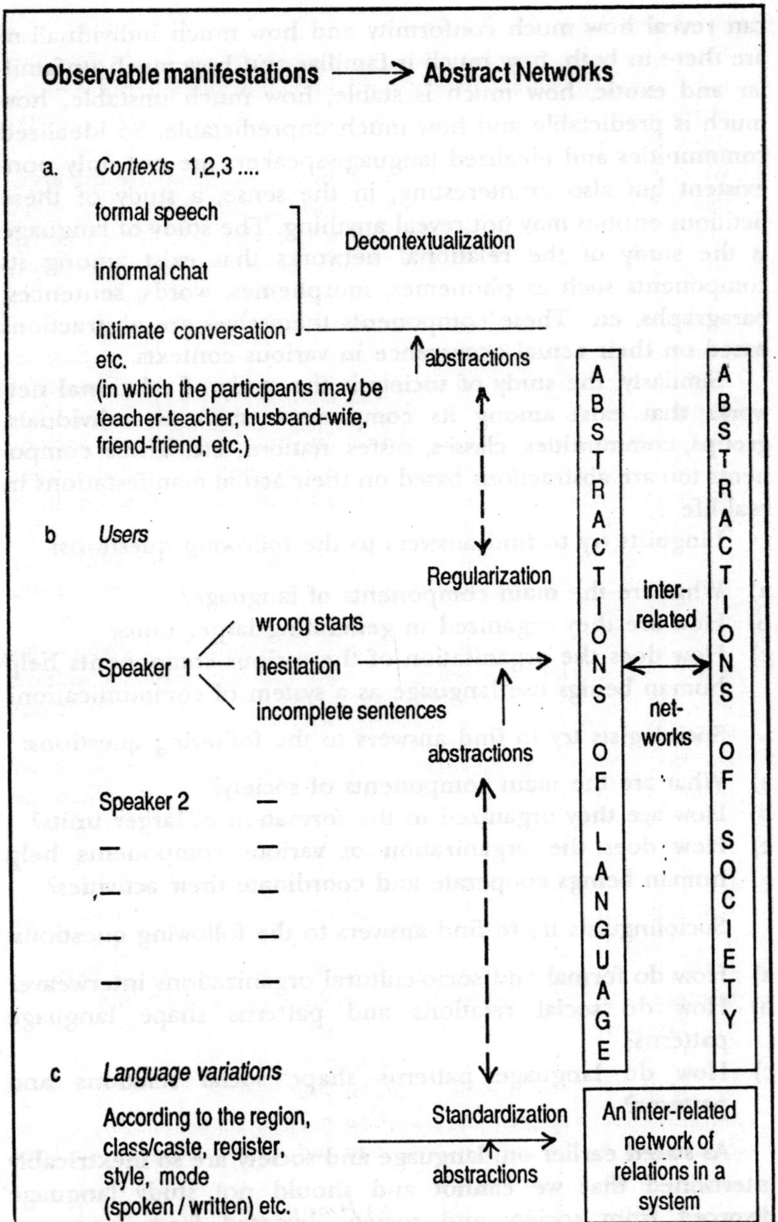

Chart 4: Theory formation processes in sociolinguistics

Questions and topics for discussion

1. One can say that every language operates by rules. There are rules for combining phonemes into syllables, morphemes into words, words into sentences, etc. Are there such rules in society? Can you think of some?
2. We can say that language is created by society. What are the arguments that can be given in support of such a statement? Can we say that society is created by language? If not, why not? If so, why so?
3. Do you think that it is possible to maintain a distinction between the *sociology of language and sociolinguistics?* In case you want to maintain a distinction, give arguments and examples.
4. The notion 'society' like the notion 'phoneme' is an *abstraction.* Explain the statement on the basis of your study of the notion of phoneme.
5. In the study of any human institution—maybe language, society, social institutions like education, law, religion, etc.—abstractions are unavoidable. Why are abstractions unavoidable? Why shouldn't we simply list what we observe?
6. If someone says that sociolinguistics is concerned with apparently trivial matters like how people talk to each other, etc., how will you react?
7. 'Colourless green ideas sleep furiously'. This sentence is given as an example of deviation—a deviation from ordinary linguistic behaviour. Are there deviations in social behaviour? Can you point out some?
8. Do you think linguistic deviation and deviation from normal social behaviour are in some ways related? What are the arguments for or against possible positions?
9. A: My Mrs. is not well; she can't come.
   B: I'm sorry to hear that, but my *family* too is not well.
   Explain the use of *Mrs.* and *family* in native and non-native varieties of English.
10. Point out the marked features of the following sentences showing interpersonal relationships in Indian socio-cultural settings:
    a) Bless my home with the good dust of your feet.
       [B. Bhattacharya : *So Many Hungers,* p.55]
    b) O Maharaj, we are all lickers of your feet.
       [B. Bhattacharya : *He Who Rides a Tiger,* p.179]
    c) Sardar Sahib, you are a big man and we are but small radishes from an unknown garden.
       [Kushwant Singh : *I Shall Not Hear the Nightingale,* p.27]

2 LINGUISTIC COMPETENCE AND COMMUNICATIVE COMPETENCE

'And 'tis remarkable that they
Talk most who have least to say.'

Prior

Focal points

I. In spite of the widespread awareness of the interrelationship between language and society, linguists have not succeeded in describing such a relationship or developing analytical procedures to account for them. Phonology, lexis and syntax which are objects of linguistic description constitute only a part of the elements in the code used for communication. The meaning(s) of an utterance (a sentence, a clause, a phrase, a word, etc.) do(es) not depend entirely on its form; a lot depends on *who says what to whom, when, where, in what manner, and with what effect.* In other words, the *context of situation* in which an utterance is said is very important in deciding its meaning.

For example, the utterance 'Can I have the salt, please?' is interrogative in form but expresses a polite request in a dining room situation.

II. Grammatical knowledge alone is not enough to help us participate effectively in communicative situations. In addition to knowing the forms of a language, one must know the following in order to communicate appropriately:

a) *The socio-cultural situation:* the attitudes, values, conventions, prejudices, and preferences of the people who use the language.
b) *The nature of the participants:* the relationship between the speaker/speakers and the hearer/hearers, their occupation, interests, socio-economic status, etc.
c) *The role of the participants:* the relationship in the social network, like father-son, teacher-student, boss-subordinate, doctor-patient, etc.
d) *The nature and function of the speech event:* whether it is a face-

to-face talk for persuasion, confrontation, etc., or a casual conversation, or a request in a formal situation, or a telephonic conversation, etc.

e) *The mode (= medium) of communication:* spoken or written or reading from a written script (= scripted speech) or unprepared speech, etc.

III. Chomsky's notion of *linguistic competence* does not capture all the factors mentioned above. Even as late as 1980 Chomsky claimed:

> By 'grammatical competence' I mean the cognitive state that encompasses all those aspects of form and meaning and their relation, including underlying structures that enter into that relation, which are properly assigned to the specific subsystem of the human mind that relates representations of form and meaning. ... ... Pragmatic competence underlies the ability to use such knowledge along with the conceptual system to achieve certain ends or purposes. ... ... I assume that it is possible in principle for a person to have full grammatical competence and no pragmatic competence, hence no ability to use a language appropriately, though its syntax and semantics are intact. (Chomsky, N. 1980: 59)

Dell Hymes (1971), on the other hand, says that one who studies language should be able.

> ...to account for the fact that a normal child acquires knowledge of sentences, not only as grammatical, but also as appropriate. He or she acquires competence as to when to speak, when not, and as to what to talk about with whom, when, where, in what manner. In short, a child becomes able to accomplish a repertoire of speech acts, to take part in speech acts, to take part in speech events, and to evaluate their accomplishment by others.

Communicative competence, it may be said, includes the whole of *linguistic competence* plus the whole of the amorphous range of facts included under *sociolinguistic-pragmatic competence* (the rules and conventions for using language items in contexts) and other factors like attitudes, values and motivations.

There are linguists like Chomsky who argue that *linguistic competence* can be separated from the rest of communicative competence and studied in isolation; there are other linguists who feel that the notion of *linguistic competence* is unreal and that no significant progress in linguistics is possible without studying the language forms along with the ways in which they are used.

IV. Social interaction can be called 'skilled work' and it requires effort; for the most part, since it is *social,* it is learned from others and social interaction is a cooperative effort. It is not innate (inborn or genetically endowed) as it is claimed to be in the case of the language faculty. The consequence of failure to cooperate successfully is described by Goffman (1957) as follows:

> A person who chronically makes himself and others uneasy in conversation and perpetually kills encounters is a faulty interactant; he is likely to have such a baleful effort upon the social life around him that he may just as well be called a faulty person.

The argument given above clearly shows that *communicative competence* is an important notion in sociolinguistics; even the ability to sound appropriately incompetent in the language when a situation demands it becomes a part of one's competence. On some occasions, one would like to sound communicatively incompetent in order to produce certain results, like a subordinate speaking in a hesitating manner to escape the anger of someone of higher rank.

V. *Communicative competence* includes everything involving the use of language and other communicative dimensions, like when to speak and when not, the level of loudness, etc. in particular social settings.

As Hymes points out *competence* is dependent upon both tacit knowledge and the ability to use it; it is related to the four features listed below:

a) whether (and to what degree) something is *possible;*
b) whether (and to what degree) something is *feasible* (in relation to the means available);
c) whether (and to what degree) something is *appropriate* (adequate, effective, happy in relation to the context in which it is used);

d) whether (and to what degree) something is *performed* (actually done and what the doing entails).

This will mean, that a native user's *communicative competence* is reflected in his/her grammatical (i.e., formally possible), psycholinguistic (i.e., implementationally feasible), socio-cultural (i.e., contextually appropriate), and de facto (i.e., actually occurring) knowledge and ability to use a language.

All these show that *linguistic competence* is largely a part of *communicative competence* and that *some aspects of linguistic competence may even be irrelevant to communicative competence.* From this point of view, we can regard linguistics essentially as sociolinguistics since the study of *linguistic competence* will form a part of the study of *communicative competence.*

The conceptualization given above will lead us to recognize that the study of language is a multidisciplinary field to which, in addition to conventional linguistics, other disciplines such as sociology, social anthropology, social history, psychology, physiology, philosophy, folklore and poetics, to name a few, are indispensable as well. Such a view will alter the very bases of linguistics.

VI. Dell Hymes' criticism of the concept of *linguistic competence* is that it is an abstraction without any relevance to actual use. The same criticism has been directed against the notion of *communicative competence.* According to Widdowson (1983), if *linguistic competence* is an abstraction of grammatical knowledge, *communicative competence* is an abstraction of social behaviour. If we say that language doesn't exist and that it happens, we give importance only to *procedural capacity* and not to the abstract ability.

The notion of *communicative competence* does not include in its purview the actual procedures which language users adopt in order to participate in language-based activities. So, along with *linguistic competence,* and *communicative competence, pragmatic competence* should also be brought into focus. *Pragmatic competence* is the one that underlies 'the ability to use language along with the conceptual system to achieve certain ends or purposes' (Chomsky 1980) and it determines how the tool can be effectively put to use; it is user-oriented.

VII. We can sum up and say that the following are essentially the components of communication and go into the building up of *communicative competence:*

a) Linguistic knowledge and the paralinguistic cues:
   i. Verbal elements (sentences, clauses, phrases, etc.)
   ii. Non-verbal elements (aspects of communicative behaviour such as facial expressions, body movement, eye gaze, gestures, proximity, etc.)
   iii. Elements of discourse and their organization in connected speech and writing.
   iv. Range of possible variants (other possible variations and their organization).
   v. Meaning of variants in particular situations.
b) Interaction skills:
   i. Norms of interaction and interpretation.
   ii. Strategies for achieving desired goals.
   iii. Perception of features (verbal as well as non-verbal) in communication situations.
   iv. Understanding appropriateness in any given situation.
c) Cultural knowledge
   i. Social structure
   ii. Values and attitudes
   iii. Cognitive scheme and the culture transmission processes.

These factors decide the communicative norms in a community.

VIII. The setting of interaction is also an important factor in defining a situation. Whether the place or the setting of interaction is a church, a temple, a market-place, or a classroom contributes to the nature of interaction and the variety of language used.

IX. Another concept useful in understanding *communicative competence* is the concept of *phatic communion.* One purpose of *phatic communion* is to avoid silence because silence where it is not required may imply hostility or embarrassment. In a prayer hall silence is the mark of respect, but when two people meet, if they remain silent, it may imply hostility. So some expressions like 'Good morning', 'How are you?', 'Ram Ram', 'Namasthe', etc.

are exchanged; they are highly conventional and when they are violated the communicative patterns are disturbed which is felt in the discomfiture of the participants in the interaction. In certain cultures, however, total silence on the part of the participants meeting in a place is welcome without any feeling of embarrassment.

Questions and topics for discussion

1. The following sentences are categorized as declarative sentences:

   I shall be thirty next year.
   You should leave this place at one.
   I would love some ice-cream.
   That plate is very hot.

   Try to list their functions like command, request, etc. in specific situations.

2. Look at the following sentences:

   It is possible that he will come.
   There is a possibility that he will come.
   There is a possibility of his coming.
   Possibly, he will come.
   Maybe, he will come.
   Perhaps, he will come.

   Do they all convey the same meaning? If there are differences, try to specify them.

3. 'You are an ass!' — Grammatically it is a well formed sentence. List some of the situations where it is treated as illformed and offensive discuss it in relation to linguistic competence and communicative competence.

4. 'I ain't done no home work' - what is wrong with this sentence?

5. Customer: Good morning. Do you have anything for a bad throat?

   Shopkeeper: Good morning, sir. Can I help you?

   What is wrong with the exchange given above?

6. 'Not now, darling!' - What are the possible socio-cultural situations for this utterance. Give at least five situations and mention what this utterance implies in each.

7. Look at the following pieces of discourse in English. Say in each case why the response is inappropriate.

   a) Doctor : Good morning.
      Patient : Good morning.
      Doctor : Feeling better?
      *Patient : Fine, thanks. How are you?

b) A : Is it possible to go there *on foot*?
*B : Yes, it is possible to go there.
c) Doctor : Has there been any case of cardiac arrest in your family?
Patient : We never had no trouble with the police.

8. There is a well known fable about three blind men describing an elephant; to one it is like a rope, to another it is flat and to the third it is like a long hose. Each one is correct but they fail to provide the picture of the animal. Describe and explain what is common to the three descriptions?
9. Sentences may be
   a) grammatically correct but situationally *not* acceptable,
   b) situationally acceptable but grammatically *not* correct.
   c) situationally as well as grammatically unacceptable.
   d) situationally as well as grammatically acceptable.

   Give two examples of each type from English and your first language.
10. What is 'communication'? Is it 'exchange of information' or communion? Try to construct a scale with two extreme ends and intermediary points in the continuum. Can it be just a linear scale or should it be multi-dimensional? First collect the dictionary meanings, including etymological meanings.
11. Some say that it is impossible or very difficult to express what you want to say; this means that there is always a gap between what you want to say and what you say. How do you capture this notion and fit it into the notion of *communicative competence*?
12. 'The true use of language is not so much to express our thoughts but to conceal them.' How will you fit it in as part of *communicative competence*?
13. 'The idea that there is no one correct English or Hindi or Tamil is horrifying; it involves the abandonment of standards and the permissive society will run riot.' How will you react to such a statement?
14. 'We practise language in the sense in which a doctor practises medicine or a lawyer practises law, and *not* in the sense in which the actors in a play practise before it is performed.' What is meant by the statement given above?

3 VARIATIONS IN LANGUAGE

'No society can make a perpetual constitution, or even a perpetual law.' — *Thomas Jefferson*

Focal points

I. Variety is the very spice of life and language is part of it. We like variety in everything including language.

Not all people in a speech community speak in the same manner; even the same person does not speak the same way in all situations.

Consider the following utterances:

What time is it?
What time do you make?
What o'clock is it?
What is the time by your watch?

Though the purpose is the same, the linguistic forms are different here. Sociolinguistics tries to account for such variations in terms of socio-cultural parameters, since the motivations for variations cannot be explained in formal terms alone.

II. In order to understand variations in language, we must understand the term 'speech community'. A very simple definition is given by John Lyons (1970:326):

> Speech community: all the people who use a given language (or dialect).

Such a definition takes it for granted that the terms *language* and *dialect* have already been defined; but the fact is that these concepts have not been defined in functional terms. It may be useful to examine some of the views expressed by linguists.

According to Dwight Bolinger (1975:333):

> There is no limit to the ways in which human beings league themselves together for self-identification, security, gain,

> amusement, worship, or any of the other purposes that are held in common; consequently, there is no limit to the number and variety of speech communities that are to be found in society.

Examined from this point of view, any community (of a city, a town, etc.) even if it is monolingual, will contain a large number of speech communities with overlapping membership and overlapping language systems. From a social point of view every individual tries to locate himself/herself in a multi-dimensional space and identifies himself/herself with a number of groups from time to time according to certain purposes and opportunities; there is a lot of mobility, not only in terms of geographical locations but also in terms of class, caste, sex, age, occupation, interests, etc.

Such an approach is advocated by Robert Le Page (1968):

Each individual creates the systems for his verbal behaviour so that they shall resemble those of the group or groups with which from time to time he may wish to be identified, to the extent that:

a) he can identify the groups,
b) he has both opportunity and ability to observe and analyse their behavioural systems,
c) his motivation is sufficiently strong to impel him to choose, and to adapt his behaviour accordingly,
d) he is still able to adapt his behaviour.

This enables us to think of *sociolect,* a concept which gives us a new insight into the traditional notions like language, dialect, etc., because it tries to relate the use of language to societal patterns.

III. It will be useful to revise some of the traditional notions at this point; for the sake of convenience, a list is given below:

a) There is no sharp demarcation between *language* and *dialect.* If two varieties of speech are mutually intelligible, they are considered dialects; if they are not, they are considered languages.

b) An individual speech act is called *parole* and the abstract system is called *langue; langue* and *parole* together constitute language.
c) Each individual has his/her own variety and that is called *idiolect* (i.e., *idio* = individual; *lect* = variety of language).
d) When two or more people share the ways of speaking, the group uses a *dialect* (i.e., *dia* = two; *-lect* = variety of language).
e) A dialect spoken in a geographical area is called a *regional dialect.*
f) Dialects can be based on social stratifications; in that case, they are called *sociolects.* There are class dialects, caste dialects (Brahmin, non-brahmin, etc.), urban/rural dialects.
g) A *prestige* dialect is a dialect accepted and emulated by speakers of other dialects (like *Standard English, Khari-boli, Andhra Telugu,* etc.). In due course the prestige dialect may acquire the status of the *standard language.* The notion of standard language may also be based on a non-regional written variety that is mostly literary.
h) Variations in pronunciation are referred to as differences in *accent.*
i) A language variety marked by certain features that are typical of certain disciplines/fields/topics, occupations and social roles played by a speaker is referred to as *register* (like the legal register, the scientific register, the journalistic register, etc.)
j) Within a register there are different *styles,* depending on the speaker's intention and individual preferences, and the relationship between the speaker and the hearer.
k) The *mode* or medium of expression may be spoken or written.

IV. There are considerable problems in demarcating one variety from another of the same type (e.g., one language from another, one dialect from another, a dialect from a language). Is there any clearcut distinction between one variety and the other? *Mutual intelligibility* is one of the important criteria that has been proposed by many in addition to the size of the variety. If speakers A and B are mutually intelligible, and B and C are mutually intelligible, C and A are not necessarily mutually intelligible; for example, a person from Rajasthan (who speaks a dialect of

Hindi) may not understand a person from Eastern Bihar (who speaks one of the Bihari dialects of Hindi), but can understand each other when they write; a person from Peking cannot understand one from Hong Kong, even though both of them speak Chinese. The Chittagong and Calcutta varieties of spoken Bengali are mutually unintelligible. Secondly, mutual intelligibility is a matter of *degree* ranging from total intelligibility to total unintelligibility; there cannot be a definitive answer to the question, 'How intelligible should they be, total or partial or how partial, etc.?' A given variety may be relatively similar to some other variety and relatively different from others. In addition, the notion of a variety is a gross idealization of the relations between varieties; speakers may be mutually intelligible or unintelligible but not varieties. The *family tree model* that is widely used in the historical study of languages (for example, Tamil, Malayalam, Kannada and Telugu as members of one Dravidian family) is based on idealization and sameness; it does not take into account the fact that one variety influences the other and two varieties may converge into one—a single variety emerging out of two or three varieties. The *wave theory*—the assumption that changes in language spread from place to place like 'waves' intersecting, converging, with many centres of influence from which ripples spread and interact, like the seeds of different species of plants sown in the field, coexisting, competing, not all the time prospering, some thriving—is more dynamic in its conception than the family tree model; the wave theory captures the notion of linguistic continua, the fact that varieties shade off into each other.

There are similar problems in demarcating registers, styles, etc.

V. In sociolinguistics, we must attempt a *social description* that will include in addition to geographical mobility, the social mobility, maybe from the 'bottom' of the social heap to the 'top'; this involves drawing a multi-dimensional map which may ultimately reject even the notion of *sociolect.* We, the social animals, are to draw the map and we are governed by social, political and cultural considerations. Wherever a line is drawn someone, somewhere, will be upset since deep emotions are involved in issues of language.

Derek Bickerton and William Stewart, in their study of creole languages have posited a *continuum* of three levels, linking *basilect* (the lowest variety) to the *acrolect* (the highest variety) through a succession of *mesolects* (the middle varieties—again upper-mid, mid-mid and lower-mid); this is true not only of creoles but of all human languages.

Secondly, we can't ignore the individual and describe idealized speech communities; idealized speech communities do not exist; only individuals do. Like the notions of dialects, registers, etc., a speech community is an idealization. This leaves us in a paradoxical situation; we have to give a social description of the individual user of a certain variety and his/her range of linguistic items as well as a description of the dynamic operation of speech communities (geographical and social) with which the individual tries to identify himself or herself according to his/her perception of the community. This is a very complex task. This means that we continue to use terms like 'variety', 'dialect', 'language', etc. in an informal way with the full awareness of their limitations as theoretical notions and that any classification of language varieties is likely to be oversimplified.

VI. *Pidgins* and *creoles* are varieties. Pidginization and creolization are processes. This study is useful in sociolinguistics for it enables us to understand language varieties arising out of language contacts.

Creolization is a term used to capture the process of the formation of a new language, when two, or more, languages mix together to form a new one. The first stage of this process is pidginization which may yield a pidgin, a limited speech code, typically used by people who do not understand each others' language; a pidgin is a mixture useful only in a limited situation; it is a link language which may not be anyone's mother tongue. After a while, the children in that speech community adopt it as their mother tongue. Slowly, it develops into a complex, independent variety, which is called a creole; *a pidgin which has acquired native users is a creole.*

Pidgins arise out of several complex social situations; it may be a conquered-conqueror situation, where the conquered tries to learn the language of the conquerer and uses it in some restricted situations, as in the case of Butler English in India; it may be the upper class-lower class situation, where the speech of the lower class is considered broken or defective.

There is no clearcut difference between pidgins and creoles; they form a cline.

VII. In our attempt to work out the sociolinguistic profile of a language, another notion that may be useful is *diglossia,* since it demonstrates the value of language variations according to the ways they function in society.

In Tamil, for example, the classical or literary form, which is considered more correct and 'beautiful' than the colloquial forms, is used in prestigious domains like public speaking, education, religion, etc; it is the High variety of the language. The Low variety, which is different from the High variety, varies from region to region; the High variety is fixed and codified in grammars and dictionaries. Such a situation is known as *diglossia.* This happens in Arabic too, where the High and the Low are used in different circumstances; they do not overlap. When Latin was the language of education and religious services in England, English and Latin were in a diglossic relationship. In India Sanskrit is used, in certain speech communities in India, for certain High cultural roles (like in religious functions) and the vernacular for the lower cultural values. These are called H(igh) and L(ow) varieties. Such cultural differentiations lead to biculturalism; where there is biculturalism in the same society it has been called *dinomia.*

These distinctions again are fuzzy at their edges, but they are useful, to study the nature of language and society and their inter-relations.

VIII. There are also non-native varieties of a language (varieties which are used as second languages) like the non-native varieties of English: Indian English, Nigerian English, Malaysian Tamil, etc. Can they be considered language variations? If we consider the position of Indian English, several problems in sociolinguistics surface. Limited contact with native users of English, the use of English in certain specifiable domains, insufficient attention paid to the spoken medium, exposure to all kinds of non-standard forms, the gravitational pull of the mother tongue, the influence of the written form in the learning of the language, the flavour of literariness, the preference for formal style and such other factors make the Indian variety of English a second language, non-native variety. Is Indian English a dialect of English? Is it a pidgin or a creole?

Attitudes to the non-native varieties are deep rooted; during the colonial era Indian English was referred to as 'Babu' or 'Cheechee' English by the English. On the other hand, Indians would like to argue that Indian English is different from the native varieties but it is not a pidgin; it is creative; many novelists and poets have tried to find a personal voice in the Indian variety; it is full of vitality; people express their feelings and experiences in it. At the same time, it must be remembered that only varieties as Malayali English, Bengali English, Telugu English, etc. are found but there is no such abstraction that can be called Indian English. Indian English may be defined in terms of a political entity called India; can we say that Indian English is the English used by one who lives in India or who holds an Indian passport (Indians' English)? What about the English of non-resident Indians? What about the English of Anglo-Indians? Such questions continue to be asked and there is no definitive answer to all these questions. A lot will depend on how we look at the term 'India'; it may be taken as a political entity, a socio-cultural entity, a linguistic entity, or in terms of notions like rural-urban, educated-uneducated, etc. There will be several answers to the questions raised and the concept of a continuum will have to be used to represent a range of varieties from native-like English to pidginized English.

IX. In all these discussions, one important issue becomes clear. Every individual has his/her private model of his/her society—he/she builds up a conception of the model of a society based on his/her experience of social interactions; similarly, each linguistic item is related to some aspect of society (i.e., the individual's conception of his/her society) and, sometimes, a group of items are related to some aspect or aspects of society. When such speculations are made, we may come to some broad understanding between language items and society without trying to be very rigid, or highly predictive, or too 'scientific'. In the study of humanities, wherever human beings are involved, the situation is always in a state of flux and no rigid codification is possible; predictions may or may not come true.

Questions and topics for discussion

1. Hindi has different terms to refer to father's brother (*chaachaa*), mother's brother (*mausaa*), father's sister's husband (*phuuphaa*) and mother's sister's husband (*mausaa*); English has a multi-purpose term 'uncle'. Can we say that Hindi is superior to English?
2. Consider the following expressions in English and Hindi:

i) come in	i. a. *andar aao*
	b. *andar aaiye*
ii) please come in	ii. *kripayaa andar aaiye*
iii) would you mind coming in?	iii. *kyaa andar aane mẽ aapko koi itraaz hogaa?*

   Why should there be different forms for conveying the same basic message, i.e., asking someone to come in? Can you explain the social motivations involved?
3. Consider the following:

English English	*Hindi*	*Indian English*
What's your name?	*aapka shubh naam kyaa hai?*	What's your good name?
	**teraa shubh naam kyaa hai?*	

   How do you explain the use of 'good name' in Indian English? Why is *shubh naam* not used with *teraa* in Hindi? Why is it that there is no expression like 'What's your bad name?' in any human language?
4. Certain expressions, like the following, are widely used in Indian English; they are not used in native varieties:
   a. The *concerned officer* will look into this matter. (instead of 'the officer concerned')
   b. The meeting has been *pre-poned* to an earlier date. (instead of '*advanced* to an earlier date')
   c. The criminal *is absconding* (instead of 'has absconded')
   d. I'm *having a car.* (instead of 'have a car')

   Do you consider them mistakes or Indianisms? Should we accept them as Indian English? If this tendency continues, do you think pidginization will set in and may lead to a pidgin or a creole?
5. It is said that Indians are fond of using high-sounding words and phrases and prone to verbosity. For example, they use 'demise' for 'death', 'witness' for 'see', 'purchase' for 'buy', etc., even in non-formal contexts. What are the reasons for such tendencies?
6. Look at the following parameters:

   Standardization - (e.g., Vernacular lacks standardization; has no written form; no dictionary; no grammar books)

Autonomy - can function independently.
Historicity - tradition of development.
Vitality - i.e., used in day-to-day interactions in a number of situations (classical language has no vitality).

a. Think of Indian English and assess its status using the parameters given above.
b. Think of your first language and assess its status, using the parameters given above.

7. What is the status of the following varieties of English used in India? Can we consider them varieties of Indian English? Do they have identificatory features (i.e., can one identify each in terms of certain marked features)?
   a. The English used by R.K. Narayan or Kushwant Singh in their novels.
   b. The English used by the Anglo-Indians.
   c. The English used in the bazaar.
   d. The English used in government offices.
   e. The English used in textbooks produced by national agencies.
8. Do you think there is a clash between English and your first language, in terms of their domains and functions in your social set up? Illustrate your answer.
9. Why do people who oppose English send their own children to English-medium schools?
10. 'Be Indian and Buy Indian'. In tune with the sentiments expressed by this slogan, can we say we have to use only the *Swadesi* variety of English, whether the world outside understands it or not? Give arguments in support of your answer.
11. Hindi treats the word for beard *daaRhi* as feminine in gender and the word for breast *stan* as masculine. Is this because of social attitudes or is this a problem of perception? Give reasons.
12. Assamese speakers say that Bengali is written in Assamese script and Bengalis say that Assamese is written in Bengali script. The script is the same. Who is 'correct'?
13. Konkani has no script of its own but it has been recognised as a language. Why?
14. Think of the life of a working person; (s)he goes to the office, the club, etc.; meets his/her friends; interacts with the members of the family, immediate as well as wider circle; meets strangers and interacts with them; goes shopping, etc. Can we put them all in one box and construct only one speech community? How many speech communities can we construct? Try to define your notion of 'speech-community' and the linguistic profile of an English-based multilingual in India or Nigeria or Hong Kong.

15. Society cannot be classified neatly into pigeonholes and defined clearly in terms of social status, socio-economic considerations, etc.; language too cannot be classified neatly into dialects, registers, etc. Then how do we study the relationships between languages and their varieties? What are the solutions suggested in the unit?
16. Some linguists like Gumperz and Fishman have extended the meaning of the term 'diglossia' to include any society in which two or more varieties are used under distinct circumstances. Does it mean that the concept of 'registers' can also be included under 'diglossia' and every society is diglossic?
17. Give examples of 'diglossia' from your language.
18. What may be the 'extended parameters' for recognizing a communication system as 'language'?

4 LANGUAGES IN CONTACT

'What is needed is common wealth *of nations.'*

Focal points

I. People are not sentence-churning machines. They are human beings who make linguistic choices and organize them for certain purposes. Social as well as linguistic structure will remain an illusion till such time as we unearth some connection between the processes that contribute to the use of language in everyday social interaction and the normative accounting schemes that are used by scholars and researchers in formulating their *idealized notions* of language and society. We assemble and create 'speech communities' through language in our social interaction; how this is done and whether generalizations are possible is the crucial question in sociolinguistics.

For the present, we shall continue to use the term 'variety' to refer to the concepts traditionally called language, dialect, register or style. We must note that the varieties get hopelessly mixed up in a number of situations. When two systems (maybe languages, dialects, or registers) are in contact, one affects the other, putting varieties at some point or the other on the scale where the two ends are 'focussing' and in 'diffusion'. *Focussing* is found where there is a high degree of *contact* as well as *agreement* among the members of the speech community on linguistic norms, and *diffusion* is found where neither of these conditions hold good.

II. In biological systems, when two 'mutually infertile' systems come into contact, a new system that is totally different is born; in such cases a divergent or evolutionary change takes place. In the case of language systems, on the other hand, there are changes leading to convergence and then leading on to divergence.

When two languages are in contact, there is a contact between two cultures, too. At the linguistic level, we call the process *bilingualism* and at the cultural level *biculturalism* or *acculturation;* if there are more, we can refer to them as multilingualism or multiculturalism. At the same time, we should remember that language is an integral part of *enculturation*; firstly, language is part of culture and they cannot be separated; secondly, language is the medium through which the users explore and manipulate the socio-cultural environment. Thus, exploration as well as transmission takes place through language. One learns to be a male or a female, a Christian or a Muslim or a Hindu, or to play the dozens of social roles chiefly through language. So, it is not possible to maintain a clearcut distinction between bilingualism and biculturalism; it depends on the focus that is given to one aspect or the other.

Hall's (1959) categorization of *formal, informal,* and *technical* levels of culture is useful in understanding the distinctions clearly.

Formal learning of culture takes place through observation and admonition, using authority. 'This is not our way', 'It's not to be done like this', 'We respect elders', etc. are some examples of how it is done.

Informal learning of culture takes place through non-verbal channels of communication, unwritten conventions, indirect responses, etc. For example, certain things are not said directly; in a classroom situation, if the teacher says, 'Would you like to stand up now?', even though it is a question, the student will not say 'no'. There are no explicit rules for informal learning.

Technical learning is what takes place in terms of rules at the conscious level. A lesson on 'etiquette' where rules for 'proper' behaviour are explained is an example of this type of learning.

The role of language in enculturation is for personal growth (to acquire knowledge, interpret the world, etc.) and for socialization (to maintain social interaction, gain acceptance etc.).

III. Who is a *bilingual*? The term has been variously defined by different linguists. At one end, the definition 'native like control of two languages' (Bloomfield) refers to people with near perfect mastery of two systems; such a bilingual person is called a *coordinate bilingual*; at the other end, there are *incipient bilinguals* (who are slightly better than monolinguals). In between coordinate bilinguals and incipient bilinguals, there are different levels of *subordinate bilinguals* with varying degrees of proficiency in the second language. These are the distinctions made in the area of individual bilingualism. We can now say that a bilingual is a person who makes alternate, effective use of two languages (or their varieties).

IV. In a community, when the privileged or dominant language is used by the privileged sections of the society and the less privileged or less dominant language is used by the underprivileged sections of the society, *language shift* can take place; the general tendency will be to move towards the dominant language and over a period of time the less dominant language may be lost. Or the users may use both the languages with different contextual functions (like English and the vernacular or Sanskrit and the vernacular in the case of some) and maintain their loyalty to their first language. This may be called *language maintenance*. In formal, institutional language learning situations, these languages are called first language (or, primary language) and second language (or, secondary language). The impact of the secondary language on the primary language leads to degrees of convergence of the secondary on the primary language.

We can study convergence in terms of certain notions like the following:

a) *Switching and Mixing*: the alternate use of two languages, like the use of English and vernacular;
b) *Interference*: the overlapping of the two or the influence of one

on the other, as the pull of the mother tongue in the learning of English as a second language; and

c) *Integration:* the diffusion of the two.

Code-switching as a communicative strategy is discussed in the next unit.

V. Another way in which different varieties may get mixed up with each other is through *borrowing*, in which a linguistic item is taken over from one variety into another; we use the term, generally, to refer to borrowing from one language into another; but items can be borrowed from one variety into another.

Indian languages have a number of words borrowed from English. It is common for items to get *assimilated*. This assimilation may be total or partial. For example, words like bulb, wire, switch, etc. have become part of the vocabulary of the major Indian languages; the word 'hospital' has become aaspatri in Tamil, a case of total assimilation; the word 'peon' has become 'pyuunu' in Telugu, a case of partial assimilation.

We can present this picture in the form of a continuum with completely unassimilated loan-words at one end and assimilated loan-words at the other. For instance, in English words like 'guru' and 'shanti' remain totally unassimilated whereas words like mulligatawny (Tamil *milagutannir*), bandicoot (Telugu *pandikokku*), bandobast (Hindi and Pers. *band-o-bast*), juggernaut (Sanskrit *Jagannaatha*) have very little resemblance to the words borrowed from Indian languages.

VI. Another important phenomenon studied along with languages in contact and bilingualism is the notion of *diglossia*, discussed in the previous unit (see Unit 3). Diglossia is the sociolinguistic aspect of the contact situation between communication systems. The term 'diglossia' was first introduced by Charles Ferguson (1959); according to Ferguson the H(igh) and L(ow) variety should belong to the same language. For example, in Tamil the items *pengal* 'women' and *aangal* 'men' belong to the H(igh) variety and *pomblenga* 'women' and *aamblenga* 'men' belong to the L(ow) variety. In Bengali, *saadhu bhaashaa* denotes the high variety and *calit bhaasha* the low one.

Later Fishman (following John Gumperz) extended the term diglossia to include any society in which two or more varieties are used under specifiable circumstances; but this broadens the scope of diglossia. One can also extend the term to include triglossia and multiglossia, where more than two specifiable distinctions are maintained.

Bilingualism is essentially a characterization of individual linguistic versatility whereas diglossia is a characterization of the societal allocation of functions to different varieties.

VII. Research in the area of language contact and bilingualism can be useful in the following areas:

a) in understanding the effect of the interaction among the various languages and varieties that come into contact and the cognitive processes and results; for example, we would like to study whether a monolingual, if there be one, can think more clearly than a bilingual. Can we say that a bilingual or a multilingual is more tolerant than a monolingual because a bilingual knows that 'reality' can be processed and expressed in more than one way and that there are different cultures and different ways of looking at the universe around us? Attitudinal studies will be very useful in understanding problems. In other words, what is the effect of bilingualism on a bilingual?
b) in understanding the problems in the area of second language teaching, language planning, etc.; for example, we would like to know whether bilingualism is desirable in the field of education, at what level to introduce a second language in the curriculum, how many languages are to be introduced, what the medium of instruction (the primary or the secondary language) should be, at what level and in what subjects (physical sciences, humanities, etc.).
c) in understanding power politics, national integration, unification of the world; for example, how far bilingualism can be exploited to bring people together and create conditions for better understanding.

VIII. In the field of *language education* in bilingual communities the following questions can be raised:

a) Language Policy
- — Should all our students be advised to go in for bilingualism/trilingualism?
- — Should the study of all the two/three languages be compulsory at all stages?
- — Should the policy vary according to the background/needs of the individual, or of the area?
- — What considerations are to be given, if the 'home' dialect is different from the 'standard' variety used in education?

b) Medium of instruction
- — Should all the students be taught at least at different levels through the medium of $L_1/L_2/L_3$ or should the medium of instruction be L_1 only?
- — If English is to be the medium of instruction, at what stage is it to be introduced? Should it be the medium only in higher education?
- — Should the medium be left to the choice of the individual or should it be uniform for an entire area? Should it be uniform for all the subjects taught?
- — What is the justification for saying that science subjects should be taught through the medium of English and social sciences through the medium of the mother tongue?

c) Language teaching methods and materials
- — Should we advocate a bilingual method? How many languages can be used in the classroom?
- — Should we produce bilingual materials?
- — Should all activities in the educational set-up be in all the languages or should there be a dominant language?

d) Other related issues
- — How should we organize training programmes for bilingual education?
- — Should parents be given the choice of selecting the languages to be learnt?
- — How does one get so many trained bilingual teachers in a country like India?
- — How do we motivate the learners to learn two/three languages?

Questions and topics for discussion

1. "And the Lord said, 'Behold the people is one, and they have all one language . . . Let us go down and there confound their language, that they may not understand one another's speech!' So the Lord scattered them abroad from thence upon the face of all the earth."
   - Genesis. Ch. II

   We can say that even the Lord is in favour of bilingualism. Do you agree? State the reasons for your answer.
2. It is generally believed that children educated in their mother tongue can think clearly without getting confused. Do you agree? What are the arguments for and against such a position?
3. Do you think acculturation is necessary for building up a unified world? Give reasons.
4. 'Monolingualism' in the modern world is a myth. Do you agree? Give reasons.
5. What kind of a bilingual are you? Give a brief linguistic profile of yourself.
6. What is the relationship between bilingualism and general intelligence? Illustrate your answer.

5 CODE-SWITCHING AS A COMMUNICATIVE STRATEGY

'These fragments I have shored against my ruins
Why then Ile fit you. Hieronymo's mad againe.
Datta. Dayadhvam. Damyata.
Shantih shantih shantih' *T.S. Eliot*

Focal points

I. Every normal, well-formed human being has at his/her disposal a repertoire of linguistic choices, from which (s)he selects for each situation type the appropriate stock of available harmonies in the appropriate key—his/her choice of items is conditioned by the topic of discourse and the networks of interlocking socio-cultural relations. Most of us are members of several speech networks. Exponents of sociolinguistics maintain that the ability to use one's language correctly in a variety of socially determined situations is as much and as central a part of linguistic 'competence' as the ability to produce grammatically well-formed sentences. What we do actually produce is a rule-governed realization of a complex network of situationally and culturally determined choices.

II. Since these choices are situationally determined, shifts in situations require shifts in language varieties. In order to understand this activity fully, we will have to examine role relationships, types of interaction, and situationally relevant domains. They may be analysed in terms of the following components and their interrelations:

a)	participants (addresser and addressee	-	their sociopsychological behaviour; their mood and their relative social positions.
b)	socio-cultural setting	-	its distinguishing features.
c)	topic of discourse.		

III. Members of social networks sharing a linguistic repertoire must (and do) know when to shift from one variety to another. One category of such shifts is that known as situational shifts. A shift in situation may require a shift in language variety. A shift in language variety may signal a shift in the relationship between co-members of a social network, or a shift in the topic and purpose of their interaction, or a shift in the privacy or locale of their interaction. It may be represented diagrammatically as:

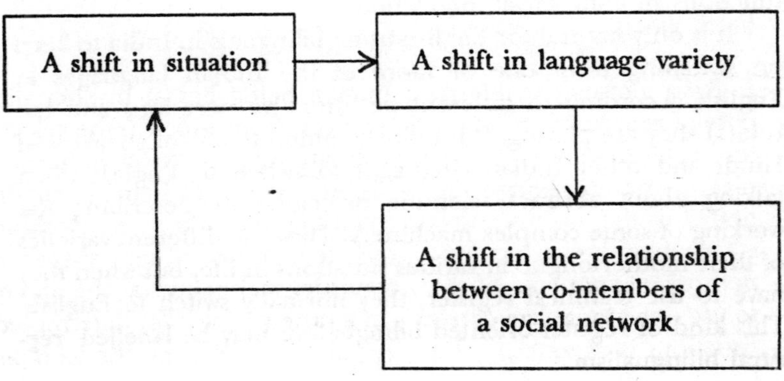

This situation is more difficult in the case of bilinguals and multilinguals who select different varieties of two or more languages to meet the requirements of different situations. Their choices are conditioned by their concepts of appropriateness and effeciveness. They tend to switch from Code A to Code B and from Code B to Code C and so on. This means that they produce a chain of codes.

It is clear then that code-switching (switching from Code A to Code B) cannot simply be a matter of free individual choice. It is a verbal strategy used by speakers in much the same way as creative artists switch styles and levels. Each type of coding or code-switching is appropriate to the topical and situational features that give rise to it. Certain topics are handled better or more appropriately in one language than in another in particular bilingual contexts.

IV. In India English-using bilinguals behave in certain distinguishing ways. English has until very recently been the language of instruction, administration, and technical education. It is even now used as the medium of instruction at the post-graduate level and also in technical education. It is commonly used as the language of all-India seminars and workshops on technical topics. Higher education has thus far meant English-based education. Most of the textbooks, reference materials and journals on technical subjects are in English. The language of conversation among the elite in clubs, officers' mess, central offices is English. English and the major Indian languages have coexisted within the same linguistic area as part of the same socio-economic complex for years. Both the codes have been serving important functions in daily social interaction.

It is only natural for English-using bilinguals in India to keep on switching from one or more of the Indian languages to English according to different performative occasions and the role(s) they are playing. It is quite common today for speakers of Hindi and other Indian languages to switch to English when talking about abstract scientific principles or describing the working of some complex machinery. They use different varieties of their mothertongue in various situations in life, but when they have to use technical register, they normally switch to English. This kind of register-oriented bilingualism may be labelled 'registral bilingualism'.

V. Let us now consider the following extracts which show different types of switching and different degrees of mixture:

Dr. Prasad : Hullo Sinha! How are you?
Dr. Sinha : I am fine. Thank you.
Dr. Prasad : kyon bhaaii! idhar nazar nahiin aate. mahiinon guzar gaye. mulaakaat nahiin huii. (My brother! How come you are not seen these days. Months have gone by; we haven't seen each other.)
Dr. Sinha : yah to tumne thiik hii kahaa. main idhar baraabar baahar hii baahar Tuar kartaa rahaa. (You are right. I have been away on tour.)

Note: Dr. Prasad and Dr. Sinha are highly educated. They belong to sophisticated upper middle class families. Their children go to English-medium schools. Their servants have been trained to address them as "saahib" and their wives as "memsaahib". They use a variety of English lexical items in their ordinary, everyday conversation in Hindi. In the extract given above expressions of phatic communion (which constitute purely operational language activity) are entirely in English. Not that they are not familiar with expressions like 'namaste' and 'kyaa samaacaar hai?', but that the formula-type expressions in English are class markers. They are supposed to place them in educated (upper) middle class. They are markers of higher education and social status. English is used as a superposed elite variety. Hindi expressions reflect personal involvement and intimacy. It is one of the marked features of English-dominated collegiate education that the bilinguals keep on throwing in complete English sentences, clauses, and phrases in conversations which are supposed to be one of the Indian languages. The chief regulators of Hindi-English code-switching or of mixture of Hindi-English styles are level of education and topic of discourse. The higher level of education and the more technical the topic of discourse, the greater is the degree of mixture and frequency of switching. It may, therefore, be said that the bilingual's switching is patterned and predictable on the basis of topical and situational features.

VI. English is used in highly formal situations to talk about technical topics; Hindi and other major Indian languages are used for intimate, informal, personalized statements. In between these two extreme ends we find different degrees of English-dominated and

Hindi-dominated mixtures. This cline may be shown as:

⟵⟶

English English dominated Hindi dominated Hindi

VII. Some of the main features of code-switching may now be summed up:

a) Intralanguage and interlanguage switching are sociolinguistic universals. No normal person, and no normal community is limited in repertoire to a single variety of code. Bilinguals and bidialectals use code-switching naturally as a verbal strategy, for the ability to switch codes controls the ability to switch roles. If people are to make themselves understood in varying contexts today, they must often switch from one code to another. Code-switching in multilingual settings is regulated by the topic of discourse and stylistic (formal-informal) considerations. "The fact that two individuals who usually speak to each other primarily in X nevertheless switch to Y (or vacillate noticeably between X and Y) when discussing certain topics leads us to consider topic per se as a regulator of language use in multilingual settings. The implication of topical regulation of language choice is that certain topics are somehow handled 'better' or more appropriately in one language than in other in particular multilingual contexts." (Fishman, 1972, p.439). Some speakers acquire the habit of speaking about topic *X* in language *A* partly because that is the language in which they are trained to deal with the topic, and partly because language *B* may currently lack as exact and as many terms for handling topic *X* as language *A* has. The speakers do not radically switch from one style to another, but they build on the co-existence of alternative forms to create meaning. Switching from one code to another is not a matter of free individual choice. It is affected by topical and situational features, which determine the speaker's choice from among a set of available codes. "One of the basic assumptions of Bernstein's theory (1958) was that Elaborated Code speakers would tend to be able to switch from one code to another according to the demands of the situation whereas the Restricted Code user would tend to be confined to one code." (Lawton, 1968: 131). We switch codes either because the topics of discourse demand different codes or because our role and the participants involved make us switch our codes.

b) The switchers use English words and expressions even when equivalents exist in Hindi. They feel that these English expressions come so naturally to them that their equivalents in Hindi might sound formal and unnatural.

c) Some of the formulaic expressions in English are now so deeply embedded in urban bilingual societies that they come out naturally in informal conversations.

d) There is so much of English around and it is so much in active use that switching from Hindi to English takes place automatically and unconsciously. Educated speakers tend to switch freely and insert entire English sentences, clauses, and phrases in their Hindi discouse. "But the lacing of L_1 utterances with L_2 items is not confined to multilingual societies. It is likely to happen wherever a foreign language is a mark of social distinction and the sole medium of language activity in certain registers" (Halliday, et al, 1964: 102).

e) Code-switching is context-governed. If the interlocutors have a degree in English and use English as their medium of lecturing or in their office work, they are likely to use information carrying items of English and the linkers of Hindi. If their topic of discourse is technical, their registral items are likely to be from English and the grammatical items from Hindi. Code-switching, one might say, is a marked badge of educated, urban bilinguals.

f) The preponderance of a particular set of lexical items of a code depends upon our emotional and intellectual attachment to the code. Bhojpuri speakers at Patna, for example, use Hindi sentences and phrases only in formal situations. In their normal intra-group conversations they always use Bhojpuri syntax and Bhojpuri lexicon. They may be said to alternate between in-group and out-group modes of expression.

g) What is significant today is not that English is used in X situations and Hindi in Y situations, but that Hindi-English is being used more and more in informal, everyday conversations. It would be interesting to examine the quantum of

English that goes into Hindi conversations and the modifications that English patterns undergo in terms of Hindi systems. Gumperz noted 'code-switching styles' of Hindi and Punjabi spoken in Delhi appropriate to specific social roles in which contact is made with the other languages. Switching between Hindi and Punjabi in Delhi gives rise to mixed styles of speech which illustrate how languages can 'seem to merge' in 'stable bilingual communities'. "One striking linguistic aspect of the code-switching situation is the fact that we find few of the strictures against structural borrowing commonly reported in the linguistic literature. Interference extends to all levels of the grammar—morphemic, morphophonemic and phonological—as well as to lexicon. It almost seems as if the two languages were gradually merging" (Gumperz, 1964:1123).

h) Code mixtures yield new collocations, such as "eDyukeshan paanaa', 'fuul banaanaa', 'reporT karnaa'... and so on. One of the regular patterns of the lexical verb in Hindi is Noun/Adjective + karnaa/paanaa/banaanaa/honaa etc. Here in each Noun/Adjective slot we have an English item.

i) The bidimensional diagram given below shows the code or codes that the speakers tend to select in the given situations: Code-switching reveals certain patterns and regularities rather than purely random or idiosyncratic manifestations:

Topic	*Manner*	*Speaker's choice*
Sermon or Prayer	Formal/Informal	Hindi
Instruction to servants	Informal	Hindi
Personal letters	Informal	Hindi/English/ Hindi-English
Speech on technical subjects	Formal	English
University lecture (technical)	Formal	English/Hindi-English
Conversation	Informal	Hindi-English
Newsbroadcast	Formal	Hindi/English
Buying and selling	Informal	Hindi
	Formal	Hindi/English

j) It has been stated earlier on that mixed languages are a natural by-product of language-contact situations. We would, however, like to mention here that the use of L_2 in situations for which the L_1 is adequately developed, and of L_2 words, phrases, and clauses in L_1 utterances where equivalents are available in L_1, tends to inhibit the progress of the L_1 towards regaining its full status in the community. It also creates socio-psychological complexes among the speakers of this mixed language. If these speakers feel ashamed of using their L_1 expressions in certain situations, it means that they have suffered a basic injury as human beings.

Questions and topics for discussion

1 "No normal person, and no normal community is limited in repertoire to a single variety of a code, to an unchanging monotony which would preclude the possibility of indicating respect, insolence, mockseriousness, humour, role-distance, etc. by switching from one code variety to another." (Dell Hymes). Do you agree with Hymes? How is this position different from Chomsky's concepts of 'ideal speaker-listener' and 'homogeneous speech community'.

2 Code-switching and code-mixing may be treated as the two ends of a cline. Give examples to illustrate this statement.

3 Our teachers in regional medium institutions are using code-switching as a strategy to teach science and technology. Give examples to prove this.

4. Give examples of the following:
   a) Code-switching (English and your first language)
   b) Dialect switching
   c) Register switching
   d) Style switching

5. Analyse the following sentence in terms of code-switching/codemixing:

   "yah insTiTyuuT apne fiild me baRaa yuuniik hai"
   (This Institute is very unique in its field).

6 LINGUISTIC AND SOCIAL INEQUALITY

'All animals are equal but some animals are more equal than others.' - *George Orwell*

Focal points

I. Very few people realise that language planning is as important as family planning in a country like India. In a multilingual country, language planning is central to educational planning and economic planning. The three major problems in our country are:

a) absence of language planning,
b) lack of political will to implement and organize policies and programmes, and
c) lack of coordination among the various agencies (the Governments at the Centre and States, universities, the Directorates, and other agencies working in the area of language teaching and language planning).

Since we have failed to have a well-defined language policy, we have no sense of direction and the gulf between the 'haves' and 'have nots' in our society has been widening.

II. The term *language planning* has been defined as follows:

> *Language planning* is a term used in socio-linguistics to refer to a systematic attempt to solve the communication problems of a community by studying the various languages or dialects it uses and developing a realistic policy concerning the selection and use of different languages.
>
> (David Crystal (1980) *Dictionary of Linguistics and Phonetics*).

Like bilingual studies, language planning has concerns about language and society at three levels: individual, societal, and governmental.

At every level decisions will have to be taken regarding

a) How many languages should be learnt/taught and in what order?

b) What should be the medium of instruction? Should it be the same for all subjects in the curriculum?
c) How should we help learners move from 'dialects' to the standard variety? and
d) Should we have the same programme for the privileged as well as the weaker and deprived sections of the community?

Documents produced by the Government of India support the three language formula for the language curriculum. But the government has not specified the details like what precisely the three languages are and at what stage each one is to be introduced and to be discontinued; there are hardly any guidelines regarding the ordering of L_1, L_2, L_3,..., the level of proficiency to be achieved in each. As a consequence, each state in India follows its own policy. The Government of Tamil Nadu follows a two-language formula (Tamil and English) and the Government of Uttar Pradesh has imposed a ban on English as the medium of instruction in schools; the Government of India has not spelt out clearly whether Maithili and Hindi could be treated as two languages or one. What is urgently needed is to specify the roles and functions of the national official language, state official language, English, and the languages of the minorities.

III. Sociolinguists like Haugen (1966, 1969) have suggested some parameters for language planning:

a) *Selection:* A particular language or language variety must be specified as the variety to be used in educational settings. It may be a variety useful for political and commercial activities. This is a political decision to be taken by the government based on consensus.
b) *Codification:* Some agency must produce reference materials (like dictionaries and grammar books) as well as teaching and testing materials so that the codified variety is properly taught and learnt. This is a process of stabilization.
c) *Acceptance:* Once the codified variety is accepted by the people, it serves as a unifying force, as a symbol; the symbolic function is in its association with patriotism, nation building, etc.

d) *Elaboration of function:* This involves the expansion of the language function and the assignment of new roles to the chosen variety; modernization of the variety such as evolving technical terms, etc.

There is ample scope for debate in this area. For example, can an academy or a government agency project one variety or one language as the standard for all? Will it be taken as 'imposition'? Hindi in Tamil Nadu is looked upon as an imposition. Coastal Andhra varieties of Telugu in the Telengana area are considered an imposition. These are very sensitive issues that are to be handled with great care and wisdom. The problem raises certain theoretical issues in sociolinguistics:

a) Can languages and varieities be standardized?
b) How can languages and varieties be used for exploitation and manipulation by interested groups?
c) Are standard languages and varieties unreal and pathological since they lack vitality, diversity, and creativity?

These are interesting questions worth studying in language planning.

IV. It is appropriate to mention the work of Bernstein here (1958, 1959, 1971); he looks at the problem of communication in a socio-cultural matrix in terms of the social classes and their use of language. He makes a distinction between the 'elaborated code' (i.e., the language) used by the middle class and the 'restricted code' used by the working class. According to Bernstein, the elaborated code is accurate and has a complex grammar but the restricted code is grammatically simple.

Bernstein has been the chief inspiration behind the theory of 'language deficit' or 'verbal deprivation' and the resultant concept of 'compensatory education'. The theory of 'language deficit' assumes that working-class children do not do well at school because they suffer from cognitive deficiencies in the absence of their access to the elaborated code; they cannot organize their experience and interpret the world the way middle-class children do. This leads to a circularity; language deprivation resulting in cognitive deprivation leads on to further language deprivation.

However, sociolinguists like Labov (1972) have attacked the very premises on which the deficit theorists rested their case. Labov, based on his empirical work carried out in Martha's Vineyard (a small island off the New England Coast in the USA) and later in New York, shows that non-standard varieties like the so-called restricted code are rule-governed systems in their own right, not poor replicas of the standard variety; in other words, the non-standard varieties are different but not deficient. Secondly, Labov shows through his samples of speech recorded in natural settings (as opposed to test situations from which the deficit theorists drew their evidence) that speakers of non-standard varieties like Black English are capable of complex, logical, symbolic and expressive speech. We tend to use the norms of the standard variety and label the non-standard ones as 'incorrect' and 'illogical'; this is the result of middle-class bias. This means that the users of the non-standard dialects are not linguistically deprived and this, in turn, means that compensatory language programmes which try to fill in the 'gaps' and try remediation are inappropriate.

This is an extreme position to take since the 'difference thesis' does not take into account social attitudes; it may be true that *linguistically* language varieties are equal and each variety is a complex system and adequate to express the ideas and feelings of the community that uses it; varieties of a language are different but not deficient. But, *socially, varieties are unequal and some are more equal than others,* because there are other socio-cultural, political and economic factors affecting our attitudes to language varieties; though not linguistically deficient, users of the non-standard varieties are at a disadvantage because their language variety (accent, vocabulary, syntax, etc.) is at odds with the norm; in order to succeed in the society in which they live the non-standard forms should be supplemented (not substituted since that will be met with hostile behaviour on the part of the non-standard speakers and hence doomed to failure) and complemented with the more widely socially-accepted forms.

Such decisions are to be taken by educationists on the basis of research and findings made available, in part, by sociolinguists. At present, we lack information about the linguistic structures characteristic of different varieties of a given language. The standard text books prescribed may pose serious comprehension difficulties to the learners who have a different linguistic background such as the non-standard variety. Teachers too are familiar with the gap between the technical vocabulary of the specialist subject and the ordinary use of language; but they fail to recognise the gap between the variety they use and the variety used by their students. We must be able to identify the features of different varieties and extend the learners' language resources to cope with the demands of such varieties in order to minimize social inequalities.

V. In multilingual societies, different languages and varieties often serve different functions, and any simple assumption regarding language and its equality or inequality will obscure sociolinguistic data.

For example, in India English is used in science, technology, international commerce and higher level academic transactions; the regional languages are used in religion, music, social gatherings, etc. In other words, English is used as the language of modernization and science and technology and other Indian languages as the language of intimacy. English and the regional languages play a complementary role in Indian society.

As pointed out earlier, all languages are equal in the sense that all human languages have a built-in potential for expressing concepts, feelings, and experiences and fulfilling all functions. But, like human beings, languages have evolved differently through processes of variation, adaptation, and selection in different socio-cultural-economic-political-technological environments. The fact that each language may have the potential to perform various functions (just as each person may have the potential to perform various functions) does not alter what they are doing at a given point of time; the distinction here is between 'can do' and 'are doing'. In terms of what they are doing, languages have different functions; in terms of what they can do they have the same potential.

For example, English, whether we like it or not, has become the language of international communication and the language of science and technology; it has been shaped so by historical forces and has developed the resources in such areas as science and technology; whereas languages like Sanskrit and other Indian languages have developed their potentialities in areas like religion, philosophy, music, dance, etc. We cannot ignore this in the name of patriotism or anticolonialism. English, for a vast majority of Indians today, is the language of science and technology. Efforts are on to develop Indian languages too in these areas. But before becoming emotional on language issues one should bear in mind the cost factor attached to developing a language. As Dell Hymes says (1973:73), 'The cost, as between expressing things easily and concisely, and expressing them with difficulty and at great length, is a real cost, commonly operating, and a constraint on the theoretical potentiality of language in daily life.' The cost of ignoring science and technology, the cost of developing technical terms and other materials like books, etc., the cost of translation, and the cost we shall be paying for imprecise expressions are to be taken into account. In the modern world complexity is part of life and one must know how to strike a balance.

At the government level, the question presents itself of how much diversity, inequality and autonomy may exist within a nation without threatening the strength of that nation and without uprooting individual identities and the identities of groups and communities. Though all societies have moved towards greater equality among their members, at any given point of time inequalities have existed at various levels according to the dynamics of the polity governing a society. In the 1980s the question of linguistic nationalities has become a thorny question even in socialist countries like Russia, where there had been systematic language planning for nearly half-a-century. Though a common language is the cement of unity in the case of a nation, we must try to find this unity in diversity; unity should not be mistaken for uniformity.

If we recognize the complementary roles of languages, varieties, registers, styles, etc. this problem of competition and confrontation can be converted into responsive co-operation. A careful study of the tensions created by language issues in any given society may give the right direction to the policies of a government. At the international level, if we take into consideration readily available international airtravel, satellite communication, mass media, etc. no country can live isolated from, or unaffected by, others. All these points have to be borne in mind when one discusses issues relating to language planning.

Questions and topics for discussion

1. Can Bernstein's notion of restricted code be related to the notion of linguistic incompetence?
2. Language prejudices play an important role in creating social prejudices. Can you illustrate this with some examples?
3. All normal people are equal with regard to their language. Comment.
4. Hudson says that there are three types of inequality:
   a) Subjective inequality—What people *think,* which may or may not be true; this may be unreliable.
   b) Strictly linguistic inequality—the effective range of a given variety of language; this may be applicable to an individual or a group.
   c) Communicative inequality—inability to interact in social contexts.

   Give examples of the three kinds.
5. Educational failure is a case of language failure—Explain and illustrate.
6. Language planning, like family planning, is an emotional issue. Explain and illustrate.
7. In a multilingual society there are tensions. Can you think of countries other than India, where there are linguistic tensions? Compare one such instance with the Indian situation.
8. How can we accommodate all dialects in language planning?
9. It is said that *language status* decisions are influenced by ideological and political considerations, powerful groups, and other forces. How will you react to such a statement with reference to the problem of official language in India?
10. In multilingual societies tensions are created basically because of the sense of insecurity; one group may invade the other and eliminate it linguistically. Whether it is an individual or a group, the problem of identity is crucial. Comment on this with reference to linguistic minorities in India.
11. 'Members of a complex society belong to groups at many different levels—the household, the peer-group, the region or city or village, the socio-economic class, and the nation, to mention a few of the groupings involved (which may cut across each other as well as being arranged in a part-whole relationship). If there is a conflict between two groupings (i.e., if the values of the nation conflict with those of regionally and socially based groups), the values of the nation may triumph at the expense of those of the less powerful group.' (Hudson). Explain this with reference to the language problem in India.

12. **Some groups do *not* believe that they speak better than others, but, on the contrary, think that they think and speak badly. Labov calls this linguistic insecurity. Can you give some examples of this type of situation in India where we say we don't speak even our mother tongue properly?**
13. **If you were appointed the Chairman of the Language Planning Commission of India, what recommendations would you make?**

7 LANGUAGE AND CULTURE

Cultures are organisms, and world-history is their collective biography.'
- Oswald Spengler

Focal points

I. Language is *culture-preserving* as well as *culture-transmitting*. That was why, Descartes said, 'Thanks to language, Man became Man.' In this very statement, Descartes has used the term *man* to refer to all human beings (men, women and children)! There are well-known statements like 'The proper study of mankind is Man' (Pope), 'The child is father of the man' (Wordsworth), 'Man is the measure of all things' (Pythagoras), etc. that reflect the patriarchal culture of the society in which 'man' is taken as a generic term; this aspect of culture has been preserved and transmitted to future generations. Though there are other forms that preserve culture, such as music, painting, etc., language is the most common and dynamic form in which culture is preserved and transmitted.

Culture has been defined as the sum of transmitted behaviour patterns, arts, beliefs, institutions, and all other products of human work and thoughts characteristic of a community or population. These characteristics are all transmitted by language; they are not inherited through the genes. An English baby taken away from the parents shortly after birth and raised in a tribal society would be, except for certain physiological features, the same as all other children born and brought up in that society.

II. Culture and language are so tightly related that they may be regarded as parts of the same thing. No case is known of either a language or a culture existing without the other. Obviously, no language can survive in isolation and no civilization can be built up without language. Cultural changes tend to occur along with changes in language; the two proceed reinforcing each other.

As Indo-Aryan dialects changed over the years into different languages like Gujarati, Marathi, Punjabi, Bengali, Assamese, etc., the cultural patterns got differentiated. Emanating from one common source, Aryan culture, there are today markedly different cultures like Gujarati culture, Marathi culture, etc. Even within one speech community, there are cultural variations—in terms of region, class, caste, profession, etc.

III. *Ethnocentricity,* or the belief in the superiority of one's own ethnic group, is manifested in the use of language; ethnocentricism is actually maintained through language by creating myth. Every culture has the process of myth creation through language.

For example, Telugu speakers believe that Telugu is the Italian of the South; the Telugu word for the neighbouring language Tamil is 'aravam', which means 'noise'. French is supposed to be a beautiful language; Tamil is supposed to have been 'born' even before the rock formations of the earth got powdered into sand; Sanskrit is the language of gods. The superiority of the male, as pointed out at the beginning, is another myth found in all languages.

IV. Some scholars have defined culture as socially acquired knowledge:

> ... a society's culture consists of whatever it is one has to know or believe in order to operate in a manner acceptable to its members... Culture, being what people have to learn as distinct from their biological heritage, must consist of the end product of learning: knowledge in a most general sense of the term.
>
> (Goodenough 1957)

If culture is knowledge in a broad sense, one can ask whether it is socially acquired knowledge. Hudson (1980) makes the following distinction:

a) cultural knowledge—which is acquired from people.
b) shared non-cultural knowledge—which is shared by all human beings but not learned from others.
c) non-shared, non-cultural knowledge—which is unique to the individual.

In this schema, some parts of language belong to cultural knowledge; some parts like dimensions, directions, etc. are not learned from other human beings; some are highly individualistic like 'I like the smell of paint, of new books', or 'I don't think that nations exist', etc.

V. It may be said that knowledge, culture, and language are interrelated on a number of dimensions. In sociolinguistics, we must try to study the following:

— How do languages and cultures differ from one another?
— Do they differ arbitrarily and unrestrictively from one another?
— Are there any universals in thought and culture that are reflected in language?

This takes us to the age-old debate between *relativists* and *universalists*.

According to the relativists each language imposes its own grid on the language users' experience and it provides a set of pigeon-holes in terms of which the users of a particular language reduce the world of experience and knowledge to order. The principle *linguistic relativity* or *linguistic determinism*, popularly known as the *Sapir—Whorf hypothesis*, tries to relate thought and conduct to language. According to Benjamin Lee Whorf (1897-1941), who was a student of Edward Sapir (1884-1939), people use their own language to put labels on all observable phenomena and they are conditioned to see only the objects and ideas that can be expressed in the language. 'We dissect nature along lines laid down by our relative language' (Whorf).

Consider the pronominal system of Telugu. It makes use of different degrees of politeness in addresser-addressee interaction as given below:

3rd person, singular, male

waaDu	very informal, intimate, impolite.
atanu	informal, not intimate, third degree respect
aayana	polite, formal, second degree respect
waaru	very polite, first degree respect.

English uses only 'he' for all the four. Does it mean that English users are incapable of expressing different degrees of politeness? Is there anything semantically lacking in the English speaker who uses only one pronoun 'you' corresponding to three pronouns—*tuu, tum,* and *aap*—in Hindi? Does it mean that English, Telugu and Hindi chop up the world in different ways?

The greetings of different cultures, viewed in their original meanings, indicate different concerns. The Arabic *salaam* means 'peace'; the English *hello* originated in 'Healthy be thou'. All these greetings express a basic concern for the other person's well-being, although some are spiritual and some are physical in content.

If one adopts an extreme version of the view that each language forces its users into a particular mental mould, the following questions arise.

a) How is it possible to translate an idea underlying a text in one language into another if the structuring of reality is totally different in each language? Does it mean that if a word is not available in a language, the concept represented by that particular word is also not available? While the Chinese make no distinction between 'he' and 'she' in the spoken language, they are obviously aware of the differences between males and females.
b) A multilingual person has control of two or more languages. He can switch from one language to another in terms of functions. How do the two languages shape his worldview?
c) It is possible that something cannot be *named* in a particular language but it can be *recognized*. English speakers can recognize and name two colours 'yellow' and 'orange'; there are languages where there are no distinct terms for these two colours. Does it mean that they cannot recognize the two colours?

d) If we extend the relativist-hypothesis upto the level of dialects and idiolects (since each person structures reality according to his/her own perception), what will be the consequences?

VI. The *universalists,* on the other hand, propose that all languages share basic common features; this implies the rejection of the assumption that languages differ in innumerable and unpredictable ways. The universalists argue that the differences among languages are found only in their surface structures and at the deeper level there are a number of similarities. Their basic assumption is that a child has an inherent, inborn, innate or genetically programmed capacity for learning any of the human languages.

For example, children all over the world learn the sounds *m* and *p* quite early but sounds such as *r, w* and *l* come later (or not at all). A universal model can be constructed that will have a 'core phonological' system for all languages. In grammar, control of irregular-verb forms is learnt after the child learns the regular forms; this principle of verb regularity can be used in constructing a 'core grammatical' system.

VII. Sociolinguistics tries to strike a balance between the two extreme positions, relativism and universalism. Human language is the product of a series of interactions between an organic entity (called the human being) and his/her environment. The organic entity (because of its particular structure which in turn is the product of historical forces in the evolution of matter) is at once the product of historical evolution and environment. There is thus, a dialectical relationship between the historical process and environmental dynamism for change; thus, language, because of its dialectical nature, is innate as well as social. A dynamic speech community and the individual interact and strike a balance between stability and change, total determinism and total freedom resulting in chaos. The meanings of linguistic items *can* and *have been* adjusted by individuals to fit their needs through extensions; it is not necessary for a whole 'speech community', in the larger sense, to agree on every item and its meaning or meanings, since there are several 'speech communities' (sub-communities) within a 'speech community'. Human beings are similar, in a broad sense, but not identical (not even in the case of twins)!

Questions and topics for discussion

1. ***Mangal sutra*** and ***kumkum*** are culture specific items. Can you think of at least five more culture specific terms from your mother tongue and attempt a description of each in English.
2. Give a list of the colour terms in your mother tongue and compare the list with the terms in English. Comment on the range of vocabulary in the two languages in question.
3. In Telugu there is no distinction between a woman and a dog because the verb ending is the same for both:

   aame vocindi 'she came'
   kukke vocindi 'the dog came'

   On the basis of this can we say that Telugu speakers do not see the difference between a woman and a dog?
4. Coastal Andhra Telugu has a special word for serving rice and it is not used for serving any other item in a meal:
   annam voDDinccandi 'rice serve' (please serve rice!). English uses the word 'serve' for all items. Can we say, on the basis of this, that Telugu is a superior language?
5. Given below is a chart of kinship terms.

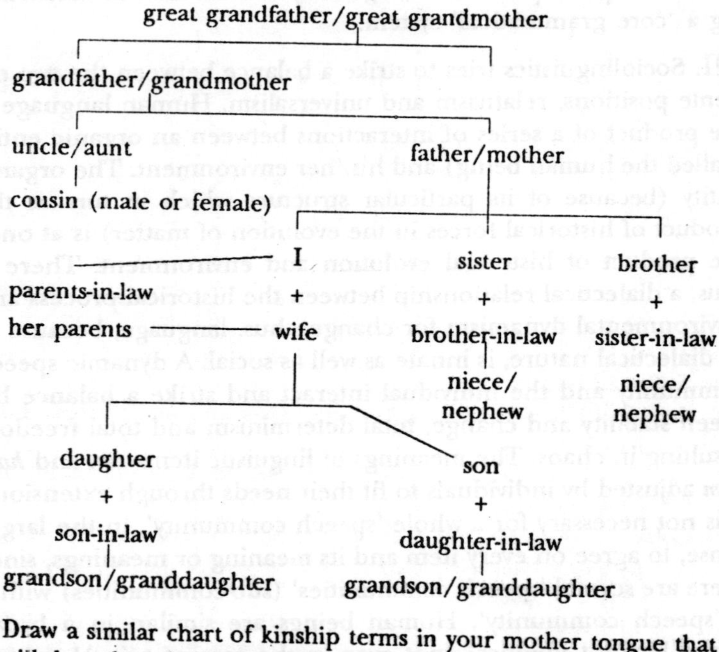

Draw a similar chart of kinship terms in your mother tongue that will show the relationships indicated. Compare the two and explain the differences, if any.

6. Most Indian languages have a network of kinship terms. They have different terms for father's sister's husband and mother's sister's husband, father's brother and mother's brother. English, on the other hand, manages with one multipurpose term 'uncle'. Does this mean that English is poorer than Hindi, Tamil, or Telugu?
7. The word 'cousin' refers to father's or mother's, brother's or sister's son or daughter. Are there different terms for these relationships in your first language? If there are, what does it show?
8. 'East is East, and West is West, and never the twain shall meet.' (Kipling). What does this indicate in terms of culture/linguistic differences?
9. a) The Eskimo has a number of words for *snow* but the English user has only one.
   b) In Arabic there are a number of words for 'camel' but English has only one.
   c) In Tamil there are a number of words for 'rice' but English has only one.

   Do these statements imply that English is a poor language?
10. 'The sexual principle, the man-woman biological difference has become an organizing principle of the most important symbolic order—language.' Explain this statement; illustrate your answer.
11. 'We don't even speak the same language' is a complaint voiced by parents about the younger generation. Can you think of at least ten examples where there is generation-gap in the use of your mother tongue or English.
12. Meaning is not in words; it is in people. Explain and illustrate.
13. " 'Stupidity' does not exist in nature; yet we think it does, because our language has put it there." Can you interpret the Sapir-Whorf hypothesis in a deeper sense to show that all of us are living in the *prison house of language*? Explain your answer with theoretical information given in the seven units you have read so far (in this chapter).

Suggested reading

Bell, R. 1976. *Sociolinguistics : Goals, Approaches and Problems*. London : Batsford.

This book gives a good introduction to the field linking up concepts and research in the field.

Cobarrubias, Juan, and Joshua A. Fishman. (eds.). 1983. *Progress in Language Planning: International Perspectives*. Berlin/New York/Amsterdam: Mouton.

The essays included here are developed on Haugen's (1966) language planning model and Kloss' (1969) distinction between *status*

Hudson, R.A. 1980. *Sociolinguistics*. Cambridge : Cambridge University Press.

This is a very useful textbook on sociolinguistics and it provides a coherent theoretical framework within which the findings of sociolinguistics may be related to a theory of linguistic structure.

Hymes, D.H. 1977. *Foundations in Sociolinguistics*. London : Tavistock Publications Ltd.

This book presents a coherent scheme in the epxression of three themes that Hymes considers 'fundamental' to sociolinguistics : towards ethnographies of communication, the status of Linguistics as a science, and Linguistics as Sociolinguistics.

Knapp, Karlfried, Werner Enninger, and Annelie Knapp-Poth-hoff. (eds.) 1987.

Analysing Intercultural Communication. Berlin/New York/Amsterdam: Walter de Gruyter.

This book addresses itself to intercultural communication which poses a challenge to many of the assumptions on which current linguistic theories are based.

Labov, William. 1972. *Sociolinguistic Patterns*. Philadelphia : Universivy of Pennsylvania Press.

The first part of the book (chapters 2-6) covers a large part of methods and findings of 'The Social Stratification of English in New York City,' and the last part continues the argument in a broader framework.

Milroy, Lesley. 1980. *Language and Social Networks*. Baltimore : University Park Press.

This book represents a synthesis of 'Labov-type' work in social dialectology, 'Gumperz-type' work in the social anthropology of language, and work in the social psychology of language.

Paradis, Michel. (ed.). 1978. *Aspects of Bilingualism*. Columbia, South Carolina : Hornbeak Press, Inc.

This book presents the picture of multidisciplinarity of studies in Bilingualism covering a) developmental, b) linguistic, c) pedagogical, d) psycholinguistic and neurolinguistic & e) sociolinguistic aspects of Bilingualism.

Pride, J.B., and J. Holmes. (eds.) 1972. *Sociolinguistics*. Penguin.

This is an interesting collection of original papers for those who want more details and more advanced articles on the state of research in sociolinguistics.

Saville-Troike, Muriel. 1982. *The Ethnography of Communication: An Introduction*. Oxford : Basil Blackwell.

This book presents a comprehensive introduction to the subject. The essential terms and concepts introduced by Dell Hymes and others are clearly explained, and related to recent theoretical developments.

Trudgill, P. 1974. *Sociolinguistics: An Introduction.* Penguin.
This is a clear introduction to the field. There is a good discussion of the relations between language and social class, and of educational issues.

Verma, S.K., and N. Krishnaswamy. 1989. *Modern Linguistics: An Introduction.* Delhi : Oxford University Press.
A very good introduction to sociolinguistics is given, though the book is an introductory course in theoretical linguistics.

CHAPTER TWO

Language and Mind

What is mind? No matter. What is matter? Never mind.

8 LANGUAGE AS A PSYCHOLOGICAL SYSTEM

'Language doesn't exist; it happens'.

Focal points

I. Descartes said, 'Thanks to language, Man became Man'. But what is language? Does it exist somewhere or does it happen? Is it a social phenomenon or an individual phenomenon? Is it used only for communication or is it used for communion? Is it logical or psychological? Questions can be multiplied but finding anwers is difficult; what is important is not the answer but the search for the answer.

Animals have their systems of communication transmitted genetically from generation to generation; they are unchanging and stereotyped. A newborn puppy, removed from its mother and other dogs and raised in a laboratory, would, after several years, be able to communicate with other dogs, though it had not in the meantime encountered others of its species. A puppy in U.P. and a puppy in London use the same system of communication unaffected by what is used by people.

Only the human baby must start from scratch and learn the language spoken by its parents and others in the community. A number of theories have been proposed to explain how this takes place. John Locke, the seventeenth century English philosopher, believed that at birth the human mind is a 'tabula rasa' or a 'clean slate' waiting for impression and experience to make their recordings there. In the eighteenth century, Johann Guttfried von Herder, a German philosopher, suggested that language was too imperfect to have been a divine gift and that it was the result of an 'instinctive impulse similar to that of an embryo pressing to be born,' which implies that it is an inherent impulse. A century later, Charles Darwin argued in his *Descent of Man* (1871) that there is only a difference of degree between the language of human beings and the language of animals. This debate continues even today. In 1957, B.F. Skinner in his *Verbal Behaviour* pointed out that language is learned from the environment, whereas Chomsky (1957), in his *Syntactic Structures* claimed that language formations do not come from a memorized stock and that the child has the *ability* to generate an infinite number of well-formed sentences that were not spoken or heard before.

Whether the built-in impulse to talk emerges from a specific and isolated section of the brain, or whether the language-faculty is a nonlocalized psychological trait exclusive to human beings, is still not known. We only know that a neural equipment that is complex is present in the human brain but, at the same time, we know that languages are learned. Children, isolated from exposure to any human language, though do not spontaneously begin to use a language, do learn to speak if supported by the environment. Early in this century, two children in India, Kamala and Amala were found living with wolves; they behaved in every way like wolves and did not speak any human language when they were located. The younger one died before any speech-training experiment was conducted but the older one lived, and eventually learned to speak a few words only. Judging from such limited studies, one can only say that if the first speech impulses of children are not reinforced through social support, the innate impulse may die; this means that human beings, though born with a language faculty, must be supported in their speech development from the very beginning by constant reinforcement from others in society.

II. A study of language in relation to society, as discussed in Chapter I, is sociolinguistics and a study of language in relation to the human mind is *psycholinguistics*. In other words, psycholinguistics is a study of the relationship between language as a network of relations and the human mind, a study that might offer fresh insights into the nature of the human mind.

The birth of psycholinguistics as a discipline may be credited to the conference in 1951 sponsored by the Social Science

Research Council that brought together several leading psychologists and linguists; the proceedings of the conference outlined a psycholinguistic reseach agenda that reflected a consensus among the participants that the methodological and theoretical tools developed by psychologists can be used to explore language and language acquisition.

The earlier phrase 'psychology of language' and the new term 'psycholinguistics' represent the shift of focus in our approaches to the study of language behaviour. Earlier, particularly in behaviouristic psychology, it was claimed that verbal responses are directly related to stimuli without any need for intervening variables such as meaning, ideas or the processing of grammatical rules; meaning was brought in only to study meaning responses to individual words, with less emphasis on the problem of meanings of sentences, statements and connected speech. To indicate a change in focus the term 'psycholinguistics' was used in the early 1950s and the new term refers to the entire approach to the study of language behaviour and the emphasis on the 'creative' aspect of the language user's ability to produce language.

Psycholinguistic studies may be broadly classified into three types according to the following questions:

a) how language is *acquired* during development,
b) how language is *comprehended*, and
c) how language is *produced*.

Of these, studies on language acquisition are referred to as *developmental psycholinguistics* and the other two as *experimental psycholinguistics*.

III. Anyone who has observed children learning languages can perceive that the processes involved in the development of language learning are quite mysterious. A baby's very first sounds can hardly be called speech sounds; the baby's cries - signal hunger, thirst, or some other discomfort, or they are a part of an instinctive testing of the muscles and organs (of speech) like the vocal cords; these cries are organically determined. After two or three months, the baby moves into the *babbling stage;* at this stage the sounds signify something. It is at this stage that the prelinguistic sounds gradually progress to imitative sounds. When the baby moves towards the twelfth-month stage, an average infant (i.e. one without any brain damage or other deformities) takes note of the speakers around him/her, usually the parents. The self-stimulating babbling gives way to stimulation from others around; by twelve months, the perceptive development progresses to the point where sound patterns made by others can be reproduced. The baby's gradual physical growth is accompanied by the equally gradual development of the speech areas of the brain and the speech apparatus too keeps on developing, slowly. At about seventeen or eighteen months, the child understands and responds to simple utterances and understanding usually precedes production of speech. Even before a child is two years old, his/her vocabulary increases considerably and (s)he can form two- and three-word utterances; we do not know much as yet about the child's full awareness of the range of meaning of each item of vocabulary. At this stage there are mostly single symbols and there is no notion of syntax. For example, 'mamagive' is a single symbol relating to 'mama give'; *maaduudh* stands for 'Mummy, give me some milk'. Sometime after the second year, the child begins to recognize that single word symbols can be broken into parts. This is the *analytic* stage; the child experiments, puts together parts and tests them on others, usually the parents. The child at this stage is not concerned with truth and only plays with words as though they are toys. Her/his linguistic behaviour is not conditioned fully by adult semantics. It is still the trial-and-error stage of learning the language and he/she is amused by the play of words and their arrangements. Along with this, the child's memory increases and, by three, longer units of increasing complexity begin to appear. It has been observed that the child internalizes his/her native language by the time (s)he is six years old; this means, the child has developed an intuitive knowledge of the rules by which the acceptable sentences never used before are generated and sentences never heard before are understood. The learning processes continue as (s)he moves about in society and constant experimentation goes on with new forms and styles. But the speed with which a child learns the language during the first six years decreases in later years and the 'hard work' that the child puts in so naturally in the early years to categorize the universe around him/her is amazing.

This is a brief profile of the language learner.

IV. This profile raises a number of issues in psycholinguistics. The number of possible grammatical sentences in any language is potentially infinite, since it is always possible for a user to produce some new combinations not used before: there is no theoretical limit to the number of new sentences that can be produced. The question that we have to answer is: how is it, then, that a child is able to internalize this kind of capability in terms of a finite number of sentences to which (s)he is exposed in the process of language acquisition? Secondly, even assuming that there are some limits to the number of possible sentences in a language, the child could not have experienced all the possible sentences in a language. This means that a child without experiencing all possible sentences is able to make a number of generalizations regarding sentences (acceptable as well as unacceptable) in that language; this 'creative' aspect of the language user's ability is to be captured and explained in any study. Thirdly, is the ability to generalize restricted only to language acquisition or is it characteristic of all human cognitive, perceptual, and even motor skills? For example, the ability to use one's car-driving 'rules' to develop a new combination of feet and hand movements when asked to drive a new car can be compared to the use of generative rules to generate new sentences. Fourthly, does the acquisition of a second language proceed along the same lines as that of the first language? To what extent does memory play a role in language learning? Such issues become the central concern in psycholinguistics.

V. It must be pointed out that in the 1950s it was the thinking of Chomsky that directly stimulated psycholinguistic experiments in the field of language acquisition. Chomsky's criticisms of the behaviouristic approach to the study of language and his view on the appropriate goals of linguistic theory made a significant contribution to cognitive psychology and his formulation of the issue of language acquisition provided a framework for developmental psycholinguistics. His framework of transformational generative grammar guided much of the first decade of research in experimental psycholinguistics.

The developments in the area of information processing pioneered by cognitive psychologists and computer scientists gave a great deal of support to Chomskyan formulations in the 1960s, but by the middle of the 1970s psycholinguistics became more a part of cognitive psychology because of the complex and competing formulations in the generativists' camp. The focus shifted from syntactic variables in sentence processing to higher level processes in the comprehension of discourses and texts and other processes such as the recognition of lexical and sub-lexical units. In addition to the study of literal meaning, psycholinguists began to study the processing of meaning in the case of idioms, metaphors, etc. The speech act theory of Grice (1967) and Searle (1969) also influenced studies in psycholinguistics.

During the middle of 1970s, the comprehension of stories and texts emerged as an important research area and a number of theoretical models were suggested. As cognitive psychologists became more interested in discourse and text studies, interest in inferential meaning, anaphora and antecedents, interpretation of anaphoric meaning, and information processing emerged as the central area in research.

In the 1980s, a more integrated approach to the study of language emerged; the term *recognition* was made broad-based to include not only word recognition but also syntactic processing, higher-order syntactic and semantic structures.

VI. Like Chomskyan formulations research in artificial intelligence has also influenced psycholinguistics. Digital computers, since they manipulate symbols, argued some theorists of artificial intelligence, provide both a theoretical and a methodological model for understanding intelligent behaviour. The symbol manipulation idea merged with the view that the cognitive system is an information-processing system to form a new information-processing approach. The most significant influence of artificial intelligence on psycholinguistics relates to the work on language understanding and knowledge representation. The computational work within artificial intelligence has also been a source of continuous influence on psycholinguistics, most significantly at the methodological level. Computer simulations have provided psycholinguistics with a powerful tool for making their theories more explicit. The computational approach has helped in clarifying the possible relationships between 'competence' and 'performance' theories. The influence of artificial intelligence on psycholinguistics continues in areas like knowledge representation, discourse structure and parsing.

Questions and topics for discussion

1. 'The essence of language is human activity — activity on the part of one individual to make himself understood, and activity on the part of the other to understand what was in the mind of the first. These two individuals, the producer and the recipient of language, or as we may more conveniently call them, the speaker and the hearer, should never be lost sight of if we want to understandthe nature of language.' — Otto Jespersen.
   Can you restate Jespersen's ideas in terms of Chomskyan terminology?
2. What is it that you know when you know a language?
3. a) A bird trainer gives a few grains to a parrot when it repeats the word he utters.
   b) A mother kisses her baby when the baby repeats the word she utters. Can you relate the two and comment?
4. Do you think that repetition has no role to play in language learning? Think of your first language and how you learnt it.
5. Do you think that parents, by repeating words and sentences, can accelerate the learning process and make a genius out of a child?
6. Long-term memory is related to the notion of rules and short-term memory to repetition. How will you react to this sort of compromise formula?
7. A child in the third year may say 'Doggie bite daddy' or 'Daddy bite doggie'. At this stage can we say (s)he is an incorrigible liar?
8. A child, in the course of about six years, is exposed to only a limited number of sentence-types; though the exposure or input is limited, the production or output is unlimited, since the capacity to generate an unlimited number of sentences is what (s)he is born with. How can we resolve this problem?
9. Can we make an exhaustive list of words, phrases, and sentences? What is the motivation for developing rules as compared to listing items?
10. 'Language learning is not like acting in a play; it is more like writing one.' What are the implications of this statement?

9 LANGUAGE ACQUISITION

'The child is father of the man'

— *Wordsworth*

Focal points

I. The child manages to internalize the linguistic systems of her/his father/mother in about six years, but philosophers, linguists, and psychologists have not been able to externalize it even in two thousand years! Although many observations have been made about language acquisition, only recently some systematic work has been done in the area.

Chomsky has argued that the linguistic input to which a child is exposed is too impoverished for him/her to bring about a correlation between a complex network of meanings and linguistic forms. So the child, according to Chomsky, ought to be in possession of some 'language universals' as 'latent knowledge structures' and that should form the basis for all our explanations. During the 1960s, Chomsky's proposals about language acquisition were contrasted with the behaviourist accounts in which language learning was explained through mechanisms such as *imitation, conditioning,* and *reinforcement.* Chomsky argued that behaviourist theories cannot account for the following:

- **i) Children clearly produce utterances that are not simple variations of sentences that they have seen or heard (e.g., 'Why daddy no go?'**
- **ii) The states that children pass through in acquiring language suggest that they are capturing 'rules' and 'systems' and not just sentences, phrases, and words. Thus, when children first learn the regular ending for the past tense in English, for example, they begin to apply the endings to all verbs, including irregular verbs (e.g., ring - ringed; hold - holded; bring - bringed). This clearly shows their capacity for making generalizations and forming rules.**

Recently, Chomsky has further refined his position and has

characterized the study of generative grammar as having effected a shift of focus in language study from *E-language* (i.e. externalized language) to *I-language* (i.e. internalized language), that is from observable behaviour to states of mind, which has made the study more mentalistic. The basic assumptions of the *mentalist* approach to language are:

a) The study of language is basically the study of the nature of the language user's knowledge of the language concerned — that is, how the user acquires this knowledge and how (s)he puts it to use.
b) The human mind is a system of computational principles *forming* and *transforming* representations (i.e. images of reality as perceived by the mind) and linguistic knowledge is a *set of such principles;* putting this knowledge to use involves the interaction of these principles with other systems of mental representations and computations.
c) Exposure to linguistic input from the environment outside is essential for the human mind to reach the state of linguistic knowledge but that alone is not sufficient. The input triggers and shapes what is already innate, a rich and complex structure.
d) Linguistic knowledge is different from the knowledge of objects in the outside world. The knowledge of the properties of objects is based on the assumption that there is an external reality and it grows along with other characteristics of human beings in the normal course of maturation.
e) Our linguistic 'performance' is a product of our knowledge of language (i.e., 'competence'), but not entirely of that knowledge alone. Our lingustic performance is the product of the interaction between the intentional systems of beliefs and goals, and the language system. Our performance will show the limitations of stresses and strains on the various systems participating in the activity of performance as well as limitations of memory, attention focus and other limitations connected with the systems of motor coordination that underlie speech.
f) I-language is, or a part of, a specific mental system which may be called the *language faculty.* The human mind is a system of many interacting modules and I-language is one of them.

Chomsky, in 1975 and 1980, proposed that there are distinct faculties for such capacities as deductive reasoning, arithmetic, problem-solving and scientific theory formation, as well as language.

Developmental psycholinguists, following Piaget, however, maintain that the mind develops as a whole rather than as a modular structure with specific capacities developing in their own ways. In Piaget's framework, a child's congnitive development, including language, is 'constructed' out of its sensory-motor capacities. The debate on mental modularity is one of the most lively debates in psycholinguistics.

II. Piaget outlines the stages of a child's development as follows:

a) Sensory-motor intelligence (0-2 years): At this stage only reflex actions are found; the reality is conceived only from the child's own point of view.
b) Pre-conceptual thought (2-4$^{1}/_{2}$ years): The child at this stage moves from sensory to inner symbolic manipulation of reality; at this stage too the child is ego-centric but understands signs.
c) Intuitive thought (4$^{1}/_{2}$-7 years): The child moves from action to perception and is still unable to identify the various members of a class; for example, all are identified as insects though they are different.
d) Concrete operations (7-11 years): At this stage, internal representations of cognitive actions come to be grouped in systems; concepts of time and space, relations of temporal order, duration, and their classifications are worked out.
e) Formal operations (11 + years): At this stage, a break with the real happens and hypotheses are worked out; propositional thinking takes place and rules and laws are sought. Some children may reach each stage early but the broad framework can be formulated.

[One can compare this with the framework suggested by Jacques Lacan, the famous French psychoanalyst, in the 1960s. According to Lacan, the child is a 'sliced' piece from an original whole; so it lacks something right at birth because of the fragmentary condition. The child at first, according to Lacan, is a human omelette which spreads in all directions resulting in the territorialization of the body; this is thought of as a mapping operation. Then, the child enters the pre-language stage (6-18 months) which is the imaginary stage; at this stage there is no social determination; there is no cultural mediation; the child is 'ideologically' neutral since there is no symbolic mediation. The third stage is called the symbolic stage where language isolates the subject from the real and the child is confined to the realm of signification; only at this stage, the unconscious comes into existence because of the subject's access to language. The inauguration of meaning, the loss of the real, the formation of the unconscious and the entry into the symbolic aggregates the lack that was present right at the birth; in psychoanalytic terms, the subject gets alienated from itself, the search for the 'other' goes on; that is called 'desire' — it is the search for the whole or the ideal. This, in brief, is another developmental, psychoanalytic model that has started influencing researches in the field.]

A discussion between Piaget and Chomsky, two great minds theorizing on issues related to human mind, was organized in October 1975 near Paris. This symposium was attended by biologists and philosophers. The following points will summarize the two different approaches:

a) *Human knowledge and linguistic knowledge:* Whereas Piaget sees the human child and his/her mind as an active, constructive agent that slowly inches forward in a perpetual bootstrap operation, Chomsky views the mind as a set of essentially programmed units, each equipped from the beginning to realise its full comolement of rules and needing only the most modest environmental trigger. To Chomsky knowledge is largely inborn, a form of innate ideas existing in the realm of nature. To Piaget, on the other hand, knowledge is *constructed* only through *interaction* between certain inborn modes of processing available to the young child and the actual characteristics of physical objects and events. Both of them differ from the traditional empiricists who regard knowledge as a product of a series of messages of *nurture* transmitted by the other individuals as one's environment etched onto a *tabula rasa,* the mind.

b) *The relationship between the child and adult thought:* Piaget believes in the unity of stages with children, and, as they become older, they attain different modes of reasoning that are qualitatively different and more and more complex. To Chomsky and his followers the above account of stages is logically indefensible. It is, in principle, according to them, impossible to generate more powerful thoughts from less powerful ones; essentially, all forms of reasoning that an individual will eventually be capable of are specified at birth and emerge through a maturational process during development.

c) *The nature of mental representations by which we conceive of our experiences including the objects and persons of the world:* The Piagetian view is that the ability to represent knowledge to oneself and others is a *constructive process* that presupposes a lengthy series of *actions* upon the environment. These actions await the completion of sensory-motor development at age two and this completion makes possible symbolic play, dreams, mental images, language, in fact the whole gamut of symbolic capacities. Chomsky expressed doubts about the legitimacy of grouping together a family of representations; he argued that language as a symbol system must be dissociated from other symbolic forms since the human child is born with a form of representation, a language of thought upon which all others are simply grafted.

d) *On thought and thought processes:* To Piaget, thought is an extremely broad set of capacities and initial mental operations underlie one's encounters with a wide range of cognitive materials and topics (space, time, mobility, causality, etc.); according to Piaget, the roots of later forms of thought (for instance, reasoning in language) can be located in earlier forms (such as sensory-motor problem solving by the one-year old).

Chomsky firmly believes that language is divorced from other and earlier forms of thinking; each intellectual faculty is a separate domain, maybe located in a separate region of the brain, exhibiting many of its own processes and maturing at its own rate; like the human heart, the human mind has its genetic timetable.

III. The debate between Piaget and Chomsky, which resulted in a number of experiments, research papers and books in psycholinguistics, also widened the scope of developmental psycholinguistics to include studies of the child's acquisition of communicative and pragmatic competence.

During the 1960s Chomsky's proposals about language acquisition destabilized the behaviourists' accounts, as it was seen earlier, and the early transformational-generative models guided much of the research in language acquisition, which primarily focussed on how children learned syntax. There were attempts to document the order in which different transformational rules were learned as well as the correlation between the derivational complexity of linguistic structure and their order of acquisition.

For example, *The man who was running fell down,* is learned at a later stage because the relative clause (who was running) interrupts the main clause; children avoid structures like this, and if asked to imitate them, often leave out the relative clause altogther. Klima and Bellugi (1966) showed three main stages in the acquisition of negative structures in English:

The first stage: No sit there. Not a teddy bear!
The second stage: No pinch me. Don't bite me yet.
The third stage: No, I don't have a book. This not ice cream. I not crying.

This shows that they use *no* and *not* consistently for negation of all sorts of utterances, placing the negative at the beginning. They had not worked out how negatives such as *no one* or *nothing* are used and come up with double negatives such as *No one didn't come in.* These details are acquired later.

In 1960s a child's language development was sought to be characterized in well-defined stages like the learning of the use of word-order to express semantic relationships, the use of grammatical morphemes to modulate meaning, the use of sentence modifiers, the use of embedded sentences, and the use of coordinate constructions.

In the early 1970s, there was a shift towards more cognitively based explanations of language acquisition. A number of researchers proposed that the child's early utterances were better characterized by basic semantic relational categories or case roles like agentive, state resulting from action, instrumental, possessor, affected by action, beneficiary, etc. than by syntactic categories alone. Does the child begin with innate hypotheses about syntactic categories? This question has time and again provoked debates on the issue.

As more attention was given to what is known as *caretaker's speech* (usually, mother's talk since she is the primary caretaker) to the child, it became clear that the propositional content and syntactic form of 'motherese' (i.e., caretaker's talk) is simplified in systematic ways; analyses of 'motherese' have cast doubts on whether the child attends to and benefits from the simplifications used by caretakers to make the structure of their language easier to the child.

Most languages contain 'baby talk' words considered appropriate in talking to young children. For example, 'baby talk' often replaces the words for animals for their sounds — miaw-miaw, etc., or by a dimunitive form of the adult word—kitty, pussy, doggie, and include kinship words like *daddy, mummy,* etc. R.Brown (1958) argued that the words parents use in speaking to young children and adults seem to use language that is characterized by 'level of utility'. They are selective — they omit some words and avoid some; they seldom correct what children have to say, but when they do, they only seem to do it to make sure that what children say has truth value (R.Brown and Hanlon, 1970). When adults talk to children, they slow down, use short forms and simple constructions, and they repeat themselves frequently since repetition allows more time for children to interpret adult utterances.

The modifications made in 'baby talk' raise some important issues. Are the modifications adults make necessary for acquisition? Are they helpful? What aspects are necessary and what aspects are helpful? Further investigations are to be carried out, though difficult, to formulate theories about acquisition.

IV. As the emphasis shifted from syntax to word meanings, it was proposed that the child's initial word meanings have unspecified features or components which are learned in some specifiable order.

Components are not tied down to narrow classes of objects or events; they can also represent features like negation, cause, etc. For example, semantic features like *male* and *female* are found not only in *father-mother, boy-girl,* etc. but also in *bull-cow, tomcat-pussycat;* features like *adult* and *non-adult* turn up in *cat-kitten, dog-puppy,* etc. Maybe, when children acquire the meaning of a word they construct an entry for it in their mental lexicon, starting with simple entries containing only a few of the components relevant, and learn more about their meanings, and how they contrast with other words by adding further components, discarding irrelevant ones, and altering components. They start from components of shape, texture, movement and so on, and move to more abstract components like male/female, animate/inanimate as they build up their mental lexicon.

More recently, this componential model has been challenged on both theoretical and methodological grounds. Both overgeneralization and undergeneralization have been shown to occur. Some recent researches propose that children's initial lexical concepts are defined in terms of prototypical features and they, subsequently, switch to a more definitional meaning. It has been observed that a 'subordinate' term that is more frequent in the child's environment is likely to be interpreted as a basic term; for example, since the dog in the house is called *Jomo,* the dog next door also becomes *Jomo* for the child. The word *dog* is 'superordinate' and *Jomo* is 'subordinate' and acquisition proceeds from subordinate categories with local cues to superordinate categories that have global cues.

V. Two distinctly opposite ways of characterizing the procedure a child adopts to acquire a language are found in language acquisition studies. They are: a) acquiring syntactic forms from meaning, and (b) acquiring meaning from forms. These have been termed (a) semantic bootstrapping, and (b) syntactic bootstrapping, respectively.

The semantic bootstrapping approach holds that the semantics of various words and sentences are discovered by observing the real world outside and that once the meanings have been culled from observation, these meanings themselves yield conjectures about linguistic classification. For example, children say 'John moves the table' and 'The table moves'; once this relationship is understood, they use the analogy in constructions such as 'The baby eats' and 'Don't eat the baby' (to mean 'Don't feed the baby'), extending the use of 'move' to 'eat'. It must be noted that the child won't be in a position to extract all the nuances of usage from all possible contexts; in other words, semantic bootstrapping is not possible in all the instances of language, and something else is used in addition to acquiring form from meaning.

The syntactic bootstrapping approach argues that if there is really a strong correlation between verb syntax and verb meaning, the child can make conjectures from form to meaning with the same procedure used for making conjectures from meaning to form. It has been shown that blind learners of age 3, just like sighted children of the same age, understand that the verbs *look* and *see* describe spatial-perceptual acts and states, and that they are distinct from the contact word *touch*. How is it, then, that blind children discover the spatial-perceptual interpretation of these words, and correctly deduce the spatial components? They neither *see* and *look* nor observe others *seeing* and *looking*. Evidently, some other procedure is used despite impoverishment. It has also been shown that the evidence provided by a mother (or caretaker) of a blind child will be sufficient for learning to take place and that direct observation of the real-world contingencies is not necessary in all cases.

This clearly shows that *semantic* as well as *syntactic bootstrapping* is not adequate to capture the process of language acquisition. A more balanced view will be that the child, to a very satisfactory degree, captures the forms and meanings of the exposure language just because (s)he can and does play off the two data bases (events and the language forms) against each other to derive the best match between them.

VI. There is also another important and related issue called 'memory'. People generally listen to speech or read something for its meaning. They try to identify references, draw inferences, get at direct meanings, and in general build global representations of the thing or things being talked (about) or described. Later when they try to remember what they heard or read, they recall certain things but forget certain other things; yet when they have to, they can recall even the details.

How far does memory play a role in language acquisition? Memorization requires concentration and this is different from remembering. Remembering requires three stages: (a) input, (b) storage, and (c) recall and output. When we are asked to read ten unrelated sentences and then recall them, we do not read them for meaning alone; we try to memorize so that we can recall them word for word. In normal situations we do not memorize such sentences.

Psychologists have distinguised between short-term memory and long-term memory. Short-term memory is a phenomenon where exact wording is stored for brief periods of time; long-term memory, on the other hand, is a phenomenon where information is stored for longer periods of time. Short-term memory tends to preserve verbatim content, as well as meaning, whereas long-term memory tends to preserve meaning. In other words, the more the listeners have had to work on an utterance, the less they have of its form and the more they have of its meaning.

In remembering, we retrieve bits and pieces from memory in order to *reconstruct* sentences; this too depends on *depth of processing* and *focus of processing* and these two complement each other. By focussing on different aspects of a sentence, people recall the sentence differently and focus involves depth of processing. There are also other factors like their knowledge of situations, beliefs, and customs that help them fill in many details in the reconstruction process.

If language and knowledge are closely intertwined, how is knowledge represented in memory? There are quite a few difficult and complex questions in the study of memory and have no clear answers.

VII. During the middle 1970s, the mathematical study of learnability was introduced into developmental psycholinguistics. In contrast to the mainstream developmental psycholinguistic research, which focussed on empirical studies of what children say, this work began with the basic assumptions, that children learn a transformational grammar based only on positive evidence, and sought to determine under what conditions, if any, a transformational grammar could be learned. The formal study of learnability has now become an important sub-area within developmental psychology.

VIII. Of late, the focus of research has shifted to the mechanisms by which children construct and modify their language. The two major issues on which researchers in language acquisition are concentrating can be stated thus:

a) Though nobody tells them or gives them evidence about utterances that are not grammatical, how do children construct a hypothesis about the nature of the language that they learn? The child manages to construct a hypothesis that is general enough to include not only notions of grammaticality but also notions of ungrammaticality.

The problem has motivated the Chomskyans to shift their view of language acquisition from 'hypothesis testing' to 'parameter setting'. According to this formulation, all the differences in the languages of the world can be described in terms of how the parameters are set. For example, 'pro-drop' (i.e. dropping the pronoun from the subject position) is a parameter specific of many Indian languages and this differentiates these languages from English.

(*neenu*)	*bhoojanam*	*ceesaanu*
I	meal	did (I)

The English VP is 'left-headed' while the Telugu VP is 'right-headed'.

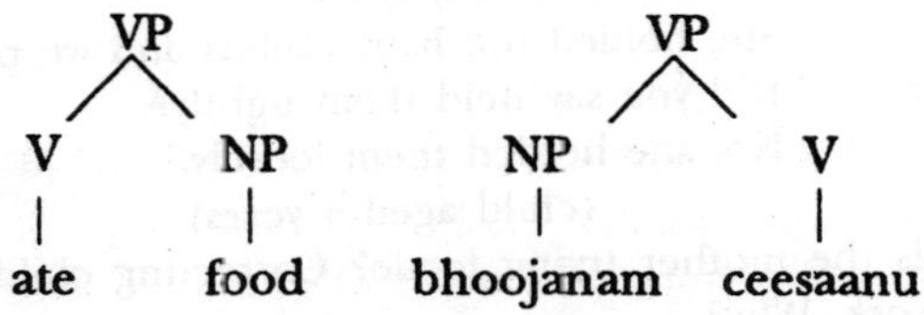

These conditions cannot be very elaborate and simply taxonomic but restricted in terms of certain parameters set for a small number of rule schemata. This is quite abstract but, according to Chomsky, the child's task is to learn how to set the parameters.

b) Secondly, how does the child recognize his/her understanding of the linguistic phenomenon? Does it happen 'on line', as part of the function of the child failing to correctly phrase a sentence? Or, does it occur 'off line' as a result of a more reflective reorganization?

Research into these questions may lead to the formulation of certain mechanisms that will provide for offline or reflective reorganization which is not done consciously. Very little is known about these processes but, as a result of the work done so far, we can at least formulate the right issues and ask certain relevant questions in the area of language acquisition.

Questions and topics for discussion

1. Look at the following data:

   Child: Nobody don't like me.
   Mother: No, say, 'Nobody likes me...'
   Child: Nobody don't like me.
   [Repeated at least eight times]
   Mother: Now listen carefully; say 'Nobody likes me'.
   Child: Oh! Nobody don't *likes* me.
   (H.H.Clark and E.V.Clark 1977:336).

   As a student of psycholinguistics, what comments will you offer on the data?

2. Consider the following:

   Child: My teacher holded the baby rabbits and we patted them.
   Mother: Did you say your teacher held the baby rabbits?
   Child: Yes.
   Mother: What did you say she did?
   Child: She holded the baby rabbits and we patted them.
   Mother: Did you say held them tightly?
   Child: No, she holded them loosely.
   (child aged 4 years)

   What is the mother trying to do? Correcting children's syntax is hard work. Why?

3. Stages in the acquisition of the past tense suffix in English:

   Stage I: Little or no use of past tense forms.
   Stage II: Sporadic use of some irregular forms like *went, broke,* etc.
   Stage III: Use of regular suffix -ed for all past forms (*goed, breaked,* etc.)
   Stage IV: Adult like use of regular and irregular forms.

   Can you think of the past tense forms in your first language and say how they are acquired?

4. Father: Say 'jump'.
   Child: *Dup*
   Father: No, 'jump'.
   Child: *Dup.*
   Father: No, 'jump'.
   Child: Only Daddy can say *dup* (Smith 1973).
   What does this data show about how children learn sounds?
5. What are the necessary and sufficient conditions for the human mind to acquire a natural language? Illustrate your answer.
6. Can we say that the human mind is nothing but a computer? If there are differences, what are they?
7. What are the substantial differences between Piaget and Chomsky regarding language acquisition? Which one do you support? Why?
8. In what ways does the notion of 'competence' differ from the notion of 'innate linguistic capacity' of the human mind?
9. What is parameter setting? Can you illustrate this with reference to some NP movement rules?
10. Chomsky speaks about rule-governed creativity. Do you think creativity is rule-governed? If so, how? If not? Why not?
11. Poets are credited with 'creativity'; all language users are also credited with 'creativity' by Chomsky. Do you think the concept of 'creativity' is the same in both the senses? Illustrate your answer.
12. If you are given a grant to work out a major project on L_1-acquisition, what plan will you propose for carrying out research? Think of some aspect of language acquisition and work out the details for that area.

10 LANGUAGE PRODUCTION

'Thou art not so long by the head as honorificabilitudinitatibus'

— *Shakespeare*

Focal points

I. People seem to be using language effortlessly but the effortlessness of language production is deceptive. There is a lot of planning involved before actual execution takes place. In planning what to say and how to say it, speakers are faced with a series of interrelated problems at a number of interrelated levels: discourse, sentence, constituents of a sentence and actual articulation. They have to structure their discourse, plan the relations among the pieces of information, decide on how to begin, what route to follow, and where to end. It means making a number of choices and putting them together. Within discourse, each sentence must be planned locally, and form the skeleton plan of a sentence. Words and phrases must be selected keeping in view 'meaning, focus, and end-weight'. Speakers must also decide on the choice of style; the levels of formality and familiarity based on socio-cultural and interpersonal relationships. Very little work has been done on the actual planning and production of language.

In the early 1970s some psycholinguists got interested in the issues related to language production, and the relations between cognitive structure and language form. This involves the study and characterization of the conceptual level semantic structures that interact with language structures to yield connected discourse. Though the problems have not been solved, the outlines of solutions have begun to emerge and there is a better understanding of the theoretical options that relate conceptual and linguistic structures.

II. Planning language production is an activity of problem solving; the speaker/writer will have to find answers to the basic question, 'what are the language devices that are to be used to convey what (s)he intends to convey in order to make the listener understand it?'

The answer requires a battery of consideration:

a) *Knowledge of the listener:* The speaker's image of the listener and what the speaker thinks that the listener knows.
b) *The social context:* Different social contexts (age, social status, social relationships, etc.) produce different linguistic items.
c) *The coooperative principle:* Speakers assume that their listeners try to follow certain principles (like telling the truth, being informative, being relevant, being clear, etc.) in the speech-act and expect cooperation; in other words, the speaker expects the listener to make an effort to understand. For example, if you try to sound ironical or humorous, or use a new word, you expect him/her to make an effort to under-

stand what you mean.

d) *The linguistic devices available:* Speakers will have to produce language only within the range of resources available, though they may not be quite adequate to express what you want to convey; we accept the limitations and try to produce language. For example, the beauty of a flower or the setting-sun cannot be fully captured in language, yet we try to express it within the devices available, accepting the constraints of the language that is used.

e) *Other considerations,* depending upon the nature of the language activity planned; they may include turn-taking, guessing intentions, mid-course correction, editing, etc.

III. The planning and production of a discourse depends on the goal—whether we want to explain something, describe something, get information, negotiate a deal, or exchange gossip. Since discourse production is a dynamic process, it does not follow rigid principles, except in very formal situations like a committee meeting. This is very difficult to study because of the number of variables involved.

Sentence planning and production can be studied in terms of the following considerations:

a) lexical selection,
b) phrasal selection, and
c) phonological coding.

a) *Lexical selection:* This depends on three factors—conceptual, syntactic, and phonological. At the core of the sentence to be planned are its propositions—ideas, concepts, feelings and emotions, units of meaning that we want to express. Once we decide on what we want to say, a retrieval system operates on an inventory of rules and forms sufficient to determine the surface forms. Studies relating to retrieval of words focus on two phenomena:

(i) The 'tip-of-the-tongue' (TOT) state in which a word, though known, cannot be recalled on the occasion of its use: The speaker is aware of this failure. Research in this area has so far shown that the initial sounds and length are the basis for the organization of the inventory of lexical forms, and, hence, are normally the effective descriptions for retrieval. More work is required in this area to have a better understanding for the retrieval phenomenon.

(ii) The 'word-substitution' state in which the failure manifests itself as the substitution of another word for the intended word: The relations between the target word and the intrusion word constitute the data for this study; the substitute has a relation—either of syntax, or form, or of meaning—to the intended word. For example, one can produce the word 'considered' instead of 'consisted', 'discussal' for 'discoursal', or 'listen' for 'speak', etc. Studies on word substitutions have shown a marked similarity between initial segments and length. This raises an important question about the role of meaning in word-substitution; if word-recall and word-substitutions are based on phonological resemblance and if there is no constraint of grammatical category, what role does meaning play in language production?

Two basic assumptions can emerge in our search for solutions:

1) Meaning and form based retrieval-processes have *separate operations*, and
2) Both the processes are *syntactically constrained*, and, therefore, part of language-specific processes; they do not determine message.

b) *Phrasal selection*: This can be approached from the following angles: (i) There are levels of organization that are required for a formal description of the language and the levels will have to be incorporated in the description of language production; (ii) There are basic phrasal, lexical and segmental linguistic categories that are necessary for processing vocabulary and the basis for the postulation of levels must be found in the production processes.

Research in the areas of sound errors, morphophonemic accommodation, word exchanges and morphemic exchanges has been very rewarding.

For example, consider the following:

1) 'even the best teams lost' uttered as
   'even the best team losts' [/z/—>/s/]
2) 'they were talking Turkish' uttered as
   'they were turking talkish' [exchange of morphemes]
3) 'mermaids move their legs together' uttered as
   'mermaid moves their legs together'

How and why do such things happen? The distribution of hesitation pauses, false starts, mixing up words, etc. in spontaneous speech provides evidence regarding speech planning and phrasal selection.

c) *Phonological coding*: Phonological planning and production have been researched with great enthusiam and the relevant evidence suggests subanalysis of words in terms of phonemes, syllables, and features. A variety of observations attests to the governing role of the syllable structure in production processes.

If we take all the three together—lexical, phrasal, and phonological—lexical processing can either be treated as a two-stage system integrated with phrasal and phonological processes or a single network representation in which form and meaning interact to govern the insertion of lexical items into phrasal environments that have phonological manifestations.

IV. The planning and execution of language production is a complicated pattern; speakers try to select words for each major constituent and, at the same time, try to execute each constituent into a single unit of delivery. This double processing makes the task complicated and leads them to hesitation, repeats, corrections. In the description, we think of various steps; the first one is to find a syntactic outline with the stress pattern, in a language like English, super-imposed on it; the second step is to select the nouns, verbs, adjectives, adverbs and the right function words, prefixes, suffixes, etc.; thirdly, the phonetic segments, the timing, rhythm, etc. are to be filled out so that the actual production takes place.

Tongue twisters, malapropisms (a type of error named after Mrs. Malaprop, a character in Sheridan's play, *The Rivals*, who tried to use high-sounding words but couldn't get them right), spoonerisms (named after William A. Spooner, an English clergyman who is reported to have made such errors often, wittily and deliberately), and such other phenomena provide a lot of useful information regarding speech production. Look at some of the examples given below:

a) Tongue twisters: She sells sea shells on the sea shores.
Six thick thistle sticks.

b) Malaproprisms: I am sure I have done everything in my power since I exploded (for 'exposed') the affair; long ago I laid my conjunctions (for 'conjectures') on her never to think on the fellow, I have since laid Sir Anthony's preposition (for 'proposition') before her.

c) Spoonerisms:
i. You have *hissed* all my *mystery* lectures. (You have missed all my history lectures).
ii. 'Bake my tike' (for 'take my bike')
iii. 'Well-boiled icicle' (for 'well-oiled bicycle')
iv. Shoving leopard (for 'loving shepherd')

The study of speech errors may reveal a lot about the production processes and there is a lot of scope for research in this area.

Questions and topics for discussion

1. Look at the following tongue-slips and say what insights they offer into the study of language production.
   a) take my tie — bake my tie
   b) Katz and Fodor — Fats and Kodor
   c) grizzly and ghastly — grastly
   d) before the place opens — before the place closes
   e) an intervening node — an intervenient node
2. List at least five examples of malapropisms from English and your mother tongue and say what insights they offer into the study of language production.

3. List at least five examples of spoonerisms from English and your mother tongue and say what insights they offer into the study of language production.
4. List at least five tongue-twisters each from English and your mother tongue and say what insights they offer into the study of language production.
5. 'After eating thirty green apples, John suddenly threw, oh, up!' — Explain why this utterance sounds odd.
6. Characterize the editing processes in the following utterances:
   a) He hit Mary — that is, Bill did — with a frying pan.
   b) I'm trying to lease — or rather, sublease — my house.
   c) I really love — I mean, despise — getting up early in the morning.
   d) It'll be done immediately — Well, in a few minutes.
7. Notice users of English come out with utterances like the ones given below. Comment on the speech 'errors' and say what insights they offer into the study of language production.
   a) Turn on the...heater switch.
   b) Turn on, uh, the heater switch.
   c) Turn on the heater...the heater switch.
   d) Turn on the stove...the heater switch.
   e) Turn on the stove switch...I mean, the heater switch.
   f) Turn on the h...h...h...heater switch.
   g) Turn on the...the...the heater switch.
   h) Turn on the sweater hitch.
8. Can you list such speech 'errors' in your first language (at least ten) and say in what ways they will be useful in the study of language production.
9. 'Colourless green ideas sleep furiously'. This is a well-known example of Chomsky to show the nature of deviation. What does this example show about the nature of language production? Explain.
10. The process of language production is psychological as well as sociological; this makes the study of language production complex and complicated. Why study it then? What insights are we likely to get in attempting the impossible?
11. Very little work has been done in the area of language production in the case of Indian languages. Can you think of any reasons for this state of affairs?
12. If you are asked to formulate a research project in the area of language production, how will you go about doing it?
13. Knowing fully well that we can never get the truth, we research. How do you resolve this paradox? What is the purpose of research in language acquisition and language production?

11 SECOND LANGUAGE ACQUISITION

'Whoever knows grammar in one language also knows it in another so far as its substance is concerned. If he cannot, however, speak another language, or understand those who speak it, this is because of the difference of words and their formations which is accidental to grammar'

- Anon., (Thirteenth Century)

Focal points

I. If languages are moulded in part by the ideas and processing capacities that all people have in common, all languages must have certain features in common, language universals. Are there language universals at all? If there are, are they helpful in the acquisition of a second language? What do we mean by the word 'grammar'? The answers to such questions may be found in research relating to second language acquisition.

The analysis of a single language has to deal with the complex network of systems of language and society. When it comes to the acquisition of a second language, apart from the factors to be taken into account in the description of one language, other parameters like the age of acquisition, the type of exposure to the second language, the learner's knowledge of other languages, and the like have to be taken into consideration; the motivation of the second language learner plays an important role in second language acquisition; a study of the 'errors' of the second language learner may be rewarding since it may provide some insights into the processes involved in the learning of a second linguistic system, universal principles governing language acquisition, especially similar error patterns that occur among learners of varying language backgrounds.

II. The focus of research in second language acquisition has shifted from the view that language learning involves learning a set of habits to the view that it involves the creative construction of a grammar, from examining the influence of the mother tongue to finding parallels between first and second language acquisition.

Recent efforts to formulate the principles of a universal grammar which constrain the range of hypotheses the child as a language learner can entertain has led to the examination of the role of such principles in second language acquisition. More precisely, the studies on second language acquisition can be grouped into the following types:

a) those pertaining to the influence of the first language on the second language;
b) those pertaining to mental representations;
c) those pertaining to universal principles.

III. *The influence of the first language: The contrastive analysis hypothesis* (CAH) emphasizes the gravitational pull of the mother tongue (i.e., the first language) on the processes involved in learning a second language: phonological, morphological, syntactic and semantic. The structuralists' assumption that the learning of a language is actually the learning of a set of linguistic habits characterizes their view of the learning of a second language too, as the learning of a secondary set of habits; this implies that the primary set of habits must interfere with the secondary set that is learnt, wherever the two sets do not have similarities. This understanding led to the comparison of the linguistic systems of the first and second languages, and to the identification of errors that could be attributed to the difference between the two systems.

For example, Hindi does not have word-initial consonant clusters like *sk, st, sn;* as a result, Hindi-using learners of English make mistakes in learning such clusters; that is why they say *iskuul,* or *sakuul,* (for 'school') and *istik* or *satik* (for 'stick'), etc.

According to the contrastive analysis hypothesis, an examination of the differences between the first and second languages should help us to predict or at least explain errors made by L_2 learners. Similarities between the two systems are assumed to facilitate learning and differences lead to interference or negative transfer. While the strong version of CAH claims that comparison of the two systems can predict a learner's errors, the weak version of the theory maintains that a comparison of L_1 and L_2 can help in understanding the difficulties of the learner.

It was taken for granted that linguists can provide 'complete' description of L_1 and L_2, at least to the extent necessary to describe the difficulties of the learner, though there are no such descriptions available; theoretical models keep on changing and only when descriptions of L_1 and L_2 are available using the same model a comparison can be effected; in addition, we need pedagogic descriptions and not just theoretical descriptions. Not much work has been done to show that comparisons can systematically explain the degree of difficulty, let alone predicting the difficulties. The criticisms against CAH reflect an inherent dissatisfaction with notions of transfer and interference; they were essentially based on form and not on meaning that led to only superficial explanations.

IV. *The mental representations:* According to the generativists, language acquisition is a creative process guided by innate, universal mechanisms. This brought with it a reaction against the view that L_1 is the primary influence on L_2. The focus shifted to errors that could not be explained on the basis of the first language. Some studies reported correspondences in the mental representations of the first and second language learners, children as well as adults. Language production was seen as a coherent system, rather than as a distortion of the second language grammar through interference from L_1. The 'creative construction' view predicts that one could find the same kind of error patterns despite the fact that the L_2 learners have different first languages, like Hindi, Bengali or Malayalam; it is also likely that the error patterns are the same as those of a child learning the first language itself. The change in focus brought about a change in the basic notion of 'errors': errors made in the process of acquiring a second language. The term *interlanguage* proposed by Selinker (1969, 1972) refers to the grammar of a second language learner, a grammar presumably distinct from that of either L_1 or L_2, but one which could be seen as a coherent system and studied as such. The terms *approximative system* (Nemser 1971) and *idiosyncratic dialect* (Corder 1971), though not as widely used as the term *interlanguage* have more or less the same implication.

If a learner's so-called errors are systematic, it shows that the learner is following a set of rules and the rules are that of a 'transitional' language similar in many respects to the target language; this 'transitional' language is not the code of a social group but it has an intermediate status between the first language and the target language. When the individual (or a group) stop learning, at least in certain areas of the language, the interlanguage gets *fossilized,* having found out they can communicate and understand without further learning (in the formal sense of the word), they have no motivation to keep it transitional.

Research in the area of interlanguage has brought into focus strategies of learning, such as overgeneralization, simplification, etc., that are processes involved in both L_1 and L_2 acquisition. In other words, the focus in research has shifted to metacognitive processes.

Another important factor that is to be taken into account is the notion of *markedness.* In a language, if construction A is rare and more difficult to learn than construction B, then A is said to be more marked. The hypothesis is that this notion of markedness also plays a role in L_2 acquisition. It has yielded some interesting results. The notion of markedness of certain constructions also leads to the notion of language transfer. Some have argued that if we take into account the relative markedness of L_1 L_2 constructions (as relative difficulty), then transfer of difficulty in L_2 learning can be predicted. In Telugu, for example; ***evaru vella ledhu*** (anyone go did not) is unmarked, for the subject (evaru) is also within the scope of the negative morpheme *ledhu.* The corresponding English sentence 'no one went' is marked for difficulty and hence the difficulty in transfer from L_1 and L_2 can be predicted.

The view of markedness makes reference only to surface characteristics of a language and allows freedom to link up a markedness relation to any difficult or rare feature; it is, therefore, possible to come up with a number of different analyses of the same facts, with different explanations and predictions.

V. *Universal principles:* An alternative to the markedness hypothesis is the one developed in recent works of Chomsky (1980, 1981). Throughout Chomsky's works, the child's task is presumed to be that of constructing a grammar of the native language based on the incomplete and somewhat misleading data to which (s)he is exposed. This task is made possible by the innate principles of Universal Grammar (U.G) which define the class of possible human languages and, therefore, constrain the range of hypotheses that a child can entertain about the structure of its language.. U.G. makes available to the child a set of *parameters* along with a knowledge of possible *settings* of these *parameters;* the child presumably starts out with the unmarked value for each parameter and resets the parameter only when confronted by data incompatible with the unmarked setting. The description of grammars in terms of parameter settings makes an explicit organic connection between developmental factors in language acquisition and distributional typological properties of languages.

An explicitly described theory of parameters will thus constitute:

(a) a theory of possible variations across languages, and
(b) a theory of first language acquisition.

Since *parameters* are presumed to be part of the child's innate equipment, identification of the marked and unmarked values of *parameter settings* would constitute a theory of first language acquisition.

The most important difference between a child's acquisition of first language and the formal learning of a second language is the assumption that in the acquisition of a first language the child has no access to negative evidence. That is, the children are ungrammatical, and tend to disregard such remarks when they are offered. In the case of an adult learning a second language, it has to be noted that the learner has passed the critical period for acquiring language naturally, and is exposed to negative evidence in the L_2 classroom. Consideration of these factors might lead to the view that second language acquisition is a very different process from first language acquisition. However, the rich evidence in support of the *creative construction hypothesis* reveals parallels between first and second language acquisition. Further more, there is a growing body of evidence that learners are sensitive to principles of U.G., even where their native language does not provide direct evidence for the applicability of these principles in particular constructions. The principles of U.G. along with language transfer can be said to play some role in L_2 acquisition.

These give rise to two alternative hypotheses:

1) One learns a second language in exactly the same way as the first, by beginning with the *unmarked parameter settings* and *resetting parameters* only when confronted with L_2 data demanding a *marked setting*. This view is most compatible with the *creative construction* approach.
2) The learner approaches the L_2 with the *parameter settings* of the L_1 and is forced to reset these when they differ in the two languages.

The parameterized approach to linguistic description has the potential to provide a framework in which the competing trends of the past decades — the focus on the influence of L_1 and the focus on the commonality of *interlanguage* patterns accross L_1 backgrounds — may find a place in a comprehensive theory of L_2 acquisition.

Questions and topics for discussion

1. 'Contemporary claims that applied linguistics can solve all the problems of language teaching are as unfounded as the claims that applied psychology can solve them, for the problems of language teaching are central neither to psychology nor to linguistics. Neither science is equipped to solve the problems of language teaching.' — Give your views on the statement given above.
2. The gravitational pull of the mother tongue is very prominent in the area of phonology. Can you list ten examples and say how the pull works in the area of phonology?
3. Look at the following utterances in the Indian variety of English. Can you explain the sources of the errors in terms of contrastive analysis hypothesis?
   a) You went there yesterday, isn't it?
   b) Why you are coming so late?
4. Comment on the CAH (Contrastive Analysis Hypothesis) from the 'relativist' and 'universalist' points of view.
5. Piaget's theory takes the organic development of language ability as a whole and takes into account 'interactionism' and 'genetic epistemology'. What do these terms mean to you? How will you apply these insights to L_2 acquisition?
6. Do you think that there are differences among the following second language acquisition processes?
   a) A native speaker of Hindi living in Patna learning Telugu.
   b) A native speaker of Telugu living in Hyderabad learning Hindi.

7. i) A : Your shoes are very nice.
   B : It's your eyes which can see them which are nice.
   ii) A : It was delicious, Mom, I hope your hands never have pain.
   B : I'm glad you like.

   Are the participants in the discourse given above native users of English? What features give you clues about them in each text?
8. A : It's a garage; come into the garage.
   B : Garage..... your.
   A : This is yours. The garage is too small.
   B : Small garage?
   A : You can come into the garage.
   B : Right. I come into the garage.

   Repetitions do play an important role in learning a language. Examine the data given above and comment on the nature of the repetition. Are there different kinds of repetition in language learning?
9. i) A : Do you think it is ready?
   B : I think is ready.
   ii) A : I don't like this story.
   B : I no liking either.

   Comment on the discourses given above from the point of view of interlanguage.
10. In second language acquisition both input and interaction are so tightly interwoven so as to seem inseparable. Krashen's Input Hypothesis does not see social interaction and language development as interwoven but sees interaction as *casually* related to language acquisition. What is your opinion? Give reasons.

Suggested reading

Chomsky, N. 1957. *Syntactic Structures.* The Hague : Mouton.

This is a classic work that ushered in the era of Transformational Generative Grammar.

Clark, H.H., and E.V. Clark. 1977. *Psychology and Language.* New York : Harcourt Brace Jovanovich, Inc.

This is a useful guide for research orientation. It contains a lot of empirical data.

Greene, Judith. 1972. *Psycholinguistics.* Penguin.

This is an introductory course on psycholinguistics with focus on theoretical and experimental linguistics. There is a full account of both the 1957 and 1965 versions of Chomsky's theory.

Newmeyer, Frederick, J. (ed.). 1988 C. *Linquistics* : The Cambridge Survey. Vol. III Language : Psychological and Biological Aspects. Cambridge : Cambridge University Press.

This book presents the recent developments in the areas of Psycholinguistics and Neurolinguistics. It is a useful reference book. The papers of M.K. Tanenhaus, M.F. Garrette, L.R. Gleitman et al., and E. Broselow will give a good introduction to the discipline.

Piattelli - Palmarini, M. (ed.). 1980. ***Language and Learning. The Debate between Jean Piaget and Noam Chomsky.*** London : Routledge and Kegan Paul.

Based on a symposium held in France, the book presents carefully edited transcription of the round table debate between Piaget and Chomsky as well as the rejoinders written after the meeting. It is essential reading for any research on psycholinguistics and developmental psychology.

CHAPTER THREE

Language as Discourse

"Words are not crystal, transparent, and unchanged; they are the skin of living thoughts, and may vary greatly in color and content according to the circumstances and time in which they are used."

- Oliver Wendell Holmes

12 TEXT AND DISCOURSE

'Every article in the constitution is to be constructed in harmony with, and, in the context of the rest of the constitution.'

- Palkhivala

Focal points

I. The study of naturally occurring connected discourse, spoken or written, is one of the most promising and rapidly developing areas of linguistics. Traditional linguistics has concentrated on sentence-centred analysis but the study of language as it is used by a community of people cannot be divorced from the societal network of relations and the psychological processes that underlie such uses of language. This is one of the primary motivations for analysing language use in terms of two interrelated notions: text and discourse.

The Chambers's Twentieth Century Dictionary (1960 impression) defines 'discourse' as follows:

discourse n. speech or language generally : conversation : the reasoning faculty : a treatise : a speech : a sermon.... v.i. to talk or converse : to reason : to treat formally... v.t.: to utter or give forth

This is too general and is not formulated in a precise sense. This does not throw any light on 'language as discourse' and 'language as text'.

We often talk of *written text* versus *spoken discourse;* this implies that discourse is interactive and text is noninteractive; at the same time, a *lecture* may refer to an event, or only to the spoken text or its written version. Secondly, *discourse* implies length, whereas a text may be very short or long. These terms have been defined by researchers in various ways.

Zellig S. Harris (1952) used the term *discourse* to mean 'a combination of sentences' and *discourse analysis* was defined in terms of its application—the breaking up of a text into its fundamental elements or component parts; but, ultimately, the focus of analysis became the sentence even in the transformational-generative grammar. Though in 1980, Chomsky proposed that 'discourse competence' is part of 'linguistic competence', there has been no serious attempt to study discourse until very recently.

II. Michael Stubbs in his *Discourse Analysis* (1983) says that 'any study which is not dealing with (a) single sentences, (b) contrived by the linguist, (c) out of context, may be called discourse analysis.' In other words, there is a shift of focus from sentences in isolation to utterances in context; to study language in use is to study it as discourse. Hymes (1971) says that there are rules (conventions) of use without which rules (formulations) of grammar will become useless.

In discourse analysis *meaning* is not seen as a static, abstract notion attached to words and sentences. Meaning is viewed as a *dynamic interactive force* constructed by the mind from language in context. The practical interpretation of utterances (i.e., 'force') rather than the mere semantic notion (i.e., 'sense') is responsible for all language based activities. In the 1980s, the analysis of meaning in the sense of 'force' formulated above was named *discourse analysis.*

III. The distinction between *text* and *discourse* is very subtle; there are slight differences in emphasis.

van Dijk (1977) uses the term *text* to refer to an abstract theoretical construct which is realized as *discourse.* Halliday (1978) talks of language being actualized in *text,* which is the opposite of what van Dijk says. Widdowson (1979) distinguishes between 'sentences in combination' (*text*) and 'sentences in use' (*discourse*), which emphasizes the need for a functional criterion as the defining condition for discourse. He distinguishes *textual cohesion*, recognizable in surface lexis, grammar and propositional development, from *discourse coherence* which operates between underlying speech acts. In de Beaugrande's (1980) framework of text linguistics 'the naturally occurring manifestation of language is text' while a 'set of mutually relevant texts' constitutes discourse; here the focus is on the conversational aspect of discourse. To Brown and Yule (1983) *text* is a 'technical term' that refers to the 'verbal record of a communicative act'; the dynamic process of creating the data (i.e. text) becomes discourse. In the discussions on narrative techniques, a distinction is made between the level of *text* and the level of *narration*; both are included in *discourse*. A very radical point of view is found in Roland Barthes (1971/1977) where he says that the text is a methodological field and that it exists only as discourse; it is experienced only in an activity, a production. According to J. Derrida (1974) the 'text is a gas', the effluvium that is not preserved, not even formed, like the excrements in decomposing organic substances; 'a text is not a finished corpus of writing, some content enclosed in a book or its margins, but a differential network, a fabric of traces referring endlessly to something other than itself, to other differential traces'.

All these make confusion worse confounded.

We have to have a working definition of these two terms *text* and *discourse*. To maintain the difference in focus between the two terms, we shall say that a *text* refers to the *linguistic entity* and *discourse* to the *dynamic processes* and *procedures*. In other words, a 'text' is the actualized linguistic entity and 'discourse' the actualization process. The focus in *discourse analysis* is on the processes of meaning making and its analysis, whereas in *text linguistics* it is on the production and interpretation of 'texts'; in this sense all rhetoric, in the classical sense, will be text linguistics since it is about the production and interpretation of texts.

In simple terms, a sign-board with the utterance 'Speed Breakers Ahead' kept in a painter's shop with many other sign-boards will be an instance of a text; the same sign-board placed on the left corner of a road in its 'appropriate context' becomes a piece of discourse since it communicates a message to the users of the road. Thus, as a linguistic entity it is a text and in this context it is realised as discourse.

IV. When 'discourse' is defined in terms of meaning-making processes and communicative functions, it implies *interaction.* Again, the term 'interaction' is ambiguous and confusing. Some use it to differentiate between oral and written 'discourse'; some others feel that both oral and written forms are interactive; the third view is that in written discourse there is *interactivity* without *interaction.* The last view needs further elaboration.

Reading a piece of written discourse and participating in conversation have to be differentiated. In reading, the reader has 'interaction' with the written discourse only at the cognitive level, while in conversation there is cognitive as well as physical and situational levels of interaction; since the reader's contribution is at the cognitive level in the case of reading, there is only *uni-source discourse development* in reading, whereas in conversation, there is a collaborative effort to produce a *multi-source discourse development.*

The difference between reading and conversation can be represented as follows:

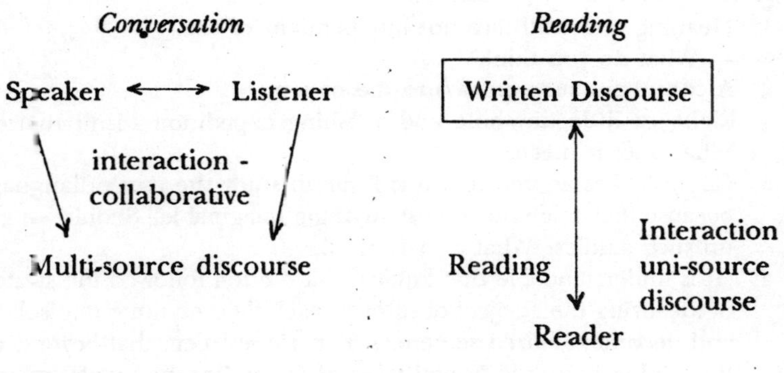

Written discourse itself may have two different structures. In a play, for example, different characters contribute to the development of discourse and make it multi-source discourse, while in a report there is only uni-source discourse structure. Where there is multi-source discourse structure there is 'interactivity', within written discourse, though there is no 'interaction'.

V. It has become increasingly clear that a coherent view of language, including syntax, must take account of what happens beyond the sentence; we must study the various functions that language can serve: promising, asserting, describing, impressing, intimidating, persuading, gossiping, arguing, complaining, protesting, and so on.

As Michael Stubbs points out there are different decisions which are to be made in analysing discourse:

i. Is idealization necessary or justifiable; if so how much is necessary?

ii. The size of units to be studied: how long?

iii. Whether the data is to be contrived/edited by the linguist or to be naturally occurring.

iv. Whether non-linguistic factors of the context are to be studied or not.

Often, we find that studies of isolated, contrived, decontextualized sentences are squeezed even into discourse analysis. If done properly, the boundaries of linguistics can be redrawn by discourse analysis.

Questions and topics for discussion

1. Meaning and truth are not independent of use.
   — What do you think?
2. A consultant surgeon says to the patient:
   Right - a little tiny hole and a fishing expedition - isn't that so?
   What does it mean?
3. Chomsky has argued that it is futile to study the uses of language, because they might be almost anything imaginable.. Should we give up such studies? What do you think?
4. "It is understandable that linguists have often followed the strategy of idealizing their object of study to exclude everything but isolated and decontextualized sentences. For it does seem that beyond the tidy and well-pruned bonsai trees of syntax lies the jungle: menus, road signs, advertisements, propaganda, guarantees, recipes, instructions, lectures, speeches, jokes, news bulletins, arguments and the like, not to mention discussions, conversations and novels."
   — Explain and illustrate.
5. **There are grounds for arguing that discourse units such as lecture, story, etc. are the upper limit of structural organization. Can you think of some arguments for supporting this statement?**

6. All linguistics is discourse analysis. — Comment.
7. Discourse analysis should be a sub-branch of linguistics. — Comment.
8. What differences can we maintain between the two terms 'text' and 'discourse'?
9. Comment on the 'sense' and 'force' of the utterances that are in italics:
   i) *Will you close that window?*
   ii) A: *I'm afraid, I'm boring you.*
   B: Not at all, please go on.
   iii) A: *I have a ticket for the theatre tonight.*
   *B: *My examination is tomorrow.*
   iv) A: Have you got Berkeley Filter?
   B: *Forty paise, please?*
   v) A: *Alcohol kills you slowly.*
   B: *I'm not in a hurry*
   vi) A: Father, I have my examination today.
   B: *Good luck!*
   vii) A: Father, I couldn't take the exam today.
   B: *Bad luck!*
   viii) Principal: What does he look like? Stupid? Intelligent?
   The Servant: Fairly intelligent I'd say sir.
   Principal: Good! *Then he's not a school inspector.* Show him in.
10. How would you characterize the discourse development in the following:
    a) listening to a radio play;
    b) watching a TV serial.
11. Think of 'texts' that become 'discourse' in a communicative context. Give five examples each from your first language and English.
12. Explain how it is difficult to develop a text grammar by extending the Chomskyan sentential grammar.
13. Probably the most common words in English are *yes, no,* and *please.* Can the eight-parts-of-speech system account for the parts of speech of *yes, no,* and *please?* Try and find out the parts of speech of *yes, no,* and *please.*
14. In social sciences like economics and politics one finds theories and practices. Is there always a match or mismatch between theory and practice? Give reasons for your answer.
15. Do you think that in all scientific theories there is idealization? Illustrate your answer.

16. What is the negative of
    a) I am a man.
    b) This is a cat.
    c) A garden has a tree.
    d) Mary is a girl.

    What are the interrogative torms or the sentences given above? Critically comment on the negative and interrogative sentences as formulated in traditional and transformational grammars.
17. Meaning is too messy for serious comtemplation.
    — Explain and illustrate.

13 DISCOURSE : THE SOCIAL INTERACTION APPROACH

"The study of language as a social pheonomenon can be a confusing but a rewarding experience, confusing because the complexities are too many; rewarding because one realizes the limitations of the 'theory-building' activity."

— *Anon*

Focal points

I. The utterance 'Will you close the door?' may be understood as a question but in a particular context it is understood to mean a request and the hearer obliges the speaker by closing the door. The appropriate context is required to bring out the 'force' of the text as well as its 'effect' on the hearer: though the meaning of a text as 'sense' may be realized without a context, it will be only 'propositional content' — what is referred to in semantic theories; it is abstract without any 'force'. The term 'force' is known as *illocutionary intent* in *Speech Act Theory* and *Pragmatics.* Meaning in pragmatics is defined relative to a speaker or user of the language, whereas meaning in semantics is defined purely as a property of expressions in a given language, without any reference to particular situations, or speakers and hearers.

The original idea in Austin's *How to Do Things with Words* (1962) and similar ideas put forward by Searle in *Speech Acts* (1969) and other papers were reformulated by Grice (1975), who has proposed a set of 'maxims' or 'conversational principles'; they are widely used to study discourse as a social interaction phenomenon.

II. Grice's *Cooperative Principle* has been often quoted and discussed in the past few years.

The principle of cooperation in exchange means that we make our conversational contribution such as is required, at the state at which it occurs by the accepted purpose of direction of the talk exchange in which we are engaged. In other words, unless we try to cooperate in talk exchange, there will not be any interaction. It is also true that this principle is often violated.

For example, in the following conversation from *Alice in Wonderland*, the Cooperative Principle is violated:

"How am I to get in?" she repeated aloud.

"I shall sit here," the footman remarked, "till tomorrow or the next day, maybe."

"How am I to get in?" asked Alice in a louder voice.

"Are you getting in at all?" said the footman.

The Cooperative Principle has four categories of maxims:

a) The maxim of *Quantity*: Make your conversation as informative as (but not more informative than) is required.
b) The maxim of *Quality*: Make your contribution one that is true and do not say what you believe to be false or for which you lack evidence.
c) The maxim of *Relation*: Be relevant.
d) The maxim of *Manner*: Avoid obscurity, ambiguity and be brief and orderly.

These principles or maxims apply variably to different contexts of language use and in variable degrees rather than in an all-or-nothing way; these maxims can conflict with one another and often they are flouted; but these principles introduce communicative values into the study of language, values that are operative in society and not moral ones imposed on society.

Along with these, Leech (1983) introduced the 'Principle of Politeness' that includes generosity, modesty, approbation, etc. and studied the interaction between the Cooperative Principle and the Politeness Principle.

III. The maxims form a necessary part of the description in that they explain how it happens that speakers 'mean more than they say' when they follow or violate these maxims. The explanation is made by means of pragmatic implications, or, as Grice called them, 'conversational implicatures'.

For example, the sentence 'Many of the delegates opposed the motion' conversationally implicates 'Not all the delegates opposed the motion', for 'many' is not the same 'quantity' as 'all'; the speaker here is assumed to have followed the 'maxim of quantity' appropriately. Such conversational implicatures are derived from the 'force' of the conversation. There are implicatures that are directly derived from the meanings of words. These are known as 'conventional implicatures'. In the sentence 'She was poor, but she was honest', the word *but* carries the implication that for a person to be poor is a good reason for supposing him/her not to be honest.

In initiating a conversation, a speaker may make some initial remarks, such as those on weather conditions. This is known as *situation monitoring* in the setting of the discourse; in such monitoring the Cooperative Principle of Grice is not followed. Day-to-day communication is far more diversified and far less transparent than what is being proposed in the studies undertaken so far. In language use many intentions are hardly ever made explicit. The 'unspoken meaning', the suppression between expression (what the speaker says) and impression (what the hearer receives), has the status of a conversational implicature in the Speech Act Theory. Implicature is often produced by the deliberate 'flouting' or 'exploiting' of any one or all of the maxims listed.

IV. The social-interaction approach to the study of discourse focuses generally on multi-source discource development since it is 'interaction-oriented'. This brings in the notion of 'relevance' which can be seen in two ways. For example, if we consider the election manifesto of a left party, the manifesto should reflect the objective conditions of the society and the immediate aspirations of the electorate/people. The manifesto should have 'relevance' in itself — each part of the manifesto should have relevance to the rest of the text; this is internal to the text — 'text-in-itself' relevance. At the same time, the manifesto must have 'institutional relevance', the relevance to the conditions of the people, society, electorate, and to the general political programme of the party, to the basic principles of Marxism, etc. Thus 'institutional relevance' is a multi-layered phenomenon.

V. The concept of relevance can be linked up with the notion of interconnection among various aspects of relevance which can be taken to mean what has been called *intertextuality.* T.S. Eliot in his 'Tradition and the Individual Talent' writes: 'No poet, no artist of any art, has his complete meaning alone. His significance, his appreciation is the appreciation of his relation to the dead poets and artists. You cannot value him alone; you must set him for contrast and comparison, among the dead. I mean this as a principle of aesthetic, not merely historical criticism. The necessity that he shall conform, that he shall cohere, is not one-sided; what happens when a new work of art is created is something that happens simultaneously to all the works of art which preceded it'. A similar view is expressed by Derrida (1979:107) when he says that the practice of 'intertextuality' is a recognition that 'one text reads another', and by Paul de Man (1979), who says that each text, no matter how complete it might appear to be, is effectively always a fragment.

In order to study relevance, we must take into account other texts too, contemporary as well as historical. For example, in the case of the election manifesto, the relevance of the manifesto of one left party is in relation to those of other left parties as well as those of different rightist parties. There is also interrelation between what happened earlier over a period of time and what is happening now. All these factors contribute to the notion of relevance.

The relationships that go into the concept of relevance must be seen at various levels. Even in the case of an advertisement, the statement that introduces the advertisement and the statement that concludes it are interconnected; this particular advertisement is related to all other advertisements in deciding its effectiveness and relevance. What is true in the case of a simple advertisement, is also true of a novel. The different sections and chapters of a novel contribute to the structuring principles of a novel; the introductory chapter has relevance to the concluding chapter; any given novel is perceived in its relation to all other novels, and this is another aspect of relevance.

That is why the notion of relevance is quite important in the study of discourse as social interaction.

VI. In human communication there is a paradoxical or a dialectical process of getting a balance between two opposing forces—the force (or forces) that compel(s) an individual to assume a social role, to accept a transindividual role which results in the modification of one's world-view in return for the common good; this is known as the 'cooperative imperative'. In acting collectively we create structures and transform them. The tendency to adapt oneself to one's milieu, the tendency to coherence and to social/global structuring processes, the dynamic character of behaviour and modifying tendency of the structure of which any individual is a part, the developmental tendency of both individual and society, the processes of structuration (continuous assimilation) and destructuration (continuous accommodation to the environment), the fact that there is no permanence to these structures which are not even fully formed because they are dynamic—all these factors, and many more, are to be taken into account in the study of discourse. That makes it difficult but challenging and interesting. A beginning has been made and more work will have to be done.

Questions and topics for discussion

1. 'How beautifully she writes!' — Comment on the ***propositional content*** ('sense') and the illocutionary intent ('force') of the utterance; specify the context in relation to the illocutionary intent.
2. Chomsky has been criticized for abstractions and idealizations. Do you think the speech act theory is above this criticism? If so, justify the claim. If not, give reasons for your answer.
3. Give five examples in actual language use for each of the following in your language and English: i) Situation Monitoring, (ii) Territorial Imperative (iii) Cooperative Imperative.
4. Explain what is meant by relevance. Illustrate your answer.
5. Take any five advertisements in English or in your first language and comment on the 'conversational implicatures' in each one of them.
6. It is claimed that communicative competence and not linguistic competence is the focal point of linguistic studies. What is your view?

7. How many kinds of competence can you think of? Make a list. Illustrate your answer.
8. Look at the data given below:

a) A : Have you seen Mr.Sharma?
B : He's in the library.
A : It's all right. I don't want to see him.

b) i. A : Would you like some tea?
B : Please.
A : (Pours out tea).
B : Thanks.

ii. A : Would you like some tea?
B : Thanks.
A : (pours out tea).

Try to analyse the exchange structure in each. How are the exchanges connected? What general and formalized statements can you make about discourse analysis on the basis of your analysis of the data?

9. If we compare natural conversation with dialogue in the theatre, what conclusions can be drawn?
10. 'Discourse analysis can get us to think of what we take for granted as everyday reality.' Explain and illustrate.
11. What are the four maxims in Grice's Cooperative Principles? Can you give examples from your first language to illustrate them?
12. A : Do you promise?
B : (Nods head)
The nod commits B to the promise although B has said nothing. One can be sorry or be grateful without saying anything. How can we account for such phenomena in speech act theory?
13. I promise you I'll be there.
I hereby promise you I'll be there.
These two sentences are not interchangable though Austin proposed the insertion of *hereby* before the verb. How can we explain the variation? Do you think Grice can help us?
14. 'There is a relationship between the speech act performed and social roles of the participants, which has been ignored in the same speech act literature.' Explain and illustrate.
15. A : Ohh I g'ta tell ya one course
B : In cred-
A : The mo- the mod- modern art in the 20th century art ...there is about eight books.
Such unplanned natural discourses contain hesitations, false starts, and other marks of 'unacceptable' sentences. While it is not difficult to show that the grammar of such natural data is different, it

is difficult to show that it is different. What is meant by this? Explain with reference to the data given above

16. Take any piece of conversation and analyse it in terms of the following components:
 opener (how the speech event is initiated), orientation (how the speaker's identiy or intention is given), act-statement (how the problem is stated), justification (reasons, arguments, etc.), remedy (solutions), closing (conclusion), valuation (the outcome).
17. 'Conversation — even academic conversation — is characterized by ambiguity, misunderstanding, meanings that insensibly change, and by what we have called 'fuzziness', all of which arise from the nature of conversation, the diversity of participants' social experience and therefore the diversity of the frames available. We must not allow the idealised unanimity to disguise from us the reality of that diversity.'
 Explain. Illustrate your answer with examples from your L_1 and English.

14 DISCOURSE: THE 'MENTAL MODEL' APPROACH

"The doctrine of innate ideas is one of the most admirable faiths of philosophy, being itself an innate idea and therefore inaccessible to disproof...".

- Ambrose Bierce, *The Devil's Dictionary.*

Focal points

I. In a conversation, in addition to the situational interaction there is 'cognitive interaction'. A hearer has to apply his/her mind to construct meaning from a 'text' in a given context. The position of a hearer in a face-to-face communicative situation like in an interview is different from his/her position while listenting to a radio play. In the former instance the hearer has to contribute to the development of 'discourse' while in the latter (s)he cannot. So is the case when one reads a text. In such cases though there is no physical, situational realization of 'interaction', there is 'interaction' at the cognitive level. In the 'mental model' approach, it is the cogitive interaction that is crucial, rather than the physical, situational 'interaction' that is given importance in the social interaction approach.

II. The construction of the mental model is viewed as part of the process of acquisition of knowledge. Firstly, the context of discourse in the mental model is a set of assumptions stored in the memory. Secondly, information not explicit in a text may be included in a representation of its content, particularly if it is required to establish links between parts of the text or among various other texts. Third, the context in which a discourse or text is interpreted and understoood determines the meanings of otherwise ambiguous expressions in it or what is not said but understood. Fourth, representations are built up as a text is read, according to certain conventions and procedures that are accepted as norms; certain kinds of expression in the text signal that new elements are going to be introduced; certain others refer back to the elements already introduced; all these involve the use of knowledge and memory. Fifth, at any point in a conversation or in reading a text, the representation that is constructed upto any given point becomes the contex for understanding what follows.

Johnson-Laird (1983) points out that participants in the same discourse may have different mental models, and each must take into account what (s)he knows about the others' models in order to make the interaction meaningful and interpretable. When talking to someone who does not know that you saw a film recently, it is unhelpful to say that 'the actors were all fantastic'.

Johnson-Laird proposes two levels of representation for discourse, one at the 'superficial propositional level' and the other at the 'mental model' level. The mental model can be viewed as a product of the interaction between 'existing assumptions' (i.e., present already in the mind) and 'new information' (that enters through the processing act).

The notion of a mental model of discourse is closely related to the proposals that have appeared recently in the literatures of psychology, linguistics, and Artificial Intelligence.

III. Text linguistics focuses on mutual relevance between/among texts as a defining condition for discourse; the social interaction approach focuses on the physical, situational context for signification and language use; the mental model (or construct) approach focuses on the 'existing assumptions' stored in memory as context for constructing representations. The concept of 'existing assumptions' can be considered equivalent to that of background knowledge' in language comprehension, which is termed 'Schema' in reading theory. One of the basic notions of the 'schema theory' is that 'every act of comprehension involves one's knowledge of the world as well' (Anderson et al 1977:369). As Carrell and Eisterhold (1988) put it, the interpretation of a text depends on the relationship between the 'existing schema' and the 'input information'.

IV. The term 'schema' (the plural form being 'schemata') has been defined differently by different philosophers and psychologists. There are three other terms used to refer to 'schema' (background knowledge); they are 'frames', 'scripts', and 'scenarios'. *Frames* are data structures stored in memory; *scripts,* though analoguous to 'frames', are 'specialized to deal with even sequences'. 'Frames' and 'scripts' are formulations of scientists working on Artificial Intelligence. 'Scenarios' are 'situation-specific' descriptions of 'settings'. The term 'schema' has been used to cover three knowledge sources and functional levels. The three functional levels of language in use are, according to Halliday, the ideational, the interpersonal, and the textual. The ideational function helps a language user to use it for all the specific purposes and situation types involving communication of experience; the interpersonal function helps one to use language for all the specific forms of personal and social interaction; the textual function is seen as a prerequisite to the effective operation of the other two. The term 'schema-directed processes' refers to the processing operations.

Carrell (1988) suggests a three-way distinction within 'schemata'. The reader's prior linguistic knowledge is called 'linguistic schemata'; the reader's prior background knowledge of the content area of the text is called 'content schemata'; the reader's prior knowledge of the rhetorical structure is termed 'formal schemata'. There are also proposals on 'culture-specific schemata'. 'Schema' is not a static phenomenon; in the processing of a 'text' readers develop a 'schema' or enrich/enlarge an existing 'schema' or prove/disprove an existing 'schema', and so on.

V. Widdowson (1983) proposes a difference between 'systemic knowledge' (equivalent to Chomsky's linguistic competence') and 'schematic knowledge' (knowledge in the organisation of utterances, as a set of expectations derived from previous experience which are projected on to instances of actual language behaviour). 'Schematic knowledge' can be equated with communcative competence. He also proposes 'procedural capacity' (the ability to effectively manage procedural work for the realisation of competence); 'procedures...are used to match up and adjust schemata in the discourse process; they are interactive, negotiating activities which interpret the directions provided and enable us to alter our expectations in the light of new evidence as the discourse proceeds.' To Widdowson, undersanding is the 'rapport' between different 'schematic' worlds.

VI. Though discourse analysis aims at the study of mental mechanisms that make it possible for people to use discourse, for practical reasons there has been a strong bias towards studying comprehension rather than production, and, in a way, a bias towards written rather than spoken language. Discourse is about the world—and often about a fictitious world—and the primary tasks of the production and understanding systems are to construct a representation of a part of the world corresponding to a given discourse or text—a mental model. Several subprocesses contribute to this operation—word recognitions, syntax, semantic interpretation, pragmatic interpretation, model construction, short-term and long-term memory, previous knowledge, etc. A theory of discourse analysis should provide models of the subprocesses responsible for carrying out these tasks, and an account of how they interact to effect understanding.

Since the early 1970s there have been hundreds of studies of the interpretation of sentences and texts. In most studies it is taken for granted that the meaning of a discourse depends on the meaning of the sentences in it; it is true that a single sentence may constitute a mini-discourse but the meaning of the discourse is not the sum total of the meaning of the sentences in it. Representations of the content of discourse are related not only to linguistic elements but also to things in the world—people, things, actions, events, processes, etc. and relations among them.

The theory of mental models, together with an account of semantic processing tries in some way to explain how information from different parts of a discourse is integrated; but we are yet to understand how world knowledge is to be related to discourse processing. Long-term memory must be highly structured if it is to be useful in comprehending intertextuality; lack of a particular item of knowledge may make a text difficult to understand and ignorance of the overall context in which a text is to be placed will have much more drastic effects.

Texts have a global structure in addition to the local structure; one suggestion is that these structures are to be studied using story grammars; but the problem is, even assuming that story grammars have been understood, that structures in stories are comprehended *primarily* from the situations that are found in the stories. In the case of a discourse, it is necessary to understand not only the structure of the discourse but also the world in which the situation is situated; the meaning of a discourse depends on knowledge about communicative acts, the society and the situation in which it takes place, and the mental make up of the participants involved in the discourse.

At present there is a growing interest in discourse production and discourse comprehension. This work is likely to continue over the next few years and may result in the better understanding of discourse processing.

Questions and topics for discussion

1. List the respective 'stored world-knowledge' which is likely to interact with the following text presented information:
   a) All men are mortal.
   b) Water condenses at 0°C.
   c) Action and reaction are equal and opposite.
   d) At times, due to inadequate supply of oxygen unburnt carbon is emitted from a kerosene stove as sooty flame.
2. Dictionaries define one word in terms of others and dictionary-makers assume that users of dictionaries have some linguistic sophistication; that is why their definitions of the most common words are not particularly helpful. But in the case of the mental lexicon of the user of the language and semantic memory, we need a very sophisticated theory. Can you point out some of the basic differences between a lexicon and a mental lexicon with reference to some common words used in your L_1 or in English?

3. 'The question of how the language processors (lexical, syntactic, and content level) work together and interact is very difficult to resolve.' Explain and illustrate.
4. 'Linguistically conveyed information is converted into internal representation, or mental model, of a situation in the real or imaginary world. The mind contains many such representations, derived from both language and perception. A theory of language production must describe how such representations are converted into speech and writing' - Explain and illustrate.
5. 'Semantics may be more directly related than syntax to cognitive abilities.' - Explain and illustrate.
6. There is something called cognitive style — the relatively stable way that people perceive, conceptualize and organize information. There are several factors that contribute to cognitive style; they can be thought of in terms of dual sets such as field dependence/field independence global/local perception of parts as related to the whole, verbal/imaginal, analytical/relational, serialistic/holistic, etc. Can we say that success in language learning depends on cognitive style? Give reasons for your answer.
7. What is the difference between cognition and intelligence? If intelligence means the ability to act purposefully, to think rationally, and to deal effectively with the environment, do you think intelligence and success in language learning are closely related? Give reasons for your answer.
8. It is clear that memory is as important to language learning as cognitive style. Try to define memory. If memory is a constructive act or process, what is its relationship with language learning? Illustrate your answer.
9. How many different levels of storage — short-term, medium-term, long-term, etc.— are there before information is truly stored in memory for use when recalled?
10. Computer memory and human memory — are they one and the same? What are the similarities and what are the differences?
11. If stored information consists of traces of previous constructive mental or overt actions, do you think there is scope for 'misprocessing' any aspect of stored information? Give some examples to show that misprocessing is possible.
2. 'Language develops on the basis of cognitive representations of experience, through the matching of linguistic forms to expectations derived from this experience.' - Explain. Illustrate your answer.

15 DISCOURSE AND NOTIONS OF TEXTUALITY

'Did you see the woods we passed by!'
'Oh no! I was counting the trees!'

Focal points

I. Only when we start analysing human language from various angles, social, psychological, textual and intertextual, we realize that we, as human beings, have mastered a very intricate system with innumerable variables; the nuts and bolts are so many that the aftermath of an intensive analysis is invariably a bewilderment leaving us 'speechless' and wondering, 'how such a small head can carry all we knew.'

We saw in the earlier units of this chapter that 'text' could be defined as a linguistic entity while 'discourse' could be defined as the process of actualizing the linguistic entity and that 'discourse' production and comprehension could be studied from both social and mental points of view. In this unit, the defining principles of textual communication—the constitutive principles that make a text a text—are given.

II. de Beaugrande and Dressler (1981) have proposed *seven standards of textuality*; they are *cohesion, coherence, intentionality, acceptability, informativity, situationality,* and *intertextuality.* These principles define textual communication and hence are *constitutive principles* (in the framework of Speech Act Theory). The principles that control rather than define textual communication are *regulative principles* such as *efficiency, effectiveness* and *appropriateness.*

a) *Cohesion:* The term *cohesion* means sticking together. There are certain devices in a text that make the items hang together; such devices that are mutually connected within a sequence contribute to the stability, economy, and efficiency of the text. Some of the devices of cohesion are listed below:
   i. *Recurrence:* Repetition of items or patterns; recurrence is often used to assert and re-affirm one's point of view or to reject something or to overcome irrelevant interruptions.

e.g., Break, break, break
On thy cold grey stones, O Sea!
— Tennyson

And miles to go before I sleep
And miles to go before I sleep.
— Frost

ii. *Partial Recurrence*: Using the same items but shifting them to different classes.

e.g. *Governments* are instituted among Men, deriving their just powers from the consent of the *governed.*
Mankind are more disposed to *suffer*, while evils are *sufferable....* Such has been the patient *sufferance* of these colonies.

iii. *Parallelism*: Similar forms recur with somewhat different content. (This is the opposite of paraphrase, where the content is the same but expressed in different forms.)

e.g. He has *plundered* our seas, *ravaged* our coasts, *burnt* our towns.

iv. *Paraphrases*: The reccurence of the same content with a change of expression.

e.g. I have never seen *a murderer*, a taker of life.

v. *Co-reference:* Use of pro-forms.
— anaphora (pro-forms *after* the coreferring expression).

e.g. There was *an old woman* who lived in a shoe. *She* had so many children to look after and the children....
Napoleon arrived at that place; *the conqueror of Austria* was in high spirits.
— Cataphora (pro-forms before the coreferring expression).

e.g. I don't know if *he* is serious, but my *roommate* wants to go there.
— *Pro-Sentence*
The earth is round. *It* is a well-known fact.
— Pro-verb — do/do so e.g. I don't *understand* you perfectly, but that's more than I *do* myself.
A : I went to the cinema.
B : So did I.
— Pro-form - such - e.g. He thinks too much. *Such* men are dangerous.

vi. *Ellipsis*: Also known as gapping; an appreciable discontinuity of the surface text; generally the omission of the verb.

e.g. Mine be thy love, and thy love's use their treasure. (The verb 'be' is needed to complete the second clause).

vii. *Junction:* Four kinds of junctive expressions.

— Conjunction: words like and, moreover, also, in addition, besides, furthermore, etc.

— Disjunction: words like or, either... or, whether or not, etc.

— Contrajunction: words like but, yet, however, nevertheless , etc; such words link units that are incompatible in the textual world.

— Subordination: words like since, as, thus, while, therefore, etc; such words link units that depend on each other; they express cause, effect, reason, plan, etc.

— Temporal expressions like then, next, before, after during, while, etc.

b) *Coherence:* Cohesion is connectivity of the surface, whereas *coherence* deals with connectivity of underlying content; in other words, coherence is concerned with the mutual accessibility and relevance of concepts and relations that underlie the surface text. In the mental model view of discourse, the language user reconstructs the continuity of the underlying content of a text; the result of his/her exploration and the representation of coherence as reconstructed by the receiver is given prominence.

There are different kinds of knowledge components that are stored by the human mind. Components of knowledge that are true for *most* instances of the concept, like 'humans usually live in communities', constitute 'typical knowledge'; components of knowledge that happen to be true of random instances, like 'some humans happen to be brown', constitute 'accidental knowledge'; components, like 'all humans are mortal', that are essential constitute 'determinate knowledge'. Such components of knowledge are stored and form part of the memory records of one's own experience. The surface expressions are taken as cues to activate the various kinds of knowledge; the receiver of a text reconstructs the content of a text, using his/her background knowledge, and arrives at the *continuity of sense.*

There are other scholars who have a different perspective of coherence. Widdowson (1979), for example, distinguishes between 'internal' cohesion and 'external' aspects of textuality; he maintains that the 'external' aspects of textuality, the link between the situation and language, are not concerned with 'internal' *grammatical cohesion* but with *rhetorical coherence* of utterances in the act of communication. For instance, in the conversation that follows there is hardly anything to make it a cohesive text except that the two utterances occur one after another.

A : Did you take the 11 o'clock train?
B : I met Sharma on the way.

To a person who has no access to the shared knowledge of 'A' and 'B', the utterance of 'B' sounds totally irrelevant. Maybe, the Sharma in question is a bore and meeting him on the way is enough to say that 'A' missed the train; or, maybe, Sharma has a car and gave 'B' a lift to the station, so that 'B' was in time to catch the train. It is clear that the coherence of 'discourse' is not always decided by the cohesion of 'text'. It is also true that hearers do not always use contextual information to maintain coherence relations; Blakemore (1988) points out that discourse is full of utterances without coherence relations, yet perfectly understandable, given the appropriate contextual information. For example, the notice 'NO SMOKING' in a cinema is perfectly understood. The connection is established at the propositional level as a consequence of the perceiver's 'search for relevance'.

That is why the concept of relevance is considered very crucial in formulating the notion of coherence. Relevance is one of the maxims in the Grician framework; though Grice does not elaborate on the simple instruction 'Be relevant', others have taken it seriously and have formulated the 'theory of relevance'. Sperber and Wilson (1979) sought to reduce Grice's maxims to a single maxim of relevance. It has been argued that in every discourse processing effort the effect achieved is a result of processing 'new information' in the context of 'existing assumptions'; so the relationship between the newly presented item of information and the context of existing assumptions can be accounted for in a *relevance-based* framework of relationships.

Thus, the interpretation of an utterance is not just a matter of identification of a proposition it expresses, but working out the consequences of adding it to a set of existing assumptions; it is the consequence that matters and not the mere identification. In other words, the language user's aim is to establish that the new information is relevant. The new information may (a) add to the existing assumptions(s); (b) provide further evidence for the existing assumption(s); or (c) contradict the existing assumption(s). In planned discourse the aim seems to be maximizing relevance over the discourse as a whole.

c) *Intentionality* and *Acceptability* are two sides of the same coin; intentionality is producer-oriented and acceptability receiver-oriented. The language producer's intentions must match with the context so that they become acceptable to the receiver. Acceptability also subsumes 'acceptance' or active willingness to participate as a collaborator in the development of discourse for the realization of a shared goal.
d) *Informativity* is a concept that is used to designate the extent to which a presentation is new or unexpected for the receiver. In order to uphold interest and fulfil an intention, text producers can create a planned flow of expectations. Informativity is not a static concept; it varies from person to person, from text to text, and context to context.
e) *Situationality* is a notion that is applied to discuss the way in which texts are correlated with discourse action and applied to a situation.
f) *Intertextuality* is seen as a key concept in fixing relevance to texts; it is also a key notion in the social interaction approach and the mental model approach. Intertextuality has become an important concept in post-structuralist thinking too. 'Each element is constituted with reference to the trace in it of the other elements of the sequence or system. This linkage, this meaning, is the text, which is produced only through the transformation of another text,' asserts Derrida (1981).

Questions and topics for discussion

1. Point out the various implications of the terms a) cohesion, (b) coherence, and (c) relevance as given in Chapter IV.
2. There was once an old farmer who owned a very stubborn donkey.

One evening the farmer was trying to put his donkey into the shed. First, the farmer pushed the donkey, but the donkey wouldn't move. Then the farmer pulled the donkey, but the donkey still would't move. Then the farmer asked his dog to bark loudly at the donkey and thereby frighten him into the shed. But the dog refused. So, the farmer asked his cat to scratch the dog so that the dog would bark loudly and thereby frighten the donkey into the shed. But the cat replied, 'I would gladly scratch the dog if only you would get me some milk.' So the farmer went to his cow and asked for some milk; but the cow replied, 'I would gladly give you some milk if only you would give me some hay.'

— Analyse the text given above in terms of the seven standards of textuality explained in this unit. Point out the problems, if any.

3. A : Do you do buttonholes?

B : She'll be back in a hour.

Comment on the text given above from the point of view of relevance.

4. In any symbolic mode of expression, we can expect hesitation, doubt, lack of clarity, ambiguity and contradictions; we can notice these in conversation as well as written texts. Do you agree? Can you give examples for each type mentioned above from the written mode, either from your L_1 or from English
5. No text is context-free — Explain and illustrate.
6. The hidden context of situation is as important as the observable context of situation. Explain the implications of the extension of 'context'. Illustrate your answer.
7. Take any short story that you like and analyse it from the point of view of textuality.
8. 'The text has no meaning in it as an intrinsic property. It is only the reader who breathes meaning into it.'

— Explain and illustrate.

16 DISCOURSE PROCESSING AND READING

'Reading maketh a ready man; ...' — *Bacon*

Focal points

I. It is said that when we read a page we read what we want to read and not what is there for us to read. Why should it happen like that? Reading is a psycholinguistic guessing game which involves discourse processing; reading is an activity in which the reader reconstructs a message which has been encoded by the writer as a graphic display; it is an extraction of meaning from print, call it construction, reconstruction, or deconstruction. The term reading refers to *reading for understanding* and not merely the physical recitation. Reading is not simple decoding but discourse processing.

II. The efforts to understand the processes involved in reading comprehension have a long history. From the efforts to discover the intentions of the writer, it has now come to finding out the interactive processes in the nature of reading—a long way indeed.

As we know, the terms 'discourse' and 'processing' have many definitions and connotations. 'Process' can be defined in terms of learning or thinking. From the behaviouristic point of view of learning, it refers to repetition of observable behaviours and their contiguities with rewards, punishments and so on. From the thinking perspective, processing refers to a mental event which is more of a problem-solving nature. A problem-solving perspective normally focuses on distinctions and changes that take place within an effort to solve a particular problem involving several mental operations which serve to connect the various aspects; since learning is only a sub-field of thinking, the focus is on the problem-solving perspective when we talk of discourse-processing.

III. Rumelhart (1977) critically evaluates the earlier Information Processing Models in their application to reading. These models have a series of *non-interactive* stages of processing, each stage doing its work independently and passing its output to the next higher stage. This does not permit the information contained in a higher stage to influence the processing in a lower stage, which is a serious deficiency. Thus, for example, recognition of letters has to take help from word-recognition (a combination of letters) and semantic knowledge influences word perception; the perception of syntax for a given word (like 'man') depends on the context in which the word is embedded (as in 'any man can do it' or 'they man it', etc.). So processing cannot be studied in terms of water-tight compartments. Rumelhart has argued that the semantic, syntactic and lexical levels have an influence on the lowest, graphemic level. This leads him to a neat formulation as given below:

> The message center keeps a running list of hypotheses about the nature of the input string. Each knowledge source constantly scans the message center for the appearance of hypotheses relevant to its own source of knowledge. Whenever such a hypothesis enters the message center, the knowledge source in question evaluates the hypothesis in the light of its own specialized knowledge. As a result of its analysis, the hypothesis may be confirmed, disconfirmed, and removed from the message center, or a new hypothesis can be added to the message center. This procedure continues until some decision can be reached. At that point the most probable hypothesis is determined to be the right one. (1977: 589-90).

Thus reading is an interactive process in which the guessing of the probable hypothesis at any given point in discourse processing becomes crucial.

IV. The earlier models looked at reading in either of the two formulations given below:

a) Reading is a decoding process of reconstructing the author's intended meaning via recognizing the printed letters and words, and building up a meaning from the smallest textual units at the 'bottom' (letters and words) to the larger and larger units at the 'top' (phrases, clauses, inter-sentential linkages, etc.). This is known as the *bottom-up* perspective of reading.
b) In the *top-down* perspective, the reader is said to be moving

from the top level of total discourse organization to the levels down below (inter-sentential, clause, phrase, words) to the level of letters.

In the interactive model the top-down and the bottom-up strategies operate interactively during discourse processing.

V. In understanding the mental processes involved in reading, the traditional notions *analysis* and *synthesis* are useful if they are understood in dialectical terms.

In the language user's mind two types of relations operate:

a) the notion of 'vertical' relations which deal with subordinate and super-ordinate categories or the relations between a category and its special cases; this is the relationship of choice which is also called *Paradigmatic Relationship*;
b) the notion of 'horizontal' relations which deals with relations within and across categories; this is the relationship of chain which is also called *Syntagmatic Relationship*.

These two relationships occupy a central position in processing and they constantly react with each other at all levels (lexical, syntactic, semantic, etc.) and across levels; analysis and synthesis involve paradigmatic and syntagmatic relationships. One can claim that all schemata involve paradigmatic-syntagmatic, analysis-synthesis interaction.

During the processing of a 'text' a reader brings into operation some schemata, which are knowledge structures. When a schema is identified or primed as relevant for the on-going processing, along with that schema the subschemata relevant to it are also primed. These elements—which can be regarded as slots in a choice or paradigmatic relationship—can accept any of the range of values compatible with their associative (chain or syntagmatic) schemata. When a reader reads a text and the schema has been primed, elements in the situation (of the coming information from the text) are bound to appropriate slots in the relevant schemata; in other words, the reader is continuously engaged in constructing the correspondence between the relevant schemata, and the 'givens' and 'knowns' of a message. This is the search for relevance through establishing relationships ('intertextuality') between the text and the existing assumptions. Thus, the comprehension of a message involves drawing information from two sources—the given message and the internal schemata—until the two are 'reconciled' as a single schema or message. The quality of associations and the network of relations among the constituents of the schemata will determine the correctness of the reconciliation of information; at the same time, the reconciliation is never static but rather dynamic, continuously being reorganised during the cognitive processing of information; this involves the constant re-evaluation of the already associated meanings or aspects of relations.

VI. If discourse processing is a search for meaning, the role of words (lexis) and the role of syntax have time and again come up in varying degrees of emphasis. Research based on the Chomskyan theory of linguistic description that focuses on syntax may be said to have the following three features:

a) The psychological reality of the theory proposed by Chomsky (the study of which is known as the 'correspondence hypothesis') and the study of the relationship between Chomsky's theory and the actual practice by language users.
b) The competence-performance factor and their correlation in the language acquisition process of children.
c) the patterns of children's grammars and the order in which the rules are acquired.

According to the 'correspondence hypothesis' the relative difficulty a learner experiences in understanding a sentence should be correlated to the number of grammatical rules necessary for deriving the surface structure from the corresponding deep structure. This position was questioned by Fodor (1969): 'Grammatical rules are themselves not a part of the recognition procedure .... The mental operations which underlie the behaviour of the speaker/hearer are not identical to, and probably do not include, the grammatical operations involved in generating sentences.' In other words, syntax alone cannot form the basis for deciding the difficulty involved in processing sentences. The criteria should be formulated with inputs from lexical, syntactic, semantic, pragmatic, and schematic aspects; syntax is not the only input, but one of the inputs.

In spoken language, the intonational pattern has many clues, apart from the very context in which an utterance occurs; on the other hand, in written discourse this information is given only marginally by punctuation. The reader must not only recognize words, but also impose correct syntactic structures on them. There are two separate aspects of syntax which are necessary for a child in order to use the language: (a) rules governing the combination of single words to form larger syntactic units like phrases, and clauses, and (b) rules governing transformations. The analytic approach to syntax has yielded a wealth of insight into language phenomena, but at the same time it has lost sight of certain questions of fundamental importance: 'What is syntax for? What is a particular syntactic rule needed for? What relationships cannot be expressed or can be expressed only very clumsily without the rules? What determines that one syntactic rule is more appropriate than the other in a particular context?'

VII. Reading in a second language has a few specific questions to pose. The most important question is: 'Are problems of second language reading those of 'language' or those of 'reading'?'

The problems that a second language reader faces may have to be characterized either as problems of 'linguistic proficiency' or problems of 'reading efficiency'; the question is being debated. In linguistic proficiency the focus is on learning the language but in reading efficiency the focus is on learning to read. A number of studies have found that success in reading in a second langauge depends crucially on one's reading ability in the first language. Goodman (1973) puts forward the 'reading universal' hypothesis and claims that the reading process will be much the same for all languages. Yorio (1971), on the other hand, claims that the reader's knowledge in second/foreign language is not like that of the native user, and so the guessing or predicting ability necessary to pick up cues is hindered by the imperfect knowledge of the second language.

The evidence supporting this hypothesis comes from research on three closely related questions:

a) Does limited proficiency in a second/foreign language restrict the reading ability in that language?
b) Does limited proficiency in a second/foreign language re-

strict readers from using very *specific types of textual information* when reading in that language?

c) Is there a 'threshold of linguistic competence' (roughly a 'take off' stage) which readers must reach in order to read successfully in a second language? If there is one how can that stage be defined and described?

Research into the first question focuses on the relationship between the level of language competence and the level of reading ability in a second language. Investigations into the second question have given a more specific version of the first question; the general findings of researches on both the questions have led some researchers to suggest that there is a 'threshold of linguistic competence' necessary for succesful L_2 reading (Devine 1988). Devine draws some pedagogic implications too:

(a) success in L_2 reading is related to the proficiency in L_2; (b) knowledge of L_2 syntax enhances L_2 reading ability (c) slow reading rate of L_2 learners can be traced to low general competence in L_2; (d) textual constraints (syntactic, semantic, discoursal), tense, aspect, modality, grammatical and lexical cohesion, etc. are some of the most significant sources of L_2 reading difficulties; (e) linguistic threshold almost varies from task to task and from reader to reader; and (f) linguistic knowledge interacts with nonlinguistic knowledge in L_2 reading.

Wolf and Walters (1988), after examining critically the Contrastive Analysis Hypothesis, Krashen's language acquisition and learning models, L_2 - Information Processing models proposed by McLaughlin, et al. propose that L_2 users search for similarities between L_1 and L_2 linguistic units and integrate information from both the languages to produce 'understanding' in L_2. This is validated by Information Integration Theory which holds that information from different sources is always integrated within the human mind according to their conceptual levels. Thus, L_1 information and L_2 information have to form a whole within the mind though they come from different sources. This theoretical understanding has to be implemented in actual L_2 learning situations in an experimental way to develop this as valid pedagogical theory.

Questions and topics for discussion

1. How would you characterize the following 'styles' of reading?
   a) Referring to a dictionary for the meaning of each new word as one proceeds with the reading of a text.
   b) Guessing the meanings of unknown words from the contexts of occurrence as one proceeds with the reading of a text.
2. Which of the two 'styles' of reading mentioned above would you advocate as a teacher of English to your students?
3. What are the differences between 'rote-learning' and the depth of processing? Do you think that 'rote-learning' has no role to play in the learning process since it is said that the depth of processing helps retention?
4. Relate the different strategies of reading ('top-down', 'bottom-up' and 'interactive') to different kinds of comprehension questions that are asked in second language text books. Give examples from a text book.
5. 'Children acquire their mother tongue by learning the sounds, letters, words, sentences and meanings in that order'. - Do you agree? Explain your answer. Relate your answer to what you read in the chapter on *Language and Mind* as well as the last unit of this chapter.
6. Explain the following behavioural patterns in terms of cognitivist understanding:
   a) As soon as a wellknown comedian appears on the stage or in a film for the first time, the audience start laughing.
   b) As soon as Kapil Dev (former captain of the Indian cricket team) enters the field to bat, the audience start clapping their hands.
   c) When we read a novel serialized in a weekly magazine, week after week we tend to predict the future developments of the story.
   d) As we read a novel we characterize only certain developments as unexpected.
   e) As one reads a page, when the last sentence on the page is incomplete one tends to complete the sentence mentally before turning the page.
7. 'Reading as a skill cannot be taught in a course! Learners can only hope to learn how to maximize the extraction of meaning from print with the minimum effort.' - Explain and illustrate.
8. Children have often been called word-learning wizards. Are words learned in the oral/aural mode learned better than words learned by reading? What conclusions can you draw from your observation of children learning words?

9. How to read a page actually means how to reap a page. Can you explain this statement from the point of view of reading comprehension?
10. Reading is the projection and fulfilment of individual desire in the interpretation of the text. Do you agree? Give reasons for your answer.
11. 'When a poet's mind is perfectly equipped for its work, it is constantly amalgamating disparate experience; the ordinary man's experience is chaotic, irregular, fragmentary, the latter falls in love, or reads Spinoza, and these two experiences have nothing to do with each other, or with the noise of the typewriter or the smell of cooking; in the mind of the poet these experiences are always forming newer wholes.' ('The Metaphysical Poets', T.S.Eliot).
    a) Discuss this view in relation to the schema-theoretic view and Information Integration Theory.
    b) Do you think it is possible to draw a line between poets and ordinary men in terms of experience and perception? Discuss Eliot's distinction between poets and ordinary men with reference to Information Integration Theory.

Suggested reading

de Beaugrande, R., and W. Dressler. 1981. *An Introduction to Text Linguistics.* London : Longman.

There is a useful summary of the work done by van Dijk, Kintsch, Petofi and others with many references to their original work. It is an abstract presentation of the area of study. There is a detailed discussion of each notion of textuality.

Blakemore, D.L. 1988. 'The Organization of Discourse.' In F.J. Newmeyer.(ed.). 1988. *Linguistics: The Cambridge Survey Vol. IV : Language — The Sociocultural Context.* Cambridge : Cambridge University Press.

This is a good introduction to the 'mental model' view of discourse.

Carrel, P.L., Joanne Devine, and David Eskey. (eds.). 1988. *Interactive Approaches to Second Language Reading.* Cambridge : Cambridge University Press.

This book presents the major developments in the area of 'Reading' in the past fifteen years. This is a useful reference book.

Gumperz, J.J. (ed.). 1982. *Language and Social Identity.* Cambridge : Cambridge University Press.

This book contains a series of case studies exploring situations of intergroup communication in modern industrial society such as job interviews, committee negotiations, court room testimony, etc.

Leech, G.N. 1983. *Principles of Pragmatics.* London : Longman.

This is a good introduction to pragmatics. The distinction between semantics and pragmatics has been lucidly presented.

Sinclair, J. McH., and R.M. Coulthard. 1975. *Towards an Analysis of Discourse. The English used by Teachers and Pupils.* Oxford : OUP.

This book presents the theoretical and descriptive problems of analysing classroom discourse.

Stubbs, Michael. 1983. *Discourse Analysis. The Sociolinguistic Analysis of Natural Language.* Oxford : Basil Blackwell.

This is a very lucid presentation of the social interactionist perspective of discourse analysis. Application of the work done by Sinclair, the Speech Act Theory, the theory of implicatures, etc. has been attempted.

CHAPTER FOUR

Language and Literature

'A linguist deaf to the poetic function of language and a literary scholar indifferent to linguistic problems and unconversant with linguistic methods are equally flagrant anachronisms.'

— R. Jakobson

17 THE LANGUAGE OF LITERATURE: FOCUS ON THEORY

'Great literature is simply language charged with meaning to the utmost possible degree.'

— Ezra Pound

Focal points

I. What makes a verbal message a work of art, a thing of beauty, a text with its own literary texture? It is a truism to say that it is the special use of language that contributes to the literariness of a discourse or text. George Steiner (1958) defines literature in negative terms as follows: (a) Literature is studied *not* for the sake of information; (b) The message in literature is *not* verifiable as true or false (because all literature is fiction); (c) Literature is *not* paraphrasable. The language of literature is not *cryptic* like the language of science; the language of literature is *delphic* (i.e., obscure, ambiguous, oracular), which is another way of saying that it is poetic or emotive.

Such statements raise more questions than they answer. Literature, primarily, is to be taken as text, as discourse; the language of literature is the medium through which a writer conveys a message about reality to the reader. Hence all that we have seen so far regarding the nature of language can be brought in to understand the following questions:

a) How do we define literature and literary qualities (i.e., literariness)?
b) What relation do we envisage between the author and the text on the one hand, and the text and the reader on the other?
c) How do we view the relationship between *text* and *reality*? (The world outside has various realities like socio-cultural, political, mental, philosophical, etc.)
d) What status is to be given to the medium of the text, language, and how do we understand the 'special' use of language?

All these are tricky questions that have no simple answers.

Roman Jakobson says: 'Poeticity is like oil in cooking. You cannot have it on its own but when it is used with other food it is more than a mere addition. It changes the taste of food to the extent some dishes no longer appear to have any connection with their oil-less counterparts.' In other words, there is some connection between poeticity (i.e., literariness) and 'reality' but at, the same time, it is not just reality; since all literature is in the form of language, there is a strong connection between literariness and language but, at the same time, it is not just 'ordinary' language; it is 'language plus'.

The impossibility of maintaining a clear-cut distinction between ordinary, day-to-day communication/language and literary communication/language has been pointed out by many. For example, if a newspaper headline like 'Bank Manager Killed' is grafted as part of a detective novel, does it get literariness since its relevance changes? Conversely, if as part of one's conversation, someone says 'For God's sake, hold your tongue and let me kiss you', does it have no literariness?

The famous example of the Ordinary Language Philosopher J.L. Austin (1962) 'I hereby pronounce you man and wife' can be grafted and made part of various situations like in a play where the 'priest' says this, or in a film where the 'priest' is forced to say this by the 'villain' in a forced wedding, or the priest is telling a lie in order to save somebody, etc. The privileged status that has been given for ages to the language of literature is now being seriously questioned and several issues in the study of literature are being examined critically and radically.

II. Even a brief survey of the traditional approaches to literary studies, called literary criticism, shows that the study of literature has been regarded as a branch of aesthetics and is concerned with the total effect of literary texts; the consequence is that literature is put beyond the scope of any linguistic or stylistic investigation. It is generally said that literature is an 'organic whole' and, therefore, form and content are inseparable; the critic, however, assumes that the artistic values of literary work are available to his/her *intuitive awareness*, which is *subjective* and *impressionistic*. In such an attempt there need not be, and usually there isn't, much agreement between two critics or between critics and readers. In such a situation the critic is always privileged. As Roland Barthes (1974:174) puts it: 'The author is a god (his place of origin is the signified); as for the critic, he is the priest whose task is to decipher the Writing of the God.'

In order to make literary criticism explicit, formal, objective, rigorous, and publicly verifiable (as far as possible as in any other humanistic discipline), the discipline called *stylistics* (which is concerned with the resources of a language code which are put to use in the production of messages) came into being.

The term *stilistik* has been in use since the early 19th century and in English it is found as early as in 1846 (Oxford English Dictionary). Stylistics 'as the art of forming good style in writing' and 'as the science of literary style' are a few of the meanings given in dictionaries. The word 'style' has quite a few meanings and the study of style various approaches:

i. Aristotle, Cicero, and Quintilian regarded style as the 'ornament of thought'; Swift's definition of style as 'proper words in proper places' belongs here. Classical works on 'rhetoric' and 'poetics' treat style as ornament and persuasion; they can be called pragmatic theories of style and often they are *normative* since they set up models of good style 'derived from the qualities of works whose success and long survival have proved their adaptation to human nature, or else being grounded directly on the psychological laws governing the response of men in general.' (Abrams 1972:12).

ii. There are also psychologically-oriented theories of style that are based on the assumption that style reflects one's personality; Buffon's definition that 'the style is the man' and Leibnitz' observation that 'languages are the best mirrors of human mind' fall into this category; style can be regarded as a characteristic manner of expression in prose or 'verse' or 'epistemic choice', a way of sorting out the phenomena of experience, a choice suggestive of and determined by habitual patterns of thought and feeling; this view of style almost borders on 'determinism'. The task of stylistics, the study of style, will then be to trace the habitual patterns of thought, the feeling signified by the language of literature.

iii. Objective theories regard literature as a 'verbal artefact', a 'heterocosm'; literary texts, according to this approach, are to be analysed in objective terms, ignoring considerations of the author, period, readers, or other external factors. Practical Criticism, New Criticism, and most sub-sects of stylistics come under this category. Practical Criticism and New Criticism focus on meaning as signified by sense, tone, feeling, intention, etc., the approach being lexicosemantic and the end being interpretation of literary texts; linguistic stylistics, on the other hand, focuses on features of lexis, syntax and phonology, the end being the description of the stylistic features of texts.

III. From the beginning, stylistics as a discipline has been polarised between two tendencies which are most clearly formulated in French *stylistique* and German *stilforchung;* the former is closely linked to linguistics and the latter to literary criticism, philosophical idealism, psychological attitudes and history. *Linguistic Stylistics,* based on linguistics, streams off into Structuralism and Structuralist Stylistics, The Prague School Stylistics, the Neo-Firthian Functional Stylistics, Transformational Stylistics and so on. *Literary Stylistics,* as advocated by Spitzer and his followers in the 1940s is more subjective than objective, more literary than linguistic. Linguistic stylistics attempts to make literary criticism as objective as possible; like Chomsky's 'linguistic competence' and Hymes' 'communicative competence', scholars and critics such as Terence Hawkes and Jonathan Culler have argued out a case for 'literary competence' and its explicit and formal description. In other words, stylistic analysis is an attempt to express in explicit terms the connection between an instance of 'actualized system' (the text that is taken up for analysis) and the 'virtual system' (the language as a whole); if the virtual system can be described, then it should be possible to describe an actualized system. Since literature comes to us in the form of texts, all the insights from sociolinguistics, psycholinguistics, discourse analysis, research in the area of reading, etc. can be used to 'read' literary texts.

IV. Among the various schools and movements in stylistics, the most significant ones are outlined below.

The publication in 1916 of the *Cours de linguistique generale* based on the lectures of Ferdinand de Saussure marks the beginning of structural linguistics. Among the many ideas expressed in this seminal work are the distinction between *langue* and *parole*, *diachronic* and *synchronic* study of language, and *paradigmatic* and *syntagmatic* relationships.

Almost at the same time the Moscow Linguistic Circle was formed in 1915 and Russian formalism flourished during 1915-30. In the initial stages the members of the Circle were preoccupied with problems concerning the language of literature and tried to build up a 'science of literature'. As a result of the political changes in the Soviet Union, some of the members moved out and Prague became the centre for the Prague School Theory of language. In 1926 the Prague Linguistic Circle met and the group included some Czech and Russian linguists. Roman Jakobson became a leading figure in the Prague Circle.

The theory of functional style is, perhaps, one of the greatest contributions of the Prague School; the basic functions are taken as the function of expression, the function of appeal and the function of reference; the first two functions serve the emotive purpose and the third one conveys the factual content. In literature, as in language all linguistic elements inter-determinate each other and each component gets its meaning only in relation to

a) all other components of the same work,
b) all other writings of the same author,
c) all the writings of the same period,
d) all the writings of the same genre,
e) all the writings that have preceded it and/or are simultaneous with it,

by contrast/tension or harmony. The network of relations are included in the study of aesthetic communicative functions of artistic expression. Thus, function was viewed as an orientation towards a certain goal. The Prague School considered all human activity poly-functional; according to them, no human activity is motivated by one function alone and many functions coexist within one human activity, though one specific function *dominates* and becomes the stimulus for ordering the hierarchy of components of any human activity. In art, the aesthetic function becomes the dominant one and the aesthetic function was seen as 'counteracting of routine and automatization' by the *foregrounding* of certain elements; in other words, using foregrounding as a device (the concept evolved by Mukarovsky) deautomatization/defamiliarization is attempted by the aesthetic function and that is the distinctive feature that marks literariness in language.

Poetic language (i.e., literary language), thus, utilizes its material primarily for the purpose of self-directedness, and not for the purpose of providing referential information; it calls attention to itself; it is self-referential; it is autonomous. At the same time, Jakobson pointed out, the literary work stood in complex relation to other uses of language, which are to be taken into consideration in the study of literature, without surrendering the autonomy of literature. Extending the same argument, Jakobson and Tynjanov pointed out that the separation of synchrony and diachrony was logically inaccurate, since every structure is in constant motion and ever-evolving — hence diachronic in character — whereas the evolution is inescapably synchronic in character. They say: 'Pure synchrony proves to be an illusion; every synchronic system has its past and its future as inseparable structural elements of its system' (Roman Jakobson and Jurij Tynjanov, 1928:37)

Following Mukarovsky's view that a work of art is a system of signs, a sign in itself, which in contrast to other signs (for example, the other uses of language) does not lay on some final, unambiguous relationship to reality, Jakobson proposed a functional model of six parameters and six functions to explain the act of communication. The six functions are shown below:

INFORMATIVE

EMOTIVE POETIC DIRECTIVE

METALINGUAL

PHATIC

They are related to verbal communication as in:

CONTEXT
(Informative)

ADDRESSER TEXTS/UTTERANCES ADDRESSEE
(emotive) (poetic) (directive)

LANGUAGE/CODE
(metalingual)

CONTACT
(phatic)

Some examples:

Addresser: typically the first person and sometimes the third person:
I request you to come and meet me.
The President requests the pleasure of your company...
Come to *mummy.* (mother calling a child using the third person instead of the first)

Addressee: typically the second person: Are you listening?

Elements of context: persons, animals or things other than the addresser and the addressee

An *utterance* that is *spoken*/uttered or a *text* that is *written* is a particular structure (the actualized instance) of the vast complex system out of which utterances and texts are built. This virtual system or the language is called *code. Metalanguage* is the language used to talk about language; terms like *noun, verb, sign,* etc.

Contact for Jakobson involves the 'physical channel' and a 'psychological connection', the most obvious being 'Hey', 'Good morning', etc.

The key to Jakobson's poetics is the term 'equivalence'; it concerns the selection and combination of items. It implies more than what is meant by proper words in their proper places since it brings similarity/dissimilarity, synonymy/antonymy, paradigmatic/syntagmatic, and normal/deviant oppositions into the notion of equivalence. The oft-quoted statement by Jakobson is: 'The poetic function projects the principle of equivalence from the axis of selection to the axis of combination.' The following figure shows how the projection is effected:

X —————————————— Y

axis of selection | axis of combination
paradigmatic | syntagmatic

Z

By making a choice along the axis XZ and putting it in the axis of XY, one is projecting equivalence from the paradigmatic to the syntagmatic relationship. In an expression like 'farm yards away', one can see how the concept of numeral quantity has been broadened by the poet by invoking the principle of equivalence:

five ten farm	yards away

The concept *automatization* can be explained, using the principle of equivalence; in normal, conventional expressions like 'ten yards away' or 'two minutes ago', the expression itself does not attract any attention since we are so used to the automatized understanding. In *deautomatization* the principle of equivalence is invoked to attract attention; when 'ten yards away' is extended to 'farm yards away' or 'two minutes ago' is extended to 'two husbands ago' or 'three children ago', the selection and combination attracts attention; it is freed of automatization or deautomatized and, thereby, *foregrounded.* By fore-grounding, we mean the use of any device of the language in such a way that its use itself attracts attention and is perceived as uncommon.

Mukarovsky observes: 'In poetic language foregrounding achieves maximum intensity to the extent of pushing communication into the background as the objective of expression and of being for its own sake; it is not used in the services of communication, but in order to place in the foreground the act of expression, the act of speech itself.' Thus, the language of literature itself is foregrounded against the background of conventional linguistic forms of expression.

The following examples will show how the principle of equivalence is extended to bring about foregrounding:

i. The nymphs are departed
Departed, have left no addresses
— T.S. Eliot, *The Waste Land*

ii. Let him easter in us.
— Hopkins, *The Wreck of the Deutschland*

iii. The just man justices.
— Hopkins, *'As Kingfishers Catch Fire'*

V. Halliday too has brought in foregrounding as part of the 'functional theory of language', he makes a distinction between 'true foregrounding' and 'mere prominence of a statistical or an absolute kind' (Halliday 1973) and comments: 'If there is such a thing as recognizable style, whether of a work, an author, or an entire period of literary tradition, its distinctive quality can, in the last analysis, be stated in terms of relative frequencies... We are probably rather sensitive to the relative frequency of different grammatical and lexical patterns, which is an aspect of meaning potential... What cannot be expressed statistically is foregrounding' (Halliday, 1973:116). For example, as the title of a poem 'To Whom It May Concern' gets foregrounded since it is not frequent in this use, though it occurs frequently on the top of testimonials.

Halliday's statistical approach to the study of style brings to focus the question of quantification of literary style. It is claimed by some statisticians that the frequency distribution of words in poems of the same size by contemporary writers can be used to decide the authorship of texts. In his book *Statistics and Truth,* Dr.

C.R. Rao cites an interesting example. On 14 November 1985, the Shakespeare scholar Gary Taylor found a nine-stanza poem in a bound folio volume that had been in the collection of the Bodelian Library since 1775; the poem has 429 words and there is no record as to who wrote the poem. Two statisticians, Thisted and Efron (1987) made a statistical study of the problem and on the basis of frequency distribution of words in poems of the same size by Ben Jonson, Christopher Marlowe, John Donne, and Shakespeare concluded that the poem fits nicely with Shakespeare's style (canon) in the usage and range of words. With the help of computers, it should be possible to study the problem of style from the statistical point of view; but there will be a lot of resistance from traditional literary thinking to any approach that is different. The statistical approach, like any other approach, will have its own limitations but a different kind of quantification may be available to the study of style which can supplement the other approaches. As Eliot points out 'About anyone so great as Shakespeare, it is probable that we can never be right; and if we can never be right, it is better that we should from time to time change our way of being wrong.'

VI. With the emergence of Chomskyan grammar, stylisticians started working on the development of a generative model of stylistics. Richard Ohmann's (1966) paper argued that generative grammar should be adopted as the basis for stylistic investigations. It was claimed that the differences between surface forms can be derived by applying transformational rules to 'deep structures' underlying 'surface forms' and that stylistic variations can be captured in terms of transformational rules. Roger Fowler (1972) proposed that notions from generative semantics can be used in stylistic analysis.

One can notice that in functional theories (like that of Jakobson and Halliday) style is taken primarily as *choice*, selection and ordering of items at various levels—lexical, syntactic, phonological, etc. In the generative framework style is taken primarily as *deviance*, which means *motivated departures* from the standard norms of a language. In both the approaches, the resulting function is foregrounding. The notion of deviance was effectively used in the transformational-generative framework because of the nature of the arrangements of the components in the theory;

once we set up a base component and specify a set of transformational rules (that will 'generate' a set of kernel and embedded/co-ordinate constructions), it is possible to say that anything not generated by the rules specified will be labelled deviant. Tall claims were made about the power of generative stylistics, but like any other approach, it turned out that the problem of studying style is much more complicated than what statistics or transformations can reveal.

VII. Some have widened the scope of stylistics by defining style as the aggregate of co-textual probabilities of its linguistic items and have argued that 'co-text includes textual as well as extra-textual context such as period, genre, dialect, and inter-personal relationship' (Enkvist, 1973).

Some researchers in the area have applied the speech act theory to the study of literature. Some scholars like Widdowson regard stylistics as the study of the social function of language and, therefore, stylistics is for them a branch of sociolinguistics. According to Widdowson, stylistics provides a basis for aesthetic appreciation by bringing to the level of conscious awareness features of the text otherwise only accessible to trained intuition. By tradition, the study of literature has been regarded as a branch of aesthetics but stylistics takes the language as primary and artistic values as incidental to linguistic description; literary criticism, on the other hand, takes artistic values as primary and refers to language insofar as it serves as evidence for aesthetic assessments. (Widdowson, 1974).

Since the 1970s a number of various other approaches like *affective stylistics, reception theory, reader-response criticism, deconstructive readings of literary texts,* developments in discourse analysis and text linguistics, to name some important developments, have given new directions to stylistics, literary criticism, and literary theories.

Questions and topics for discussion

1. Very often the common man or woman shows a remarkable ability to read between the lines; in other words, they have the ability to see what lies between expression and impression. How can we make use of this ability in reading literary texts?
2. What factors contribute to one's literary competence?

3. Jakobson says 'Poetry is organized violence on ordinary speech'. What is your opinion?
4. "A linguist deaf to the poetic function of language and a literary scholar indifferent to literary problems and unconversant with linguistic methods, are equally flagrant anachronisms"—R. Jakobson. Explain the significance of the statement. Give examples to illustrate your point.
5. We often talk about good style/bad style, formal/informal style and say everyone has his/her own style. Do these labels reflect some basic notions in stylistics? Give reasons for your answer.
6. 'Poetic function is not the sole function of the verbal art but only its dominant, determining function, whereas in all other verbal activities it acts as a subsidiary, accessory constituent.' — Explain and illustrate.
7. 'One can play a 'public literary game' or a 'private literary game' mobilizing the facts of a language.' — Explain and illustrate.
8. 'To interpret our own reality through schemas which are alien to us only has the effect of making us even more unknown, even less free, even more solitary.' — Gabriel Gracia Marquez. Comment on this with reference to the teaching of literature.
9. 'Every attempt at reading a literary text leads to an 'erasure'; it is 'always another, yet the same'. Based on your *own* experience of reading texts, try to justify the statement given above.

18 STYLISTICS : FROM THEORY TO PRACTICE

'The act of reading has become the primary focus of literary theory.'

Focal points

I. We will analyse how 'Leda and the Swan,' a 'mighty sonnet' has been read by Hoyt Throwbridge (1953), Leo Spitzer, M.A.K. Halliday (1966), and H.G. Widdowson (1975). The first two fall into what is called *literary stylistics,* the third into *linguistic stylistics,* and the fourth into discourse analysis.

Leda and the Swan

A sudden blow : the great wings beating still
Above the staggering girl, her thighs caressed
By the dark webs, her nape caught in his bill,
He holds her helpless breast upon his breast.

How can those terrified vague fingers push
The feathered glory from her loosening thighs?
And how can body, laid in that white rush,
But feel the strange heart beating where it lies?

A shudder in the loins engenders there
The broken wall, the burning roof and tower
And Agamemnon dead.
Being so caught up
So mastered by the brute blood of the air,
Did she put on his knowledge with his power
Before the indfferent beak could let her drop?

— W.B. Yeats

i) Throwbridge (1953) uses a Longinian method in his analysis of the poem. Longinus' (a Greek thinker of, perhaps, the 1st century A.D.) treatise *On the Sublime* outlines the essential features of *sublimity,* the quality in writing from which the 'greatest poets and writers have derived their eminence and gained an immortality of renown', which effects a conquest of the reader or hearer ('transport') by uplifting the mind by its overpowering force, by 'filling it with joy'.

Sublimity arises from five spring-heads — *elevated thought* and *passion* (the qualities of mind in the writer as manifested in the text) and *figures, diction,* and *composition* (the verbal means by which thought and passion are communicated). The latter three are aspects of style which refer to departure from normal syntax, deviation, grammatical combinations (*figures*), choice of words, use of metaphors and elaboration of language (*diction*), and arrangement of words in rhymes and harmonies (*composition*). Throwbridge uses Yeats' poem to exemplify Longinus' theory and as a result the analysis becomes a Yeatsian confirmation of Longinus.

The subject of the poem, the rape of Leda described in the octave bringing out the sexuality of the event without the brutal details, is the helplessness of the human victim in the face of the super-human power and the strangeness and the wild beauty of the attacker. In the second part, Helen's birth, the war of Troy, and the murder of Agamemnon are all given in a line and a half, thus opening to the mind a vista of history, a grandeur of vision achieved partly due to the tragic quality of the events in history and partly due to the implicit allusion to Homer. In the last verse, the swan clearly becomes a God. The later part of the poem sweeps us up and our passions are modulated in harmony with thought.

At the level of figure, the sonnet employs the 'incomplete sentence' effectively in the opening line, thus pushing the reader in the middle of an action. Equally obvious is the handling of tenses—the shift to the past tense in the last sentence from the earlier use of present tense—which is meant to emphasize the meaning of the event. Interrogation or questioning expresses a bewildered helplessness, an anguished pity for the unfortunate girl. The last question leaves the readers in uncertainty; it leaves the answer open. It is an oracular question.

At the level of *diction,* there is clarity because of the use of common vocabulary. Metaphors like 'feathered glory', 'white rush', etc. add to the effectiveness of the narration. The fall of Troy is conceived with Helen in Leda's womb in an interesting way—'the broken wall.... Agamemnon dead' *Composition* contributes to the music of mobility and dignity combined with expressive vigour and flexibility.

Throwbridge shows that Longinus offers a method for analysing literary texts and that 'though not a key to open all doors, his sytem is a useful tool, to be ranged with others in the repertory of criticism.'

ii) Spitzer in his comments on Throwbridge's Longinian analysis of Yeats' poem says that we should 'search for the characteristic in each poem instead of offering laudative statements which may apply to quite different poems as well.' While the observations of Throwbridge 'may be not without value, they fail, scattered as they are in different paragraphs, to integrate into one coherent picture of a temporal-positional sequence', which is the most 'portentous event of the rape of Leda by the Swan-God'.

According to Spitzer, the poem 'develops within a stretch of time' that is marked by the temporal adverb 'still' (l.1) and 'before' (1.14), capturing the event of the rape within this stretch of time. The beginning ('A sudden blow' — a sudden invasion from nowhere of the cosmic space), the continuation (with the pervasive penetration of the bird-God into the 'loosening' body of the girl) leading to the moment of procreation ('A shudder in the loins engenders there...') and the ending with the post-orgiastic weakening of the grip of the invader (that 'let her drop') arrests time to create history. The 'syntactically brusque beginning of the poem indicates the rendering of an event without prehistory, itself creating history.' The temporal adverb 'still' (l.1) shows that the incident has already begun before its beginning (within the space of the poem). The short time sequence of the act and the short form of the sonnet that contains it are interrelated while the sweep of the historical consequences extends far beyond the framework of the sonnet.

Spitzer observes that the victim's experience has no rhythm, for throughout the poem from line 3 on she is represented as 'caught'; she is still 'caught up' in line 11. The positional relationships between the swan and the victim as depicted in the poem show that she seems reduced to a local indication: *there.* The antecedent of *there* is *body.* The adverb *there* would mean 'in the medium or substance' and derives its pathos from the opposition between the passive female body and the world-shaking events of history that will be begotten 'there'. The double miracle, temporal and spatial, that has taken place then and there mirrors itself in the wording of the line. Leda, as she feels the full bodily impact of the divine beast, is only a channel through which the forces of history pass, or a place ('there') in which they work. The objective visualization of history culminates in the predicative expression: 'Agamemnon dead'—a Roman newspaper headline, as it were.

Spitzer argues that in the 'last lines we are offered the essence of the tragedy of procreation by rape'. 'With this one word, 'put on', rich in Christian connotations, there emerges the *toto coelo* difference between the pagan and the Christian climate.' the expression 'before ... could let her drop' underlines the demonic compulsions to which the divine bird himself is subject.

Of the three questions in the poem, the first one is entirely empathetic (How can those...?); the second question (...how can body...?) comes from a sympathetic observer making a generic reference; the third question is an entirely objective one asked by the poet whose reflective mood has increased as the personal event of the rape recedes into history. 'One may assume that the poet, being a mortal human himself, feels able only to ask a question about the commerce of man with the divine; but this question... betrays to us his grave fear that it is possible for the gods to engender brutally, in the human flesh, with sovereign disregard for the human mind.' Both Throwbridge and Spitzer have looked at the marked features of language carefully and systematically in order to interpret the poem.

iii) Halliday (1966) analyses *Leda and the Swan* but his principal purpose is to illustrate the application of the categories and methods of his theory to the analysis of literary texts. He has tabulated the results of his investigation of the verbal groups in the poem, thus:

		Items in verbal group functioning as 'predicator' in clause structure				Items in nominal group (i.e. not functioning as predicator)
	1	2	3	4	5	6
a	Independent	Dependent		Qualifying (rank shifted)		(inapplicable)
b	Finite	Finite	Non-finite	Finite	Non-finite	"
	hold push feel engender put on	lie let	drop catch up master		beat (2) caress catch lay	stagger loosen burn break

(a) Clause class (b) Group class

Halliday proceeds no further beyond the analysis; he makes an observation on the lexically more effective verbal items.

This kind of analysis gives us the linguistic data but unless it is related to the 'reading' of the poem (if not to the interpretation of it) it remains unrelated to the understanding of the text.

iv) Widdowson (1975), evaluating the analysis of Halliday, observes that Halliday stops with 'textual analysis' and does not go to 'discourse analysis'. According to Widdowson, the nominal groups in *Leda and the Swan* point to things supposed to be actually present in the immediate context of utterance. This suggests that Yeats is describing an actual picture or one which is clearly delineated in his mind as a precise vision; expressions like the *staggering girl, her thighs caressed by the dark webs, those* in *those terrified vague fingers* have a definitive indicating function.

v) Geoffrey Hartman analyses *Leda and the Swan* in the post-structuralist framework (Atkins 1985) and points out that seduction, in fiction or life, seems to contain, paradoxically, the promise of mastery. He points out the perplexities in the poem to show how we become unsure of the poem's real frame of reference.

II. Widdowson (1974) evaluates some models of stylistic analysis of the late 60s and early 70s. They are summarized below:

Sinclair, J. McH (1966) has analysed Philip Larkin's poem *First Sight* by applying Halliday's categories of linguistic description. In his analysis, Sinclair mentions two aspects of linguistic organization which play an important role in the study of literary texts; they are *arrest* and *release*. *Arrest* occurs when a predictable syntactic pattern is interrupted by interposed linguistic units, thus delaying the completion of the pattern. In,

Lambs that learn to walk in snow
When their bleating clouds the air
Meet a vast unwelcome...

the noun phrase ('Lambs that... snow') is interrupted by an arresting adverbial ('When their...air'), thus arresting the pattern NP+VP.

Release occurs when a syntactic structure is extended after all the grammatical predictions have been fulfilled. Thus, in 'They could not grasp it *if they knew*', the conditional clause is the releasing element since the preceding clause is already grammatically complete.

Sinclair too, like Halliday, analyses literary texts to illustrate a particular system of analysis.

III. Geoffrey Leech (1965) has analysed Dylan Thomas' *This Bread I Break.*

This Bread I Break

This bread I break was once the oat,
This wine upon a foreign tree
Plunged in its fruit;
Man in the day or wind at night
Laid the crops low, broke the grape's joy.

Once in this wind the summer blood
Knocked in the flesh that decked the vine,
Once in this bread
The oat was merry in the wind;
Man broke the sun, pulled the wind down.

This flesh you break, this blood you let
Make desolation in the vein,
Were oat and grape
Born of the sensual root and sap;
My wine you drink, my bread you snap.

— Dylan Thomas.

Leech's approach to stylistic analysis differs essentially from that of Halliday and Sinclair in that it aims at relating linguistic description to literary interpretation. Leech shows how the former has to be linked up with the latter. He highlights three 'dimensions of meaning' — *cohesion, foregrounding*, and *cohesion of foregrounding* — as important features of literary expression and suggests that for this reason descriptive linguistics cannot simply be applied indifferently to literary texts as to other texts. In the interpretation of a literary text, according to Leech, the three dimensions mentioned above have to be studied closely.

a) *Cohesion:* The intra-textual relations of a grammatical and lexical kind which knit the parts of a text together into a complete unit of discourse and which therefore convey the meaning of the text as a whole are termed *cohesive devices.* This is true of any text as pointed out in the chapter on Discourse Analysis. But in the poem under discussion, there is cohesion in terms of similar ranges of occurrence in collocation as seen in *lexical sets* like *bread - oats - crops, wine - tree - fruit - grape - vine - drink, day - night - summer - sun,* etc.

b) *Foregrounding:* This is a predominantly literary feature. In the poem referred to above, expressions like 'the oat was merry' in which a 'noun' which normally has the feature of inanimacy is given an animate, and more exactly a human feature, thereby creating a deviation which is *foregrounded* against normal expressions like 'the man was merry' 'the farmer was merry' and so on. Similarly, the construction 'broke the sun' is *foregrounded,* for the environment 'broke the ....' restricts the choice of noun to the class of nouns which have the feature of 'frangibility' as in the cases of 'cup', 'plate', 'clock', etc. This *foregrounding* —'broke the sun'— is against the background of normal choices mentioned above. *Foregrounding* occurs here because the semantic features of an item in the code do not correspond with those which are bestowed upon it by the contextual environment in which it appears. Another manifestation of *foregrounding* which Leech points out is the instance of renouncing a wider choice (which is permitted by the code) to produce uniformity. The construction 'Man in the day and wind at night' is one such instance. Here there is a syntactic equivalence between the two prepositional phrases. A similar syntactic parallellism occurs in the last line of the poem: 'My wine you drink, my bread you snap'. Setting up intra-textual syntactic equivalence is also a feature of *foregrounding* in that it introduces patterns of language which are not expected in normal use.

c) *Cohesion of foregrounding:* The deviations in a text can form intra-textual patterns when they are related among themselves, to produce *cohesion of foregrounding.* Thus, for example, the deviant expression 'broke the sun' is foregrounded against normal usage but takes on a normality in the context of the poem as a whole, because it is related to deviations of a similar kind like 'broke the grapes joy', 'pulled the wind down', etc. Similarly, inra-textual patterns are formed by the cohesion of the foregrounded expressions 'the oat was merry', 'desolation in the vine', and 'sensual root'.

IV. Samuel Levin's (1964) *Linguistic Structures in Poetry:*
In this book, Levin develops the notion of equivalence as outlined by Jakobson and exemplifies its operation at the phonological, syntactic and semantic levels to create structural features that distinguish poetic discourse from other kinds of discourse. Levin distinguishes two types of equivalence—the *positional equivalence* (Type A) and the *natural equivalence* (Type B).

A) Elements that share the same potentiality of occurrence in a given environment are said to have *positional equivalence.*
   e.g. i) The prefixes *di-, re-, per-, ad-, in-, sub-* and *con-* are positionally equivalent because they may occur in front of the stem '*-vert*'
   ii) environment: 'I saw him at—'
   positional equivalence class: 'night', 'seven', 'your house', 'the end of last semester', etc.

B) Elements that share common semantic features, when they "overlap in cutting up the general 'thought-mass'" are said to have *natural semantic equivalence.*
   When elements 'overlap in cutting up the phonetico-physiological continuum' they produce *natural phonological equivalence.*
   e.g. *Natural Semantic Equivalence:*
   Relation of synonymy — 'happy' and 'gay'
   Relation of antonymy — 'happy' and 'sad'
   Natural Phonological Equivalence:
   'Full fathom five thy father lies'

full
fathom
five
father
] naturally equivalent initial consonants

five
thy
lies
] naturally equivalent medial vowels

'fathom' (i) naturally equivalent syllable structure
'father' (ii) the first and second syllables have the same initial segment in each case

The third notion which Levin introduces is that of *coupling*. This is said to occur when one type of equivalence converges with another to produce 'the structure wherein naturally equivalent forms occur in equivalent positions'. In the following line (Pope's)—'A soul as full of worth as void of pride'—'full of worth' and 'void of pride' are positionally phonologically equivalent to the extent that they have the same rhythmic structure. The *positional equivalence* converges with the *natural phonological equivalence* to form a *coupling*. This *coupling* is reinforced by the fact that 'full' and 'void' which share exactly the same environment are *naturally equivalent semantically* in that they are antonyms and phonologically in that are monosyllables.

Levin, unlike Leech, does not apply his analysis to the interpretation of the poem. His interest rests in revealing how the language in the poem is patterned: 'The analysis is therefore not an attempt at a full-scale interpretation; it is an attempt to reveal the role that couplings play, in the total organization of the poem.' In this respect, his approach to *stylistics* is similar to that of Halliday and Sinclair.

V. Thorne, J.P. 'Stylistics and generative grammars' (1965)

In this paper, Thorne is concerned with the problem of accounting for the kind of deviant sentences which commonly occur in poetry within the grammar of a language, since grammar, as a device for generating all and only the well-formed sentences of the language in question, will not be capable of assigning analyses to deviant sentences. If the capacity of grammar is extended to generate the deviant sentences in question (poetic texts) innumerable deviant sentences which do not form part of poetic discourse will also be generated. Thus, if the grammar of English is modified to generate the line 'He danced his did' (E.E. Cummings), sentences like 'We thumped their hads' would also be generated, which are deviant without the justification of being observed as significant units of meaning in the context of a poem or other literacy texts. If the grammar is extended to generate 'The oat was joyful' (Dylan Thomas) unwanted generations like 'The potato was joyful', 'The barley was disconsolate', 'The maize was amazed' and so on will follow.

The solution that Thorne proposes is that a poem should be thought of as being a sample of a different language from Standard English and the task of stylistics is to be seen as writing a grammar which will describe the structure of this unique language. That is, the extra-textual relations that obtain between the language as a code and the language as represented in the context (of the literary text) should be ignored, and stylistics should concentrate only on the intra-textual relations, the relations that emerge within the context (of the literary text). Thorne acknowledges that his approach relies a great deal on intuition. 'Reading a poem, it is suggested, is often like learning a language. When we learn a language we develop the capacity to have intuitions about its structures.'

Thorne illustrates his approach by applying it to E.E. Cummings' poem 'anyone lived in a pretty how town' which shows a very high degree of deviance from the standard language. In his discussion on Donne's poem 'A nocturnal upon S. Lucies day', he points out that a grammar for this text would have to include rules quite contrary to those of Standard English by which normally inanimate nouns are given the feature of animacy and the reverse. This grammar, therefore, will generate sentences like 'Yea plants, yea stones detest and love' and reject 'I laugh' or 'you love' as ungrammatical. He also points out that in this grammar the sentence 'were I a man' (which occurs in stanza four of the poem) is equivalent to 'were I a stone' in standard English.

All these attempts outlined above give us some idea of how to do stylistic analysis. (Please note that only some of the models have been given above). A system-based approach to the study of the language of a literary text and its correlation to literary reading and appreciation can be useful in making us better readers.

Questions and topics for discussion

1. Read the following poem carefully:

A Coat

I made my song a coat
Covered with embroideries
Out of old mythologies

From heel to throat;
But the fools caught it,
Wore it in the world's eyes
As though they wrought it.
Song, let them take it,
For there is more enterprise
In walking naked.

— Y.B. Yeats

Can you now answer the following questions?

a) 'I made my song a coat'
Does it mean one of the following?
i. I made a coat for my song. (like 'He made *her*/I.O a cup of tea.'/D.O.
ii. I made my song into a coat (like 'She made him/O a good husband.'/O-Comp
iii. I became a coat for my song. (like 'She made him/O a good wife.'/S-Comp
Are all the readings possible?

b) Which is covered with embroideries that are made of old mythologies — my song or a coat or both? The outer ornamental cover, that which can be seen, the decorative outfit—will it normally collocate with *a coat* or a song? In poetic reading what are the possibilities?

c) 'From heel to throat'—Why not 'head to foot'? Why is there a change in the normal order?

d) 'But fools caught it'—What is the antecedent for *it*—*my song* or *a coat* or both? 'Wore *it*', 'as though they wrought *it*', 'let them take *it*'—in each instance—What is the antecedent for *it*? What is the effect of the continuous anaphora for *it*?

e) What is the reference for 'they'/'them' in 'they wrought it', 'let *them* take it'?

f) '*Wrought* it' — Why is the archaic word used? What does it signify? Why not use a contemporary word 'made'?

g) 'But the fools caught it' — What does the use of the contrajunctive 'but' convey? Why are they called fools?

h) 'Song, let them take it' — Is the poet addressing the song—'Song! don't worry; let them take it'? Or has he shifted the word song to the front for the sake of focus/topicalization? Is 'song' in the vocative or indicative mood? Which reading, *according to you*, is 'intuitively satisfying' (whatever it means!).

i) 'There is more enterprise in walking naked'—Why has he used the word 'enterprise', which belongs to the commercial register? Can you compare the use of 'wrought' and 'enterprise'?
Who is walking naked — my song or the coat or both? What is the

meaning of the word *naked* — without clothes, without the coat?

j) Can you look at the tenses used in the poem? What does the movement from the past to the present show?
There is movement from the past to the present and then to a tenseless gerund *walking* in the last line. Does this mean anything?

k) Whose song is this? 'My song' — Does it convey any empathetic feeling to you?

l) Is there only one reading for the poem? Multiple readings and the pluralistic approach leave us guessing. Does the vagueness (including amibiguity) add to the charm and beauty of the poem? What is very transparent and 'crystal clear' is not attractive; only that which is hidden arouses curiosity and the sense of exploration. Do you agree? Do you enjoy explorations?

2. Look at the following lines:

Tyger, Tyger, burning bright
In the forests of the night:
What immortal hand or eye
Could frame thy fearful symmetry?

a) Why is the word 'Tyger' spelt differently? Can you think of the possible reason(s) for the change from *y* to *i*?

b) 'In the forests of the night'—Is this construction like 'in the forests of Assam'? Is it like 'in the forests during/at night'? Can you think of a parallel construction with 'of', similar to 'In + def. article + noun + of + def. article + noun', that conveys a meaning similar to 'in the forests of the night'?

c) 'What immortal hand or eye' — Why has the poet left out the 'mind', which is very important in framing a 'symmetry'? Does it signify anything to you?

d) 'Could frame....' — What does the word *could* mean? Does it mean ability? 'What funny ideas *could* make you do that?' — What does *could* convey here?
Etymologically *can* comes from *cunnan*, which meant 'have learned', 'come to know', 'have power', 'know how', 'know', 'understand'; it is also related to *con* — 'cunning', 'learning', 'skilled', 'clever', etc. With this added awareness, can you look at *could frame* and see what readings you get?

e) '...frame thy fearful symmetry?' - What type of question is it? Is it a question at all?

f) 'Tyger! Tyger!'—What personal/connotative meaning is evoked in your mind by the word 'tyger'?

g) Can you think of some tiger stories to illustrate the fearful image evoked by these lines?

If you are still interested in exploring 'the forests of the night' read the entire poem and see how many readings you can get.

3. Attempt a stylistic analysis of the following text. (Please specify the model that you are using).

"Fourscore and seven years ago, our fathers brought forth on this continent a new nation, conceived in liberty, and dedicated to the proposition that all men are created equal. Now we are engaged in a great civil war, testing whether that nation, or any nation so conceived and so dedicated, can long endure. We are met on a great battlefield of that war. We have come to dedicate a portion of that as a final resting place for those who here gave their lives that that nation might live. It is altogether fitting and proper that we should do this. But, in a larger sense, we cannot dedicate — we cannot consecrate — we cannot hallow — this ground. The brave men, living and dead, who struggled here, have consecrated it far above our poor power to add or detract. The world will little note, nor long remember, what we say here, but it can never forget what they did here. It is for us the living, rather, to be dedicated here to the unfinished work that they have thus far so nobly advanced. It is rather for us to be here dedicated to the great task remaining before us, that from these honoured dead we take increased devotion to that cause for which they here gave the last full measure of devotion; that we here highly resolve that these dead shall not have died in vain—that this nation, under God, shall have a new birth of freedom, and that government of the people, by the people, for the people, shall not perish from the earth."

4. What devices are used in the following expressions?

a) When to the sessions of sweet silent thought.

b) Thou foster child of silence and slow time.

c) I caught this morning.

d) Or leave a kiss but in a cup.

e) Though wedded we have been
These twice ten tedious years; yet me
No holiday have seen.

f) To smash the simple atom
All mankind was intent.
    Now any day
    The atom may
Return the compliment.

g) Where wealth accumlates, and men decay.

h) I'll give my jewels for a set of beads,
My gorgeous palace for a hermitage,
My gay apparel for an almsman's gown,
My figured goblets for a dish of wood,
My sceptre for a palmer's walking staff,

My subjects for a pair of carved saints
And my large kingdom for a little grave,
A little, little grave, an obscure grave.

5. "Any unbiased, attentive, exhaustive total description of the selection, distribution and interrelation of diverse morphological classes and syntactic constructions in a given poem surprises the examiner himself by unexpected, striking symmetries and anti-symmetries, balanced structures, efficient accumulation of equivalent forms and salient contrasts, finally by rigid restrictions in the repertory of morphological and syntactic constituents used in the poem, eliminations which, on the other hand, permit us to follow the masterly interplay of the actualized constructions."

— Jakobson, R.

Do you think such an analysis is possible? If not, why not?

6. In the medical sciences an organism is dissected and ripped open to understand how its components work. There is nothing wrong in dissecting a poem to understand what it means and how it works. Actually, this purposeful dissection is stripping it naked to lay it bare because 'there is more enterprise in walking naked'. Can you defend a meaningful stripping approach to stylistics?

19 AFTER STRUCTURALISM

There will be time to murder and create.
And time yet for a hundred indecisions,
And for a hundred visions and revisions,
Before the taking of a toast and tea.

— *T.S. Eliot*

Focal points

I. Ferdinand de Saussure's *Course in General Linguistics* (1916) laid the foundation for the study of language in the twentieth century and provided the basic concepts for a theory of structuralism and structuralist literary theory; structuralist poetics is the application to literature of the ideas about language since literature is language.

Saussure began by fencing off language, defining it as an

object to be studied as independent from both the users of language and the world of outside reality; language, he said, is a system of signs and the linguistic sign 'is a two-sided psychological entity' composed of a 'concept and a sound-image': 'I propose to retain the word *sign* to designate the whole and to replace *concept* and *sound-image* respectively by *signified* and *signifier*.' Saussure made a distinction between *la langue* (the system, the institution called language which is a set of impersonal rules and conventions) and *la parole* (the actual manifestations of language in *speaking*, which is taken as primary); thus *langue* is transindividual and *parole* is individual. The most important implication of this distinction is that for the study of meaning there must be a *system* that allows it to have meaning; *language is a system of interrelated units and the value of the units is determined by their places in the system at a given time and in a given state.* Saussure did not reject the value of historical (diachronic) linguistics, but asserted that 'the diachronic perspective deals with phenomena that are unrelated to systems although they do condition them'; thus, he laid the theoretical foundation for synchronic or 'structural' analyses.

Saussure's declaration that 'in language there are only differences without positive terms' means that a sign has no meaning in itself but has meaning only in relation to other signs in the system; in other words, meaning depends on the system, on the oppositions and contrasts within the system. We can find a similar set of assumptions in the structuralist poetics of Roman Jakobson, in the anthropology of Levi-Strauss, in the psychoanalytic theory of Freud, in the sociology of Durkheim, in Bloomfieldian linguistics, in Chomskyan transformational-generative grammar, in New Criticism and Practical Criticism, in Firthian and Neo-Firthian linguistics including the speech-act theory—all of which contributed to the growth of structuralism.

As Jonathan Culler points out in the preface to his *Structuralist Poetics* (1975), three characteristics of structuralist literary theory clearly stand out. Firstly, it is not primarily interpretive; it does not offer a method which, when applied to literary works, produces new and hitherto unexpected meanings. 'Rather than a criticism which discovers and assigns meanings, it would be a poetics, which strives to define the conditions of meaning.' Secondly, structuralist literary theory does not focus on individual works, but attempts 'to understand the conventions which make literature possible', the *langue* of literature, its 'literariness', in the words of Jakobson. Thirdly, it would 'attempt to specify how we go about making sense of texts, what are the interpretive operations on which literature itself, as an institution, is based', in other words, it would focus on the activity of reading.

A method of literary study that declares itself not concerned with interpretation, with individual works or with historical developments but with the act of reading, can ignore the author, the author's intentions, and the historical and biographical details. The New Criticism, with its focus on the close reading of the text, autonomy of literature and objectivity for criticism announced 'The Death of the Author'. W.K. Wimsatt, Jr., and Monroe Beardsley in their essay 'The Intentional Fallacy' (1948) argue that the intention of the author is neither available nor desirable as a standard for interpreting literature; the argument is if the intention is manifested in the text, the statement about the author's intention is superfluous, and if the intention is not manifested in the poem, the statement is to no purpose.

The linguistic model that defines language as an independent system and a sign as arbitrary in essence but as fixed convention (the relation between concept and expression being decided not by nature but by culture) led the structuralist critics to describe 'the system of conventions which enable poems to have the meaning (the range of meanings) they do.'

What has been described so far about the development of structuralist poetics can be broadly shown as in Chart 5.

II. The French philosopher, Jacques Derrida too declares that 'there is nothing outside the text' but, for him, 'the text is a gas'. One can see that in the first statement Derrida appears to be within the structuralist paradigm by making the text or the language an independent, autonomous system but he knocks the foundation out from under the structuralists, even while standing on their shoulders, by declaring that the text is a decomposing organic substance, an effluvium! This is exactly what Derridean deconstruction does; it takes the binary oppositions, stated or described *in the text*, shows how one term of the opposition has been privileged and the other hierarchically subordinated to the other, reverses the hierarchical position of the terms, shows the mutual dependence and interpenetration of the opposites, over-

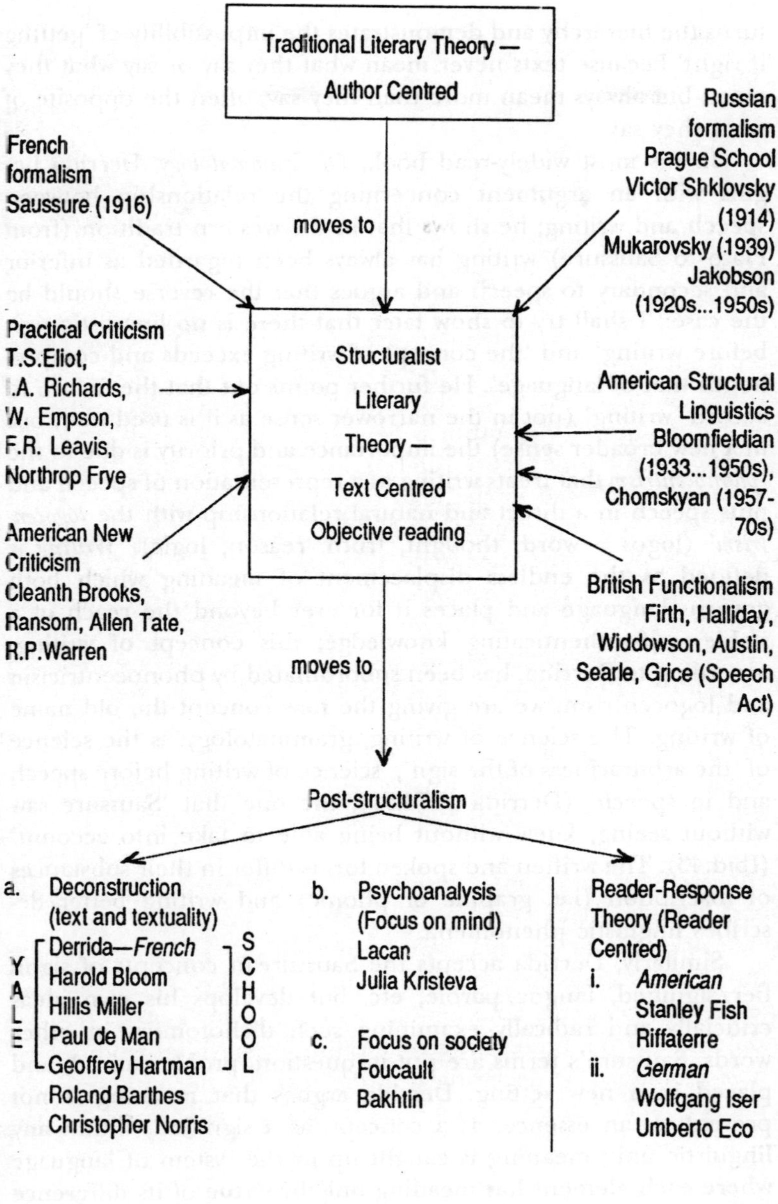

Chart 5: **A broad representation of structuralist poetics**

turns the hierarchy and demonstrates the impossibility of 'getting it right' because texts never mean what they say or say what they mean but always mean more than they say, often the opposite of what they say.

In his most widely-read book, *Of Grammatology*, Derrida begins with an argument concerning the relationship between speech and writing; he shows that in the western tradition (from Plato to Saussure) writing has always been regarded as inferior and secondary to speech and argues that the reverse should be the case: 'I shall try to show later that there is no linguistic sign before writing' and 'the concept of writing exceeds and comprehends that of language'. He further points out that the failure to accord 'writing' (not in the narrower sense as it is used now, but in a new broader sense) the importance and priority is due to the '*phonocentrism* that treats writing as a representation of speech and puts speech in a direct and natural relationship with the *logocentrism*' (logos = word, thought, truth, reason, logic). *Writing* is defined as the endless displacement of meaning which both governs language and places it for ever beyond the reach of a stable, self-authenticating knowledge; this concept of writing, according to Derrida, has been subordinated by phonocentricism and logocentrism; we are giving the new concept the old name of writing. The science of writing, grammatology, is the science of 'the arbitrariness of the sign', 'science of writing before speech and in speech' (Derrida 1974:51), the one that 'Saussure saw without seeing, knew without being able to take into account' (Ibid:43). The written and spoken forms differ in their substances of inscription (i.e. graphic or phonic) and writing better describes linguistic phenomena.

Similarly, Derrida accepts the Saussurean concepts of signifier/signified, langue/parole, etc. but develops his own ideas criticially and radically examining such dichotomies; in other words, Saussure's terms are put in question, problematized, and placed in a new setting. Derrida argues that meaning is not present, as an essence, as a concept, as a signified, within any linguistic unit; meaning is caught up in the system of language where each element has meaning only by virtue of its difference from the other elements of the system. This is what Saussure says: 'In language there are only differences without positive terms'; at the same time, Saussure talks of 'signified', the concept. After pointing out the contradiction in Saussure, Derrida argues that between the signifier and the signified (if there be one), the word and the thing, the expression and what is expressed, there is the space, the gap, where the thing signified is lost; in fact, there is *no thing*, 'nothing'. There are only signs of signs; there are no signifieds. Saussure's desire for scientific understanding within a closed structure, the cultural heritage that tries to conceive of meaning as positively present within language, and the logocentric tradition forces him to say that the sign is a *positive* fact.

For example, what is the 'signified' for the signifier 'meaning'?; in other words, what is the meaning of the word 'meaning'? The answer is: 'nobody knows what meaning is or how to define it.' The Concise Oxford Dictionary gives the following entries:

meaning	:	what is meant, significance
meant	:	what it means
mean	:	signify, have in mind, intend
significance	:	being significant
significant	:	having a meaning

One can mark the circularity of 'signifiers' and how the 'signified' gets lost in the interval between signifiers; meaning slips beneath the circularity of signifiers. The belief that there is/was a reality is the illusion on which we construct our metaphysical notions of presence, origin, truth, etc. There is nothing (*no thing*) real behind the sign (word) *mother*, the only origin of 'mother' is a *trace*, which is to say there is no origin, no point at which the sign 'mother' is anything other than a sign of a sign. The sign of a sign is for Derrida a *supplement* that not only adds itself to and replaces what it represents but also effaces its supplementary role.

Derrida coins the term 'differance' to capture the notion of difference among signs and the *endless deferral*/deferment (postponement) of the arrival of the meaning of the word of the thing itself. According to Derrida 'language is structured as an endless deferral of meaning and any search for the essential, absolutely stable meaning must therefore be considered metaphysical; there is no final element, no fundamental unit, no transcendental signified that is meaningful in itself and escapes the ceaseless interplay of linguistic deferral and difference. The free play of signifiers will never yield a final, unified meaning that, in turn, might ground and explain all others' (Norris 1982). There is no origin of meaning except the trace or difference that makes signs iterable and makes them differ from and defer that which they represent. The strange being of the sign is that half of it is always 'not there' and the other half 'not that'; in other words, the structure of the sign is determined by the trace of the other which is foreever absent; meaning is not present, as an essence, within any linguistic unit; therefore the search for meaning, truth, presence, being, is a fool's errand.

[It is worth noting at this point that notions like plurality, indeterminacy, circularity, and the 'impossibility of getting it right' are expressed in *anekaantavaada,* the epistemological view of Jainism, a protest movement against the supremacy and teachings of the Vedas that believe in the transcendental Supreme Reality, the one and only 'Shining One'. *Anekaantavaada* views reality as being pluralistic, many sided or expressing itself in multiple forms and holds that whatever we say about reality is only probable or relative. One can at the most say 'maybe' or 'perhaps' and no one can assert that reality is determinate or 'absolutely this or that'; there are then, different points of view (nayavaada) and each is conditional (syaadvaada). This doctrine of 'perhapsism' and many-sidedness is very different from Western thinking as well as from other Indian systems of thought. The Jain doctrine of many-sidedness is found in the well-known story of the blind men and the elephant. Mahaaviira emphasizes the impossibility of getting it right since reality is everchanging, dynamic and complex and any search for the absolute is futile. So all 'salvation' must be 'self-salvation' and the only course is self-illumination.]

III. Derrida's ideas on language have influenced the practice of criticism in many ways. 'As a mode of textual theory and analysis, contemporary deconstruction subverts almost everything in the tradition, putting in question received ideas of the sign and language, the text, the context, the author, the reader, the role of history, and the forms of critical writing.'

Roland Barthes in his essay *From Work to Text* (1971) points out clearly how different the concept of text is. The New Criticism and Practical Criticism have emphasized the importance of every detail in the text but the deconstructive view of the text is very different. The text, according to Barthes, is a methodological field... The work can be seen in bookstores, in card catalogues, and on course lists, while the text reveals itself, articulates itself.... The text is experienced as an activity, a production.... The text practises the infinite deferral of the signified.... The text is plural.... (*etymologically the text is a cloth; *textus,* from which text derives, means 'woven')... there is no grammar of the text.

If texts are heterogeneous, a deconstructive reading brings out contradictory readings, readings that oppositionally engage each other with no final analysis that leads to a more absolute truth of meaning. For example, de Man's reading of the closing lines of Yeats's poem 'Among School Children':

> O chestnut-tree, great-rooted blossomer,
> Are you the leaf, the blossom or the bole?
> O body swayed to music, O brightening glance,
> How can we know the dancer from the dance?

The concluding question has traditionally been taken as a statement of 'the potential unity between form and experience, between creator and creation', thus presupposing an 'organic unity'. The last line has been read figuratively, as a rhetorical question, rather than literally since it is taken for granted that the figurative reading is more 'knowledgeable'; but, de Man demonstrates that the opposite is just the case; the figurative meaning is easier and more naive than the literal reading of the question, which 'leads to greater complication of theme and statement.... the final line is read literally as meaning that, since the dancer and the dance are not the same, it might be useful, perhaps even desperately necessary—for the question can be given a ring of urgency, 'Please tell me, how *can* I know the dancer from the dance' — to tell them apart.' (Paul de Man, 1979. *Allegories of Reading,* p.11).

Two contradictory readings of an entire poem thus hinge on the interpretation of the last line. 'The one reading is precisely the error denounced by the other and has to be undone by it.' Of late, several poems, stories, and novels have been read using this 'double logic' to show that unresolved ambiguity is the very basis of meaning; the incompatible and yet mutually dependent interweaving of pluralistic perspectives constitutes the very basis of signification. Deconstructionists have shown the interrelation between the 'creative' and critical texts to show the literary nature of critical texts and the critical nature of literary texts.

The value of deconstructive reading emerges from its lack of an absolute, transcendental value; it helps criticism to continue to ask questions without accepting the dogma of a fixed standard of appropriateness, an established appropriate power of authority, a closure that would deny the very possibility of criticism. Thus deconstruction makes us aware of the risk involved in critical endeavours that accept 'appropriate' readings and takes us perpetually through the wilderness of interpretation since a text is a vast shifting fabrication.

IV. If deconstruction leaves us in despair by giving the 'final no' to meaning, there are others called reader-response theorists who try to bring in the reader as the central character in the drama of critical enterprise.

Umberto Eco distinguishes between 'open' and 'closed' texts. A 'closed' text, such as Superman Comics, can be read by almost any reader who knows the language and interpreted in a multitude of different ways; an 'open' text, on the other hand, requires a 'Model Reader as a component of its structural strategy.' According to Eco, 'when reading *Ulysses* one can extrapolate the profile of a 'good Ulysses reader' from the text itself.' Roland Barthes distinguishes between 'writerly' and 'readerly' texts. Writerly texts, he says, are the ones that 'make the reader no longer a consumer. but a producer of the text' and 'they promote an infinite play of signification where there is no transcendental signified.' Readerly texts are ones that 'can be read, but not written': they are 'products' that leave the reader 'with no more than the poor freedom either to accept or reject the text.' Michael Riffaterre, in his *Semiotics of Poetry,* and Wolfgang Iser, in *The Implied Reader* and *The Act of Reading,* also try to show how texts set up certain requirements for the reader or guide the reader by filling in the gaps. From this point of view, the reader brings a large stained-glass that has patterns and many colours to the text, which is another such glass; (s)he juxtaposes them face to face and sees the patterns and colours formed by the combination of the two. The text is just an object without a preceiving subject and it is the reader who constructs the meaning, thereby becoming the second author.

As Paul de Man points out the situation is further complicated by the fact that the reader is no more constant than the text. Each time the reader interprets the text he changes it, and every change in the text makes a subsequent change in the reader; the process is endless. In addition, there are all kinds of readers—biased readers, sensitive readers. Super-readers, naive readers. superior readers and any reader may be biased, sensitive, naive, etc. with reference to a given text at a given point of time. Even though reader-response theorists are primarily concerned with synchronic readings, the focus on the role of reader reintroduces the historical dimension. Understanding is also a temporal act and every act of understanding by a reader brings its own history and context. Even from this perspective there is no ultimate meaning.

V. The next logical step is offered by Stanley Fish, who too proposes that the proper subject of interpretation is not the text but the reader. The activities of the reader, according to Fish, include the following:

> the making and revising of assumptions, the rendering and regretting of judgements, the coming to and abandoning of conclusions, the giving and withdrawing of approval, the specifying of causes, the asking of questions, the supplying of answers, the solving of puzzles. In a word, these activities are interpretive—rather than being preliminary to questions of value—and because they are inerpretive, a description of them will also be a description of a moving field of concerns, at once wholly present (not waiting for meaning but constituting meaning) and continually in the act of reconstituting itself.
>
> (Fish 1980: 158-159).

If meaning-making is conceived of as the reader's business, one must answer the questions: What kind of reader? Are all readers readers? Can even ridiculous readings be accepted? Does it mean every reader at any given point of time can come out with absurd readings? Are there no canons of acceptability?

In trying to answer such questions, Fish ends up saying that *interpretive communities* make the texts have the meanings they do. In this *institutional theory of interpretation,* the concept of 'interpretive communities' becomes crucial. He says that 'interpretive communities' are 'made up of those who share interpretive strategies' and argues that there is stability of interpretation among different readers (if they belong to the same interpretive community) and not because of a stability in the text. This doesn't mean that the majority is always right; it *can* be right and their judgement is probably correct.

The conception of 'interpretive community' puts the experiencing-of-the-text and meaning-making out of reach to the individual reader; in other words, the community is privileged over the individual. The mechanism of adjudication will put the interests of the individual subordinate to the power of the authority that decides appropriateness, the interpretive community becomes another avatar of the 'community of critics'. Secondly, communities do not experience meaning; only individuals do.

VI. As has been shown, post-structuralist thought reflects as well as causes a swing in modern thinking from a stance of theoretical certainty to uncertainty. At least several questions have been asked about the author's intention, the autonomy of the text, the role of the reader, the nature of language, and the source and nature of meaning with no definitive answers. Post-structuralist thought undoes the very comforts of mastery that underlie the illusion that all is well in heaven.

Questions and topics for discussion

1. Look at the following 'text':

   In the beginning God created the heaven and the earth. And the earth was without form, and void; and darkness was upon the face of the deep. And the Spirit of god moved upon the face of the waters. And God said, 'Let there be light'; and there was light. And God saw the light, that it was good: and God divided the light from the darkness. And God called the light Day, and the darkness he called Night.

   a. Several dichtomies are set up in the passage:

      heaven/earth
      spirit/form
      light/darkness
      day/night

good/....(implied)

- In each pair which one is privileged?
- Are there traces of one in the other?
- Explain the notion of supplementarity with reference to these pairs.
- Is there a transcendental 'signified' for each item or pair? If there be one, can you specify it in absolute terms?
- Can you reverse the hierarchy in each pair by giving arguments?

2. Look at the following text:

So God created man in his own image... And the Lord God caused a deep sleep to fall upon Adam and he slept: and he took one of his ribs, and closed up the flesh instead thereof; and the rib, which the Lord God had taken from man, made he a woman, and brought her unto the man.

And Adam said,
'This is now bone of my bones
And flesh of my flesh
She shall be called woman,
Because she was taken out of Man.'

Therefore shall a man leave his father and his mother, and shall cleave unto his wife: and they shall be one flesh. And they were both naked, the man and his wife, and were not ashamed.

Using deconstruction as a tool (setting up hierarchical binary distinctions, finding traces and supplementarity, reversing the hierarchy, finding contractions, etc., attempt a feminist reading of the passage.

3. Literary theories can be roughly classified as follows:
   a. author-centred type
   b. reader-centred type
   c. code-centred type
   d. reference-centred type
   e. context-centred type

   Give examples for each type with the names of the scholars and their important works.
4. A language cannot be reduced to a code, any more than it can be reduced to a grammar. Explain and illustrate.
5. What does Derrida mean by the word 'writing'? What are the different systems of writing? Is Derrida justified in using the word 'writing' in a general sense?
6. What do the following terms mean? Give examples for each.
   a. deviational stylistics
   b. statistical stylistics
   c. contextual stylistics

7. 'Far from reducing the text back to detached fragments, it (i.e. deconstruction) inevitably constructs again in a different form what it deconstructs. It does again as it undoes. It recrosses in one place what it uncrosses in another. Rather than surveying the text with sovereign command from outside, it remains, caught within the activity it retraces.' — J. Hillis Miller
— Explain and illustrate.
8. 'The concept of the definitive text belongs only to religion or to exhaustion.' - L. Borges. Comment.
9. Try a deconstructive reading of the poem *A Coat.*
10. Derrida says there is nothing outside the text and Beckett says there is nothing within the text. Both are right depending upon what we mean by the text. What is your opinion?
11. 'A 'text' is henceforth no longer a finished corpus of writing, some content enclosed in a book or its margins, but a differential network, a fabric of traces referring endlessly to something other than itself, to other differential traces.' - Derrida.
Explain and illustrate.
12. Geoffrey H. Hartman has looked at Yeats's 'Leda and the Swan'. He points out, "The poem effects a displacement from 'Leda' and 'Troy' to a nonproper, that is unlocalized event that cannot be given a name or one name...., we become unsure of the poem's real frame or reference. Who is the being so caught?"
Leda is not named within the poem. Who is seducing who? Can you look at the poem from the post-structuralist point of view?
Try to point out the contradictions that you perceive in the 'text'.
13. 'A poem should not mean but be.' Explain and illustrate.

20 NARRATOLOGY

'Bees do not regale one another with reminiscences of the nectar they found last week, nor discuss together the nectar they might find tomorrow.'

Focal points

I. If you see something, say an accident, it cannot be described as a 'narrative'. The word 'narrative' is used here to mean something that is narrated, told; it has a tale, a text, a narrator and a narratee/a listener/a reader. In a general sense, all human experience is narrated in language; all of us tell tales, all kinds of tales; we discourse all the time.

In *descriptive discourse* we describe something—a person, place, or thing; in *expository discourse* we explain and inform someone about something in a matter of fact manner; in *argumentative discourse* we try to convince or persuade others. In *narrative discourse* or narration we are concerned with action, with events in time, with life in motion. Narration, which is a kind of discourse, answers the question: What happened? Narration is like the motion pictures; it keeps moving in space and time. In a narrow sense, it is used to refer to the discourse of fiction, narration in stories.

Consider the following text: 'Roses are red, violets are blue, sugar is sweet, and so are you.' This does not constitute a narrative because it does not answer the question 'What happened?' On the other hand,

> Two little kittens, one stormy night,
> Began to quarrel, and then to fight

is a piece of narrative discourse because it is concerned with action, with events in time. The question is what makes a piece of discourse narrative? How and why do people understand a text as narrative? How many kinds of narrative are used in language? *Narratology* tries to find answers to such questions by studying primarily the discourse structure of fiction.

II. It was Todorov (1969), the French structuralist, who proposed the name *narratology* to the study of narrative. Since then a number of models of analysis and theories of narratology have been proposed by French, German, Russian, and Anglo-American researchers and theorists.

Gerald Prince (1987) in his *A Dictionary of Narratology* defines narratology as follows:

> Narratology studies the nature, form and functioning of narrative (regardless of the medium of representation) and tries to characterize narrative competence (the ability to produce and understand narratives). More particularly, it examines what all and only narratives have in common (at the level of story, narrating, and their relations) as well as what enables

them to be different from one another, and it attempts to account for the ability to produce and understand them.

He further adds, that defining narratology as the 'study of narrative as a verbal mode of representation of temporally ordered situations and events' is very narrow and that it 'disregards the level of story in itself (it does not attempt to formulate a grammar of stories or plots, for instance), and focuses on the possible relations between story and narrative text, narrating and narrative text, and story and narrating.'

Narratology has to be differentiated from *thematology* or the study of themes; theme is an idea frame, a semantic macrostructure which expresses (in general and abstract terms) the concepts that are actualized in a text. Theme is different from *plot;* plot is an action frame, the sequence of events as they are available in the narration of fiction; a *story,* on the other hand, is the chronological sequence of events which may or may not coincide with the plot. Theme is different form the *thesis* of a work; the thesis of a work proposes an answer for questions raised.

III. The attempts to identify narrative modes of expression is as old as criticism. The distinction between *mimesis* (showing) and *diegesis* (telling) in Plato's *Republic* was taken up by Aristotle in his *Poetics* and has remained a basis for discussion and description to this day.

Propp's *Morphology of the Folk Tale* (1968; originally publised in Russian in 1928) may be taken as the starting point for the contemporary approaches. Propp's *Morphology* of the Russian fairy-tale is basically an inventory of all and only the fundamental events (called *functions*) that he identifies in his study of 115 Russian fairy-tales. According to Propp, an *act* has to be viewed in terms of its significance for the course of the *action* in which it appears; in other words, an act is to be considered in terms of the role it plays at the action level. Propp showed that the same act can have different roles (which is subsumed under functions) in different tales. For instance, 'John killed Peter' may be an act of villainy in one tale and the hero's victory in another; conversely, different acts can have the same role in different tales. For example, 'John killed Peter' and 'The dragon kidnapped the princess' may both constitute villainy. For Propp, *functions* constitute the fundamental components of the underlying structure of any Russian fairy tale. He listed 31 faily-tales developing functions and seven basic character types like villain, hero, helper, false hero, princess, etc.

The following story written by a 7-year-old child with Proppian functions appended on the left may serve to show how Propp's taxonomy handles simple tales.

Initial situation	1.	Once upon a time there was a bunny named Benjie
Magical agent	2.	and she had magic powers.
Departure	3.	One day she was walking in the woods and
	4.	a bunny boy appeared
Transference	5.	and they went together for a walk
Reconnaissance	6.	and a man appeared with a big net
	7.	and he got the two bunnies and went in a big ship
Villainy	8.	poor bunnies
	9.	They were caught now.
Struggle	10.	But right then the girl bunny tripped the man
Villainy nullified	11.	and they got free once again.
Reward	12.	So the boy bunny thanked the girl bunny for saving him.
	13.	The boy bunny asked the girl bunny to marry him
Equilibrium	14.	and she said yes
(happy ending)	15.	So they had six bunny babies
	16.	and they lived happily ever after.

(from King and Rentel, 1982.
In Christie et al, 1984)

Is it possible to analyse more complex tales, using this model? It may be if we ignore varying details of stories. A structuralist/ morphological approach has to *reduce,* ignoring the non-essential details; but the problem is what is non-essential is very essential to the understanding of the story. Like in structural linguistics (phonology and syntax), Propp was interested in identifying the essential conditions within which story meanings can arise.

IV. Roland Barthes (1966) in 'Introduction to the structural analysis of narratives', a study of prose narrative, emphasizes the need for a hierarchical typology of units and proposes three major levels of narrative structure:

a) functions (as in Propp)
b) actions (by which he refers to characters)
c) narration (equivalent to discourse).

Barthes posits a relation between sentence and discourse: 'discourse is a long 'sentence'...just as a sentence...is a short discourse.' The first level of function is divided into two: (a) functions proper (the Propp-type functions) and (b) indices; functions proper are of two types: (a) *cardinal* function or *nuclei* (which are like 'kernels') which are the real hinge-points of narratives, and (b) *catalysers* that fill in the space between two nuclei and function as satellites. Indices are sub-classified as (a) indices proper and (b) informants.

Jonathan Culler's (1975a:138) objection to Barthes' model is quite simple but fundamental: 'It remains strangely atomistic, through the lack of any specification of what one is moving towards as one collects kernels and satellites and groups them into sequences.' Secondly, Barthes does not give importance to narration; the focus is on semiotics.

For Barthes narrative analysis stops at the level of discourse; from there it is necessary to shift to another *semiotics.* Barthes (1970) proposes certain codes for analysing stories and Silverman (1983) exemplifies them in a lucid manner in her *The Subject of Semiotics.*

i) The *Semic code:* It functions to define persons, objects and places; it is useful for grouping a number of signifiers around a proper name or another signifier (as though it is a proper name) and the signifiers grouped function like a collective signified to the proper name or its surrogate. For example in Hardy's *Tess,* a character called Durbeyfield is described as follows:

> On an evening in the later part of May, a middle-aged man was walking homeward from Shaston to the village

> of Marlott, in the adjoining Vale of Blakemore or Blackmoor. The pair of legs that carried him were rickety, and there was a bias in his gait which inclined him somewhat to the left of the straight line. He occasionally gave a smart nod, as if in confirmation of some opinion, though he was not thinking of anything in particular. An empty egg-basket was slung upon his arm, the nap of his hat was ruffled, a patch being quite worn away at its brim where his thumb came in taking it off.

Before the proper name is supplied, *middle-aged, empty egg-basket, rickety-legs, shabby hat, bias in his gait,* etc. are given to create a collective signified.

ii) The *hermeneutic code:* This is entrusted with the responsibility of articulating and resolving the enigma (something that is mysterious and difficult to understand)—formulation of the enigma, request for an answer, snare, equivocation, jamming, suspended answer, partial answer and disclosure. These elements can be combined in assorted ways.

For example, in Stevenson's *Dr. Jekyll and Mr. Hyde,* we have the following description of Mr. Utterson (who has something to utter/tell):

> Mr. Utterson, the lawyer, was a man of rugged countenance that was never lighted by a smile: cold, scanty, and embarrassed in discourse; backward in sentiment; lean, long, dusty, dreary, and somehow loveable. At friendly meetings, and when the wine was to his taste, something eminently human beaconed from his eye; something which indeed never found its way into his talk, but which spoke not only in these silent symbols of the after-dinner face, but more often and loudly in the acts of his life. He was austere with himself; drank gin when he was alone, to mortify a taste for vintages; and though he enjoyed the theatre had not crossed the doors of one for twenty years.

The theme for the enigma is created in the description of Mr. Utterson; the conflict—self-indulgence and self-denial—is created; later Mr. Utterson says 'If he is Mr. Hyde, I'll be Mr. Seek.'

Similarly, in the description of Mr. Hyde's house, we find the enigma.

> Even on Sunday, when it veiled its more *florid charms* and lay comparatively *empty* of passage, the street *shone* out in contrast to its *dingy* neighbourhood, like a fire in a forest.... showed no windows, nothing but a door on the lower story; and a blind forehead of discoloured wall on the upper....

The mystery is built up.

A trap (snare) is created when Utterson asks Poole, the servant about Hyde: 'O, dear no, Sir. He never dines here....Indeed we see very little of him on this side of the house; he mostly comes and goes by the laboratory.'

Equivocation contains a snare and a truth. When the body of Hyde is discovered, Utterson remarks: 'Hyde is gone to his account; and it only remains for us to find the body of your master.' Utterson is already in the presence of that body and has no need to search for it. Thus it is a snare.

Jamming can take place in the form of, for instance, the death of a key witness or something missing, etc. A suspended answer or a partial answer may be given.

Disclosure is the closure and end of signification.

iii) *The proairetic code:* This is the code of actions, the sequence of events within a story; it is the 'glue' which binds the events together.

iv) *The symbolic code:* This represents polarities and anti-theses that cannot be reconciled, for example, the sexual difference that goes beyond the biological difference.

v) *The cultural code:* This may be represented in the form of good and evil, humanity and bestiality, day and night, body and soul, etc. These are fragments of ideology whose effect is felt in all the other codes. In Stevenson's *Jekyll and Hyde,* we have: 'Man is not truly one, but two', which shows that man is a house divided against itself; it may represent the Christian fall. Jekyll was slowly losing hold of his original and better self and becoming slowly incorporated with his second and worse. The cultural codes provide the means whereby the information contained in the authoritative texts like the

Bible, the Gita, etc., finds its way into the novels, poems etc., which perpetuate that order.

V. Bal (1985) in her *Narratology: Introduction to the Theory of Narrative* lists the main processes involved in the concrete, textual level realization of what has been described so far at the abstract level; the list may be useful for understanding even the other models proposed.

a) The events are arranged in a sequence (the plot) which can differ from the chronological sequence (which is the story or the narrative content).
b) The amount of time allotted in the text to the various elements of the story is determined with respect to the amount of time which these elements take up in the story. (That is to say, the actual time allocated to presentation of each event or state in the text is determined by how long these events or states last in the story.)
c) The actors are provided with distinct traits and are individualized and transformed into characters.
d) The locations (settings) where events occur are also given distinct characteristics and are thus transformed into specific places.
e) In addition to the necessary relationships among events, actors, location, and time, all of which are described in the layer of the story, other relationships (symbolic, allusive, etc.) may exist among the various elements.
f) A choice is made from among the various 'points of view' from which the elements can be presented.

VI. The most influential theorist of text-time is Gerard Genette. Genette's (1972) *Narrative Discourse* is a classic text of French structuralism and textual narratology.

The first distinction in this model is between *logos* (that which is said) and *lexis* (the manner of saying); lexis is then split into *diegesis* and *mimesis. Diegesis* is divided into *description* and *narration,* and narration is divisible into *narrative* (report) and *discourse* (comment). This can be shown as in Chart 6.

There are different levels of diegesis (which presents 'everything that happened' but only everything that a teller decides is worth telling — a reporter who is able to reflect, recognize, decide upon the point of the story). Narrators can be extradiegetic, not part of any diegesis. For instance, in the *Mahabharata,* Veda Vyasa is extradiegetic in most of the sequences; similarly, Sanjaya, who narrates the great war to the blind king is extradiegetic to that piece of narrative. Vyasa, as a narrator, plays several roles in the *Mahabharata.* When the wives of Vichitraveerya become widows without children, Vyasa is requested by Queen Satyavati to marry the widowed queens. Vyasa rules out marriage but bestows them with children. Here Vyasa, who is part of the narrative is the narrator, but he is *intradiegetic;* in his capacity as a character in the event he is narrating, he becomes *homodiegetic.* In the battle sequences, there are different narrators; so the narrative of the battle has *heterodiegetic* narrators.

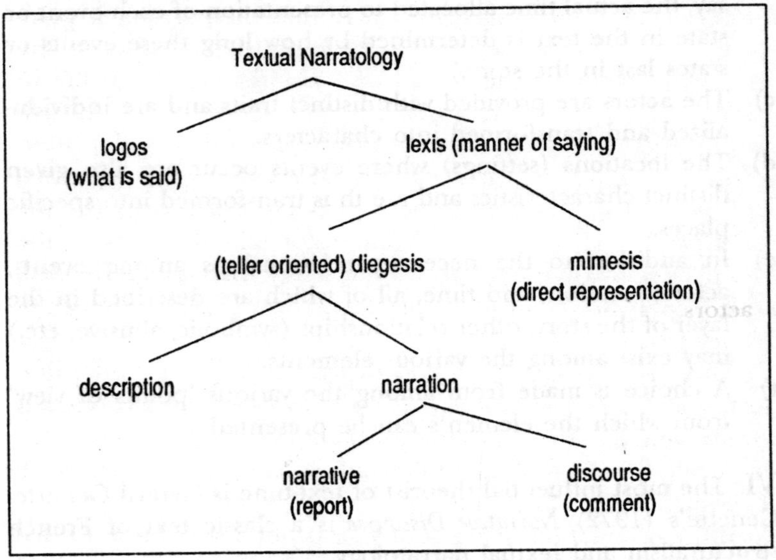

Chart 6: Textual Narratology

This brings in the problem of perception. As Bal points out: 'Perception depends on so many factors that striving for objectivity is pointless'. Genette's terms of the inescapable adoption of a limited perspective in narrative, a viewpoint from which things are seen, felt, understood, and assessed, is *focalization,* which is equivalent to the Anglo-American term *point of view*, the orientation from which the story is narrated. We can think of a broad division between third-person and first-person narratives, and then divide the third-person narrative into sub-classes. In a third-person narrative, the narrator is someone outside the story who refers to all the characters in the story by name or as *he, she, they*. Fielding begins *Tom Jones* thus: 'In that part of the western division of this kingdom...there lately lived, and perhaps lives still, a gantleman whose name was Allworthy...'. In a first-person narrative, the narrator speaks as 'I' and is himself/herself a character in the story: 'If you really want to hear about it, the first thing you'll really want to know is where I was born, and what my lousy childhood was like...'

Third-person points of view may be: (a) the omniscient point of view in which the narrator assumes that (s)he knows everything about the events and characters; thus the narrator is privileged. Within this mode, the narrator may be *intrusive* in the sense (s)he evaluates the actions and motives of human life in general; the intrusive narrator is authoritative. Jane Austen, Dickens, Hardy, Tolstoy, and others have used this mode. Alternatively, the omniscient narrator can be *unintrusive* or *impersonal* who merely presents the characters talking and acting; (b) the *limited point of view* in which the narrator tells the story in the third person, but confines himself/herself to what is experienced, thought, and felt by a single character, or a limited number of characters.

There are also *self-conscious narrators* who take the reader into confidence about the various problems involved—either seriously or for comic purpose and *unreliable narrators* whose point of view is very different from those of the author. This may take the form of irony.

If the orientation or point of view is not associable with that of any character within the text, the focalization (point of view) is external; internal focalization occurs inside the setting of the represented events, and almost always involves a character. Similarly, the focalized (someone or something that is the object of the process of focalization) can be of two types—viewing from outside or from within. In viewing from outside only the visible, external phenomena are reported; in the latter facts about feelings, thoughts and reactions of one or several characters are reported. Molly Bloom in *Ulysses* is both internal focalizer and focalized from within.

Genette also formulates the relations between events and their telling via categories derived from the grammar of the verb, *tense* (narrative time: order, pace and frequency), *mood* (forms and degrees of representation: dramatic or narrative mode, direct or indirect speech reporting), and *voice* (active or passive relation of the narrating subject with his own story; levels of embedded narration).

VII. By now it must be obvious that this business of specifying and making explicit the process of narration is remarkably complex. Chatman (1978), Prince (1982), and Rimmon-Kenan (1983) have identified six *participants* in the process of narration. This classification is useful in understanding time, focalization (point-of-view) and narration and how they are related.

The diagram below shows the optional (shown within brackets) and obligatory participants:

The Text

Real author (the one in flesh and blood) →	Implied author (the one constructed or inferred by the reader) →	(Narrator) (the one who tells the tale; may be present; e.g. 'you don't know about me') →	(Narratee) (like the studio audience in a TV show; they laugh but are rarely seen; the 'you' in 'you don't know me') →	Implied reader (imaginary reader) →	Real reader (the one in flesh and blood)

The author (as different from the person) and the real reader are extratextual participants; but the narrator (if there is one) and the narratee (if there is one) are real enough textual entities. Chatman says: 'It is as necessary to distinguish among narratees ... as it is among narrator, implied author, and real author.'

Wayne Booth (1961) wrote:

> As the author writes, he creates not simply an ideal, impersonal 'man in general' but an implied version of himself that is different from the implied authors we meet in other men's works....the picture the reader gets of this presence is one of the author's most important effects. The pictures we have of authors are always constructions, and all authors are inferred authors.

VIII. In the eighties, story narration has been approached (as has discourse analysis) from the psycholinguistic angle too. The main interest of such studies lies in exploring the 'psychological reality' for stories and their narration. There have been attempts to expand the analogy between sentence grammars and story grammars. It has been pointed out that we juxtapose episodes to produce meaning just as we juxtapose sentences and that children's narrative ability in both the length of narratives produced and their structural complexity increases visibly like in the case of complexity of sentences; roughly akin to coordination and subordination in sentence formation, there is increased elaboration and embedding in narratives. At the same time it has been pointed out that the semantic and syntactic aspects are more intertwined in stories than in sentences because story categories are more dependent on context than are lexical or syntactic categories.

A vast body of psycholinguistic research into our mental modelling of story grammars tends to show that we construct schemas, or frameworks, of archetypal stories, which we hold in our minds, and that we use these frameworks as a mental aid when we attempt to comprehend or recall particular stories. One of the significant contributions of story grammars to the study of stories is the attempt to define the 'storiness' of a story. de Beaugrande (1982) proposes the following features of a 'non-story':

a) in purely formal terms, a non-story would violate the rules of the grammar of a language;

b) a non-story may be incomprehensible because its constituents are 'out of reasonable order or are lacking in any temporal and causal relatedness';
c) a non-story may be comprehensible, but only with substantial cognitive strains;
d) a non-story may be comprehensible, but only if the audience are willing and able to carry out substantial rearranging and inferencing;
e) a non-story may be comprehensible, but devoid of all interest, so that nobody can endure it.

He extends the logic of sentence grammars to story grammars thus:

> ...whether or not a definitive definition of the grammatical sentences can be devised, it is the acceptable sentence that concerns human language users. The same point can be made for stories.

The focus, thus, has shifted from how the text is organised (structuralist narratology) to how readers assess the 'story-worthiness' of stories.

IX. The post-structuralists have critically examined many of the assumptions of the structuralists including the concept of a narrative. Barthes (1971) declared: "The text no longer has the sentence for its model." The post-structuralists have argued that the element of 'play' is present in the notion of structure itself and that structures undergo change—there is more than one structure in a structure; in other words, structure itself is pluralistic. If narration is desedimented, it will produce meaning(pluralistic) that means something to everybody. A centre which arrests and founds the free play must be decentred so that it does not become determinate; in fact, one cannot determine a centre.

For example, in the *Mahabharata*, the heterogeneity and contradiction are multiplied as much as possible; it expands to four, five, six times its original size. At every point decentring takes place; it is very difficult to set up dichotomies like hero/villain because every character is 'flawed' and no one is privileged.

There is an on-going production of meaning through constant decentring and destabilizing. So many voices are heard; it is a veritable 'babel'. It is a writerly text in the words of Barthes. There is a lot of scope for research in the area of narratology within the framework of post-structuralist thinking.

The movement from the taxonomic, static, structuralist models to a more dynamic, developmental approach will take us to the study of the *parole* of narratology. If we assume that texts are not only differential and historical but also deferantial (in the Derridean sense) and that they are not structures of presence but traces and tracings of otherness... shaped by the repetition and transformation of other textual forces, there is a lot of scope for penetrating the narrative textuality resulting in cross-fertilization. Even notions like intertextuality can be expanded to bring in intra-lingual textuality (texts in the same language) as well as interlingual textuality (texts across languages) to build up a richer narratology.

Questions and topics for discussion

1. Two little kittens, one stormy night,
   Began to quarrel, and then to fight.

   One had a mouse, and the other had none,
   And that's the way the quarrel begun.

   'I'll have that mouse,' said the bigger cat,
   'You'll have that mouse? We'll see about that!'

   'I WILL have that mouse,' said the older one,
   'You SHAN'T have the mouse,' said the little one.

   I told you before 'twas a stormy night'
   When these two little kittens began to fight.

   The old woman seized her sweeping broom,
   And swept the two kittens right out of the room.

   The ground was all covered with frost and snow,
   And the two little kittens had nowhere to go.

   So they laid them down on the mat at the door,
   While the old woman finished sweeping the floor.

   Then they crept in as quiet as mice,
   All wet with snow, and as cold as ice.

For they found it much better, that stormy night,
To lie down and sleep, than to quarrel and fight.

— Old Rhyme.

Comment on the *narrative* structure of this poem.

2. Read the following story and comment on its narrative structure:
I wrote to the zoo to send me a pet.
They sent me an .... (picture of an elephant)
He was too big! I sent him back.
So they sent me a .... (picture of a giraffe)
He was too tall! I sent him back.
So they sent me a .... (picture of a lion)
He was too fierce! I sent him back.
So they sent me a .... (picture of a camel)
He was too grumpy! I sent him back.
So they sent me a .... (picture of a monkey)
He was too naughty! I sent him back.
So they sent me a .... (picture of a frog)
He was too jumpy! I sent him back.
So they sent me a .... (picture of puppy)
He was perfect! I kept him.
(Use Propp's functions or Barthes' functions and analyse the text; then, use Genette's model.)
3. Identify the cardinal function in the narrative of the *Mahabharata*; locate the catalysis for the cardinal function. How are they related to the *Gita,* the discourse of ideology, in the *Mahabharata*?
4. Nancy would set her bundle on the top of her head, then upon the bundles in turn she would set the black straw sailor hat which she wore winter and summer.
-Who speaks, in the sense 'narrates' in this story?
5. Problems for practice:
Attempt an 'intertextual reading' for Melville's *Moby Dick* and Hemingway's *The Old Man and the Sea* focussing on the following: the narrator-narrative relationship, the point of view and the episodic structuring. (Note: 'Intertextual reading' is not mere comparison of the two pieces, but the super-imposition of one text on the other and reading the implications.)
6. Make the great fish that the old man, Santiago, killed the narrator of *The Old Man and the Sea* and write the story in about two pages and compare its structure with that of the original.
7. Attempt an analysis of a short story using the parameters suggested by Genette as given in the unit.
8. 'The medium is the message'. — Explain and illustrate.
9. Stories for and by children are remarkably complex; still children

all over the world enjoy stories irrespective of the culture in which they are embedded. Does it mean that the context of imagination and the context of narration are more important than the context of culture? Give your opinion.

10. Stories for, by, and with children can tell us a lot about the narrative development and language development in children. The distinctive features of children's narrative development can be used for language teaching. Give your comments on this.

Suggested reading

Barthes, Roland. 1966. In English 1977. 'Introduction to the structural analysis of narratives.' In *Image-Music-Text.* London : Fontana.
This paper is by now a classic example of the type of analysis practised in the early stages of French Structuralism.

Barthes, Roland. 1970. In English 1974. *S/Z.* New York : Hill and Wang.
This book marks Barthes's transition from structural to textual analysis. Through a study of Balzac's 'Sarrasine', Barthes presents the codes underlying both the production of texts and their reading. It advocates plurality and reversibility.

Chatman Seymour. 1978. *Story and Discourse.* Ithaca, New York : Cornell University Press.
It is a synthesis of various theories of narrative in literature and film, discussing events, characters, time, point of view and narration. The section on character, criticizing the reductive treatment of character by formalists and structuralists and suggesting an analysis in terms of a paradigm of traits, is important.

Culler, Jonathan. 1975. *Structuralist Poetics.* London : Routledge and Kegan Paul.
This gives a pre-deconstructionist treatment of structuralist theory, with distinct reservations (in the final chapter) about Derrida's then increasing influence.

Fish, Stanley, 1980. *Is There a Text in This Class?: The Authority of Interpretive Communities.* Cambridge, Mass.: Harvard University Press.
This is a collection of Fish's major essays from 1970 to 1980, documenting his move from 'affective stylistics'—in which the text was all determining—to a more radical theoretical position in which a text is the product of the interpretive procedures brought to bear on it.

Freeman, Donald C. (ed.). 1970. *Linguistics and Literary Style.* New York : Holt, Rinehart and Winston, Inc.
This book contains essays on the theory of linguistic stylistics, the methodology of linguistic stylistics, approaches to the study of prose style and approaches to metrics. The book reflects the thinking of

the 1960s which has come to be questioned now.

Genette, Gerard. 1972. In English 1980. *Narrative Discourse.* Inthaca, N.Y. : Cornell University Press.

This is classic text of French structuralism combining theoretical and descriptive poetics. The section on temporal frequency and the distinction between focalization and narration is a contribution to the field.

Iser, Wolfgang. 1974. *The Implied Reader: Patterns of Communication in Prose Fiction from Bunyan to Beckett.* Baltimore : Johns Hopkins University Press.

This collection of essays works toward a theory of reading through close analyses of novels.

Journal of Pragmatics, 6 : 1982. North-Holland Publishing Company.

This is a special number on story grammars. It contains many useful articles on the subject.

Leech, Geoffrey N. 1969. *A Linguistic Guide to English Poetry.* London; Longman.

This is an introductory course in stylistics and contains a general scheme for the discussion of the language of literary texts in the framework of the 1960s.

Norris, Cristopher. 1982. *Deconstruction : Theory and Practice.* London : Methuen.

This is a concise introduction to the development, ideas and uses of deconstruction.

Rimmon-Kenan, Shlomith. 1983. *Narrative Fiction. Contemporary Poetics.* London/New York : Methuen.

This is a very good text book for an introductory course on Narratology. A fairly comprehensive survey of the developments in the field in the past two decades has been presented in a lucid style.

de Saussure, Ferdinand. *Course in General Linguistics.* Trans. Wade Baskin. 1959. New York : McGraw-Hill.

This is Saussure's major text as compiled by his students; it is a cornerstone text for the development of structuralism and semiotics.

Wales, Katie. 1989. *A Dictionary of Stylistics.* London and New York : Longman.

It is a useful reference book.

Widdowson, H.G. 1975. *Stylistics and the Teaching of Literature.* London : Longman.

Differentiating between the study of literature as text and as discourse, the book discusses issues like the nature of literary communication, and literature as subject and discipline. There are also exercises in literary understanding.

CHAPTER FIVE

Language and Pedagogy

'Every teacher is a language teacher'

21 EDUCATIONAL LINGUISTICS

"Curriculum defines what counts as valid knowledge; pedagogy defines what counts as valid transmission of knowledge; and evaluation defines what counts as valid realizations of this knowledge on the pupil's part."

— Michael Stubbs

Focal points

I. The following statement of S. Pit Corder (1974) raises an important issue:

> **Applied linguistics is the utilization of the knowledge about the nature of language achieved by linguistic research for the improvement of the efficiency of some practical task in which language is a central component.**

Does this mean that linguists present their study of the nature of language based on their linguistic research and applied linguists utilize this knowledge? Or, does it mean that applied linguists study the nature of language in the context of the classroom because language is central to classroom interaction? It has been stated again and again that a phenomenon must be studied in the context in which it happens. In order to study language—language in use—the right laboratory is the classroom and not any other place; the right person is the classroom teacher, who becomes an applied linguist as a researcher and explorer when (s)he puts on the other hat.

Children spend about a thousand hours per year (at the rate of five hours per day for about two hundred days in a year) in school, which amounts to about twelve thousand hours by the time they leave the higher-secondary (10+2) stage. And for most of this time the learner is not only exposed to language throughout the curriculum but also uses it; whether it is subject teaching and learning where the focus is not on the language (which makes language learning communicative and effective) or whether it is teaching the language, learners interact with one another and with the teachers using language. In addition, the school environment offers an educational atmosphere without the uncertainties and interferences that mark the environment outside in the real world. Thus, there are real laboratory conditions available in classrooms for the applied-linguistic-teacher to do all kinds of studies and experimentation. It has been rightly pointed out that 'the medium has ten thousand hours to convey the message' (Jackson 1968); at the same time, the medium itself is evolved in these ten thousand hours as part of the message-medium complex.

Teaching and learning comprise language activities such as lecturing, explaining, paraphrasing and summarizing, listening, writing, etc. In other words, language plays a central role in the process of education. Language is used in all kinds of social and personal situations and no study of language can ignore language as it is used by learners in the classroom, in the home, and in the peer group, which is the most powerful linguistic influence on learners. As Halliday (1978) points out, 'language is too rich, complex, subtle, and messy' ever to be captured in a single theory; there can be several theories of language and different kinds of linguistics; educational linguistics attempts to develop a model of language that is relevant to language teaching and learning.

II. Educational linguistics is interested in exploring the complex relation between language and education without oversimplifying them. Several important questions can be asked: Does a child's language affect his/her success or failure at school, thereby affecting his/her success or failure later in life? If so, how? Is it true that 'educational failure is linguistic failure'? In what sense? How is it that some who fail in the school examinations are very successful in the outside world? How does a teacher's language affect a pupil's learning? What do we mean when we say that some pupils are 'linguistically inadequate' or 'linguistically deprived'? What kind of language is used by teachers and learners? In what ways is it related to the use of language outside the classroom? Does a child's home dialect or language bear any relation to his or her educational ability? Does teaching mean only talking? Can we say that every teacher is a language teacher? Can we separate teaching facts (say, in chemistry or geography) from teaching the language of the subject? Does the subject-specific language have no relation to everyday language? If so, what kind of relationship does it have? The answers to these questions, and many more, should be based primarily on naturalistic observation, recording, and analysis of language in real classroom situations. Michael Stubbs (1976) points out in *Language, Schools and Classrooms*:

> The work must be based on a linguistically adequate analysis of what is said. This means both being *explicit* about the relation between language forms and language functions and also analysing the language as *linguistic* systems. It is not enough, however, for the analysis to be rigorous in a mechanical way; what is required is an analysis of the *social meanings* conveyed by language and an analysis of people's *attitudes* to language. Finally, if we are to understand the general principles underlying the sociolinguistic forces at work in schools, the analysis of language in educational settings must be related to what we know of sociolinguistic behaviour in other settings. These demands are stringent.... And the demands must be made if we are to progress beyond linguistic folklore, personal opinions, unsupported speculation, pseudo-theories and an accumulation of interesting anecdotes, none of which, in themselves, can lead to real understanding.

This clearly shows that there is a lot of scope for work in the area of educational linguistics.

III. Any inter-disciplinary enterprise is obviously difficult. Educational linguistics has to bring in sociolinguistics and a view of the social conditions of language use since the school is a social institution; it has to bring in psycholinguistic perspectives since individuals are involved in language acquisition and production processes; the fusion of language and thought, the matching of linguistic competence and communicative competence involves *transfer competence*, which provides a new basis for inventing new modes of thought that serve as a means for going beyond experience, beyond what is taught and learnt. Since texts are used in the class there are implications of discourse analysis; the study of literature and stylistics has to be brought in; a number of general principles of education and methodological issues about language teaching are to be studied. Thus, educational linguistics is a not just sociolinguistics or psycholinguistics or language teaching but truly a joint venture.

Secondly, we don't have at the moment an adequate theoretical knowledge about the use of language in classroom situations; formulating the problems, collecting the data devising methods for analysis and description, and several other issues are to be clearly formulated. The use of language in a classroom is different from the use of language in a shop or department store. The conventions in the classroom are different from those in real-life situations. There is need for more research in this area.

IV. There is a great deal of fragmentation among the different aspects and branches of language teaching, and even a sharp opposition between mother tongue/first language and foreign/second language teaching. The increasing specialization and fragmentation tend to ignore the common conceptual basis of the different aspects of language education which can be the basis for 'language across the curriculum'.

At present there isn't any meaningful integration of the various aspects of language teaching. The teaching and testing of the mother tongue is disorderly; the aims are not clearly stated and often they are taken for granted. There is very little realization that there are variations in the use of what is called the mother tongue and that there are differences between the spoken and the written forms. What is generally taught in the schools and colleges in the name of the mother tongue is what is taken for granted as the standard language, which is quite often the written, literary form, without any realization that the pupil who comes to learn the 'standard language' is in the grip of the home dialect, which is his/her mother tongue. Thus, in trying to teach the standard language, the teacher is actually trying to teach a secondary language and the differences between the dialect and the standard language are often ignored. For example, standard Hindi maintains a distinction between /bh/ and /v/ but in the dialects it is not commonly maintained; /v/ is often replaced by /bh/; if a learner fails to learn this distinction in the standard language, the learning of the distinctions in the second language will be affected, with the result 'very' may be pronounced 'bhery'. The same is the case with the 's'/'sh' dintinction. Many forms and nuances that are found at the lexical and grammatical level in standard languages (maybe Hindi, Tamil, Telugu, or Bengali), are not found in the dialects. These facts are to be recognized in the teaching of the mother tongue and the teaching of the mother tongue may have to be regarded as the teaching of a second dialect.

Several distinctions have been made in the area of second language teaching, taking English as a typical case because of its world-wide use. A distinction is made between foreign language teaching (FLT) and second language teaching (SLT); it is taken for granted that in FLT cultural and creative aspects get the focus, whereas in SLT the instrumental and communicative aspects get the focus. Distinctions like English as a foreign language (EFL), English as a Second Language (ESL), English as Mother Tongue teaching (EMT), English as a Second Dialect (ESD), English for Specific Purposes (ESP), English for Academic Purposes (EAP), English for General Purposes (GPE), English for Science and Technology (EST), English for Speakers of Other Languages (ESOL) as a cover term for both EFL and ESL (the testing part is called TESOL), English as an International Auxiliary Language (EIAL), English as a World Language (EWL), etc. are talked about. Often these distinctions blur some of the crucial issues in language teaching and learning. For example, in a special purpose course, say Hindi for chemists, French for caterers, or English for engineering, it is likely that native users themselves may not be fully competent in the variety of language required for a particular purpose. Many such assumptions have been questioned and there is a lot of rethinking taking place now.

V. In the Bullock Report (1975), there is a suggestion regarding language across the curriculum. It is an important suggestion since it raises a central issue in language teaching. The designing of the curriculum must take into account several aspects of language teaching and learning. There is a lot of confusion in the use of the terms 'aims' and 'objectives' (as pointed out by Widdowson 1983:20). 'What the learner has to do with the language once (s)he has learned it' will specify the 'aims'; on the other hand, 'what the learner has to do *in order to learn*' defines the 'objectives', better termed 'language pedagogic objectives'. Another concept that is used is 'learners' needs', which is equally vague and confusing. There are different layers of 'learners' needs'; the society imposes some of its needs on the learners and it is based on 'social needs' that evolve in the interactional network of society. Societal needs have to be studied carefully by the educational linguist taking into account the role of a particular language in the socio-economic political-temporal-ideological-cultural context of the society.

For example, Indian languages and English have certain complementary/supplementary roles to play in the Indian social context; there is no conflict, as visualized by some, between the two. Indian languages are the languages of intimacy (for Bengalis it is Bengali, for Malayalees it is Malayalam, etc.) and English is the language of modernization and technology. This can be seen in the roles they play in the society. English, which is not the language of agriculture in India, is the language of agricultural universities; English, which is not the language of day-to-day business in the market place, is the language of business management courses in universities; English, which is not the language of daily transactions with the workmen in a workshop, is the medium of instruction in Indian Institutes of Technology and other engineering colleges. English, which is 'a window on the world', is not the language of religion for the vast majority in India. The complementary role of English and Indian languages must be properly understood in order to formulate language policies in India, which, in turn, should be reflected in the curriculum.

As pointed out in the unit on Linguistic and Social Inequality certain decisions regarding language planning will have to be taken at the political level by governments and ministries.

As Pit Corder points out:

> Decisions at this level are of general nature; whether languages are to be taught; which languages are to be taught; and how much money is to be available for training and paying teachers...in many multilingual states in Africa and Asia the decisions about which languages to teach and at what level in the educational system to teach them are difficult ones and are made, at least in part, on the basis of studies made by sociolinguists into the distribution and various functions of different languages in the community, and the role that these languages have in the political and commercial life of the community and its contacts with the world outside. This is an area of linguistic studies sometimes known as *language planning*.

The curriculum designers need all these inputs so that they can formulate the aims properly. Educational linguistics has to do with the devising of a curriculum, syllabuses and materials for carrying out the intentions of education authorities whether local or national but there must be a constant interaction and proper coordination between language planning and its implementation. Curriculum designing is like town planning; it needs a lot of coordination among the various subjects and languages to be taught. As Pit Corder says,

> ...syllabuses relate to specific languages to be taught to more or less specific groups of learners for more or less specific purposes within more or less specific limitations of time and money. Textbooks and teaching materials of all sorts are the concrete realization of the syllabus plan.

It is like planning the construction of individual units within an overall plan. Thus, the curriculum designers will have to interact with the planners on the one hand and the syllabus makers, materials producers and teachers on the other.

This involves the understanding of the practices inside the classroom since 'objectives' constitute a link between 'aims' and 'practices'. In the last fifty years or so classroom practices have undergone a sea change. We have moved away from the teacher-centred (convergence) to learner-centered (divergence) methodology. The current thinking is that teaching language (or for that matter, teaching any subject) is not a unidirectional process of 'pouring knowledge from a full vessel into an empty one'; it is, in fact, a bidirectional process, an interaction between teachers and learners in an atmosphere of 'give' and 'take'—the teachers not simply 'giving' but also 'receiving', for the learners make a significant contribution in this process. It is very clear from the various studies that language teaching-learning is a multidimensional and interdisciplinary activity. There are dimensions like *organizational* (concerned with physical and administrative facilities such as the size of the class, status of the language, educational and linguistic policies, facilities for research, development, coordination and information about language teaching, etc.), *technological* (facilities for the use of mass media such as radio, television, language laboratories, etc., the inherent advantages and limitations of the audio and video systems in language teaching), *psychological* (motivation, aptitude, language behaviour, problems of interference, relations between maturation and language learning, built-in language learning mechanism, etc.), *sociological* (concerned with attitudes to language and languages, code-switching and code-mixing, etc.), *pedagogical* (concerned with the principles of language learning and language teaching), and *linguistic* (concerned with the description(s) of the language to be taught, contrastive analysis of the patterns of the languages in contact). There are also other factors that affect the language teaching-learning activity such as the nature and quality of the medium of instruction, the quality of teaching, teacher competence and commitment, sociolinguistic barriers between schools and pupils, the 'hidden curriculum' (tacit values and attitudes concerning appropriate behaviour which every pupil must learn if she/he is to be successful at school—messages that are not explicitly transmitted in the content of a curriculum), etc.

VI. The educational linguist is a contributor as well as a coordinator of the whole language teaching enterprise. Pit Corder (1973) rightly points out:

> He does not control it, nor does the class room teacher, nor, for that matter, does the headmaster or the Minister of

> Education. It is a cooperative venture. The better each contributor's understanding of the principles upon which decisions are made at all levels, the better chances the whole operation has of being successful. But we must expect that all along the line compromises will have to be made. For example, psycholinguistic knowledge might suggest that there is some optimum age for beginning the study of foreign languages. Political and economic considerations might indicate that it was undesirable on a cost-benefit analysis to devote the necessary funds to providing qualified teachers at that level. The two principles would be in conflict. The final plan would represent a compromise. All the contributors to a total teaching operation are involved in its success: society, as represented by the education authorities, the applied linguist and the classroom teacher.

The complex interactive process in the whole operation can be diagrammatically represented as in Chart 7.

The educational linguist is a coordinator and contributor of the whole operation since language is all-pervasive in every aspect of this operation.

VII. The general remark is: 'Teachers are practical, down-to-earth people, who don't need all this theorizing.' Halliday (1982) dismisses this view as mental laziness; if teachers do not have a grasp of the general principles and processes, they are condemned to mechanical teaching; all teaching, knowingly or unknowingly, is based on some theory, whether it is behaviouristic or mentalistic or 'inexplicit staffroom folklore'. It is better to have an explicit formulation and discussion of what these theories are, and of what would be the best for a particular purpose.

At the same time, as Michael Swan (1985) points out:

> We realize we have been translating too much; so translation is banned completely. Grammar explanations are seen to have been over-valued; so grammar explanations are swept away. Generation A spends half its time doing structure drills; for generation B structure drills are anathema. Contrastive studies promise the moon and the stars; when the moon and the stars are slow to arrive contrastive studies disappear from

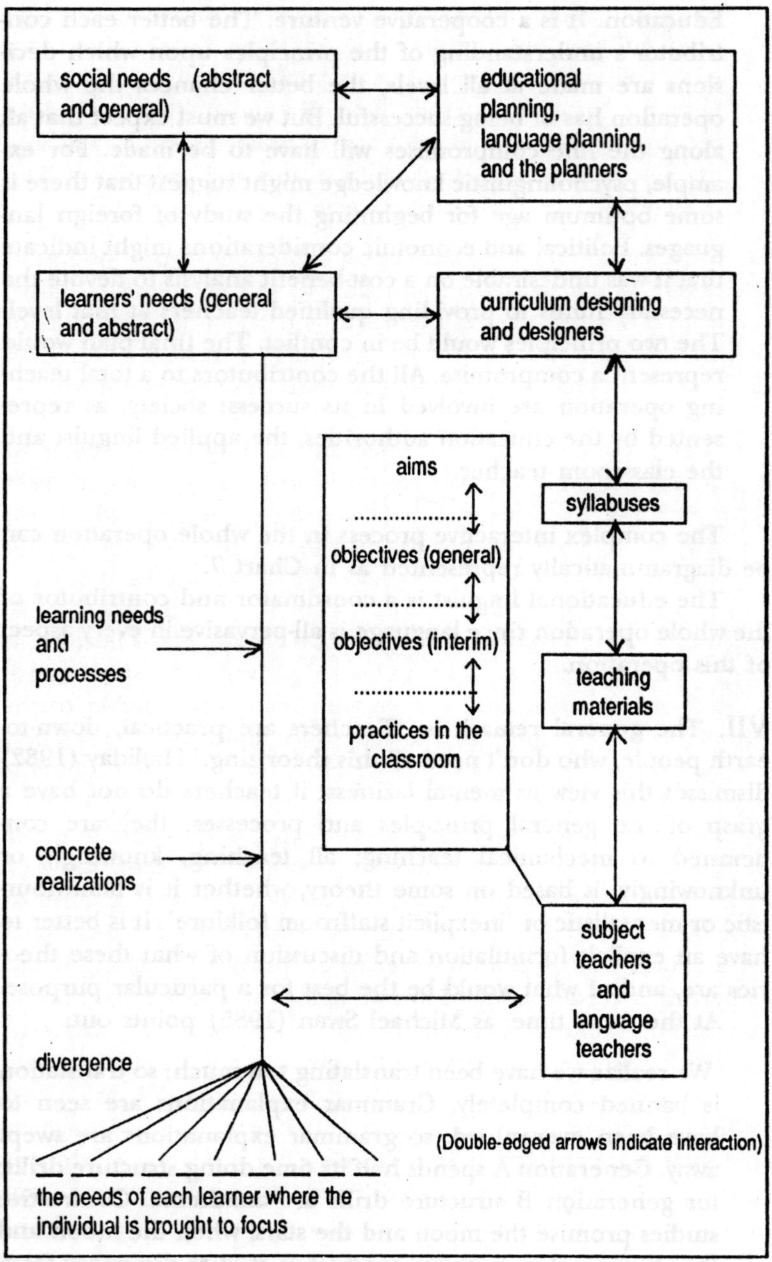

Chart 7: Interactive processes between learning and learners

> syllabus design as if they had never been. One approach fails to give sufficient importance to phonetics; the next approach does nothing but phonetics....Each time this happens the poor language teacher is told to junk a large part of his or her repertoire of materials, activities and methods (because they are no longer scientific) and to replace them by a gleaming new battery of up-to-date apparatus and techniques. The students, as a rule, learn about as much as before.

It is true that the 'terminological explosion' causes 'pollution problems' in the field. As a reaction to the changing fashions, some see teaching as an intuitive skill and reject the possibility of objective criteria for success in teaching. Teachers of English literature, in particular, feel that analysis destroys literature.

> This view, however, is a rejection of only certain types of analysis, since it forgets that traditional literary criticism uses terms such as *metaphor, synechdoche, trope, genre,* etc. which are just as much jargon to outsiders as are *phoneme, syntagmatic structure* or *sociolinguistic variable* (Michael Stubbs 1986).

Halliday (1982) argues that linguistics is *uncomfortable* because it destroys fondly held myths about language, and *subversive* because it forces us to come face to face with many unpalatable truths about social inequalities in contemporary multicultural societies.

Lawton (1981) argues that teachers need to do the right things, to do them for the right reasons, to be aware of what they are doing, and to be able to explain to the society what they are doing; they must be able to counter criticisms of their practice when they are under attack and show that they have a sense of accountability. Some things can be explained in theoretical terms; some can be proved in terms of 'results'. Teaching is not imparting a certain body of knowledge; it is a social act. Society consists of different consumers and there must be different models for different consumers; the chalk-and-talk method alone will not work. The models for the consumers are to be developed in the classroom itself. All educationists agree that language is somehow a crucial factor in a child's education but we do not have sufficient data about the different types of classroom language, the nature of classroom discourse, the language environment in the classroom/in the school, about teacher-talk. child-child talk, etc. Michael Subbs (1976) says:

> It is theoretically unsound to make generalizations about language in education which cannot be related to how language is actually used in schools and classrooms. But it is equally unsound to make intuitive inferences on the basis of isolated observations and anecdotes about language use. without considering the sociolinguistic context of schools and classrooms.

What we need is R & D — research for development, research and development, and development through research in the classroom, outside the classroom and for the classroom.

Questions and topics for discussion

1. 'We lack basic descriptive information about the kinds of teacher-pupil interaction in small rural schools.' Why do we need this information? Can't we take decisions without it? Give reasons for your answer.
2. 'Classroom discourse is different from other discourse types.' Can you think of some aspects where it is different? Illustrate your answer.
3. 'Don't shout! Don't talk! Silence!!!' — Are these instructions counter-productive in a language class? — Explain your answer.
4. 'It is important to distinguish between language in education and linguistics in education' (Stubbs 1986). Explain and illustrate.
5. 'Where the medium of instruction is English, every teacher is a teacher of English.' Explain and illustrate this statement.
6. In real life we use language for a real purpose : searching for information, asking someone for something, etc. What are the purposes for which we use language in the classroom? Try to make a list.
7. 'How children talk to other children when no adults are present is part of the important research to take decisions about language in classrooms.' Can you explain why it is important? Illustrate your answer.
8. How do you collect the data for 'action research'? Can you suggest some ways?
9. There is no point in interviewing teachers and pupils and asking them about language teaching, their attitudes, etc. or distributing questionnaires; these do not reveal much. Can you explain the reasons for this?

10. In formal chalk-and-talk classrooms, the teacher-talk pupil-talk ratio is about 90:10 or at the most 80:20. In any class, subject class or language class, do you think that this is the right ratio? Give reasons for your answer and suggest ways for reversing the ratio.
11. i. 'To find the difference of fractions with different denominations, we change the fractions into equivalent fractions with the same denominations.'
    ii. 'The objects shown above i.e., an ice-cream cone, a joker's cap, a radish, the pointed tip of a pencil represent a cone.'
    iii. 'The primary unit of time is a second and sixty seconds make one minute. All good watches have a second hand too.'

    The specimens given above are taken from a mathematics book meant for English medium schools. Do you think a teacher of mathematics can teach the 'subject' without English? Find out the words, whose meaning(s) are crucial for the clear understanding of the concepts involved in understanding the subject. Explain why they are crucial.
12. i. 'The sun is relatively very close to us. The nearest star, the sun, is nearly 150 million kilometres from the earth. Although this appears to be a great distance, it is nothing as compared to the distance of other stars.'
    ii. 'The apparent movement is different from the level movement.'
    iii. Some substances are identified due to their appearance.'
    iv. 'Scientists look upon work in a different way. People do many things called work; people may say they are 'at work' when doing their job in office. Children say that they are 'working' when they do their home-task.'

    These are specimens from a science book for English medium classes. Can we teach English through science effectively? (It is said that only when the focus is not on language, language is learnt effectively. Use this argument to support your answer.)
13. The social studies teacher in an English medium school can teach English more effectively than the teacher of English. Explain this statement; illustrate your answer.
14. 'Second-language teaching in India has been less successful than it might as a result of the restricted variety of linguistic contexts with which students are provided.' Explain this with reference to the teaching of English as a second language in India.
15. To what extent do education systems and the roles and functions of languages in a multilingual setting impinge upon our understanding of language learning and language teaching?

22 APPROACHES TO LANGUAGE TEACHING

> *'If you are teaching John Greek, you must know John, you must know Greek, and you must know how to teach John Greek.'*

Focal points

I. H.H. Stern in his Preface to *Speaking in Many Tongues* (1972) by Wilga Rivers says:

> All language teaching inevitably, tacitly or openly, implies a theory of language and a theory of language learning. Every language teacher must somehow have an answer to two questions: What is the nature of language? And, what is the nature of the language learning process? It is therefore not surprising to find language teachers responsive to the disciplines which discuss such questions: linguistics and psychology, above all, and more recently, psycholinguistics and sociolinguistics. But the relationship between the practice of language teaching and the underlying disciplines presents problems.

Chomsky in his address at the Northeast Conference (1966) said:

> I am, frankly, rather skeptical about the significance, for the teaching of languages, of such insights and understanding as have been attained in linguistics and psychology....It is possible—even likely—that principles of psychology and linguistics, and research in these disciplines, may supply insights useful to the language teacher. But this must be demonstrated and cannot be presumed. It is the language teacher himself who must validate or refute any specific proposal.

Language pedagogy, in fact, is much older than what has now come to be known as linguistics. Even during the first century A.D., Quintilian's ideal 'good man skilled in speaking' and the four qualities of style—correctness, clarity, elegance and appropriateness—to be cultivated in order to achieve that ideal had certain language teaching principles in it; Quintilian stressed the usefulness of paraphrasing a given text as a means of assisting the learner both to analyse the structure of a text and to experiment in turn in the form of abridgement. Together with the above exercise, he advocated translation since these exercises were given to Greeks learning Latin.

Ascham's *Schoolmaster* (1570) gives a 'pedagogical plan' for using the Quintilian model. Ascham's methodology consists of *Imitatio* (writing texts on the model of the great authors), *Translatio*, *Pharaphrasis* (reformulation), *Epitome* (summarizing), *Metaphrasis* (transforming a text from poetry to prose and vice versa), and *Declamatio* (public eloquence). All these are clearly intended to develop and refine the learners' sensitivity to language use. Ascham made the learning of grammar subservient to the study of original texts; Joseph Webbe (1560-1633) dispensed with grammar altogether and made communication skills and grammar through use the central focus of his language teaching method. Comenius (1592-1670) advocated the concept of natural pictures for teaching languages and believed that language should not be the object of learning but the outcome, the product.

During the same period William Lily's popular grammar, also known as the 'Royal Grammar' because of the royal support it received, *A Short Introduction to Grammar* (1540) was published to establish a uniform method of grammar teaching in schools; this book continued without a rival for over 250 years until the end of the eighteenth century and brought with it all the Latin rules and the study of sentences at the expense of the text.

Thus, one finds two trends of thought on the role and function of language studies in the late 16th and 17th century thinking on language education. In the history of language teaching in the west, the eighteenth century is quite eventful. The development of trade and communication, new colonies, social ambition, and such other factors brought into focus the way in which language was used 'with propriety' and a demand for 'fixing' usage. French and Italian Academies were set up; Jonathan Swift in 1712 called for 'A Proposal for Correcting, Improving and Ascertaining the English Tongue'; Johnson's *Dictionary of the English Language* was published in 1755; Robert Lowth's *A Short*

Introduction to English Grammar with Critical Notes came out in 1762. It almost replaced Lily's grammar; Lowth used his footnotes as a form of 'error analysis' to discuss examples of 'bad English' in the English of Pope, Swift and Addison, among others. The publication of several school grammars and dictionaries like Webster's (1828), exercises based on sentences, the concept of correct grammar and 'doing grammar', and the growth of grammar schools contributed to the evolution and establishment of the 'grammar-translation method'.

II. Howatt's *A History of English Language Teaching* (1984) gives a detailed account of the factors that contributed to the *grammar-translation method.* Howatt points out:

> The grammar-translation method was devised and developed for use in secondary schools. It could even be called 'the grammar school method' since its strengths, weaknesses, and excesses reflected the requirements, aspirations and ambitions of the nineteenth century grammar school in its various guises in different countries. It began in Germany, or more accurately, Prussia, at the end of the eighteenth century and established an almost impregnable position as the favoured methodology of the Prussian *Gymnasien* .... The origins of the method do not lie in an attempt to teach languages by grammar and translation, these were taken for granted anyway. The original motivation was reformist. The traditional scholastic approach among individual learners in the eighteenth century had been to acquire a reading knowledge of foreign languages by studying a grammar and applying this knowledge to the interpretation of texts with the use of a dictionary .... The grammar-translation method was an attempt to adapt these traditions to the circumstances and requirements of schools. It preserved the basic framework of grammar and translation because they were already familiar both to teachers and pupils from their classical studies.

In India too, language studies were based on the *kaavya* (literature) - *vyakarna* (grammar) tradition; classical languages like Sanskrit, Persian, Tamil were all studied, using grammar and translation for learning languages. This provided the basis for teaching European languages too when languages like English, French, etc. were brought to India along with their established grammar-translation method. There was a perfect match between the age-old Indian tradition and the imported tradition in the nineteenth century.

The special status given to the *sentence* in grammar did not fit in well with the translation exercise that is based on texts; grammar was sentence-based and translation was text-based/discourse-based; and there was no theory of language to link these two and produce some principles that could be called a method. The combination of brief presentations of grammar points and extensive translation practice as a distinct teaching strategy was applied in language courses like Ollendorff's which became popular around 1840. The sequential arrangement used by Ollendorff in his lessons 'became standard, followed by a vocabulary list and translation exercises. At the end of the course translation of connected prose passages was attempted' (Kelly 1969). 'Ollendorff's method was praised by contemporaries as an active, simple, and effective method, because as soon as a rule had been presented it was applied in short translation-practice sentences' (Stern 1983). Though some practitioners of this method like Ahn (1796-1865), Claude Marcel (1793-1876) and others used translation exercises at the sentence level, grammar and translation were considered a necessary preliminary to the study of literary works, a valid mental discipline in its own right. It was mostly the practice that made the method useful. The material for translation was graded from simple to more complex texts and grammar was presented in some organized sequence in the textbooks that used the traditional/grammar translation 'method'. The texts from reputed authors, their literary or religious content, the massive practical nature of the activity, the study of etymology of words backed by the historical linguistic tradition, and the importance given to the traditional method in the school curriculum and the examinations made it a powerful tool in the hands of ambitious school masters.

By the end of the nineteenth century, the grammar translation method grew into a jungle of obscure and rigid rules, endless lists of classes and exceptions, literary archaism, snippets in philology, and above all it turned into a fossilized appoach without any feeling for people who use language, their communicative needs, and changing social conditions. Neglect of the spoken aspect of language and its practical and conversational use, over emphasis on academicism, the growth of the new class of learners without the 'grammar school' education, industrialization and mass communication, and several other complex factors resulted in the Reform Movement of the late nineteeth century.

III. Henry Sweet's *The Practical Study of Languages* (1899), the formation of the International Phonetic Association (IPA) and the publication of its journal in 1889, and the attempts of several individual reformers like Jacotot, Marcel and others, resulted in the Reform Movement. The primacy of speech, the importance of the connected text, and the priority of an oral methodology in the classroom can be thought of as reactions to the rigidity of the traditional/grammar-translation method.

Henry Sweet (the model for Shaw's Henry Higgins in *Pygmalion*) can be thought of as the founder of 'modern methodology'; his book contains chapters on the teaching of phonetics and the spoken language, methodological principles covering the major areas of language learning—grammar, vocabulary, the study of texts, translation, and conversation. Otto Jespersen's (1904) *How to Teach a Foreign Language* advocates the use of contextualized learning material. All the proposed reforms were referred to under a variety of names: 'reform method', 'natural method', 'phonetic method', etc., but the most important label that was used to describe the features of this approach was the term '*direct method*'. A clear statement of this method is given in the six articles of the International Phonetic Association (IPA).

The 'direct method' argued against the use of translation. The following principles and procedures were used in this method:

i. All classroom instructions are to be given only in the target language.
ii. Only day-to-day vocabulary and sentences are to be taught.
iii. Oral communication skills are to be built up in a carefully graded progression organized around question-and-answer exchanges between teachers and learners in small intensive classes.

iv. Grammar is to be taught inductively.
v. New teaching points are to be introduced orally.
vi. Concrete vocabulary is to be taught through demonstration; objects, pictures are to be used; abstract vocabulary is to be taught through association of ideas.
vii. Both speech and listening comprehension are to be taught.
viii. Correct pronunciation is to be emphasized.

We get a similar picture in the Berlitz system. Titone (1968) cites the following guidelines used in the U.S.A. by Maximilian Berlitz (1852-1921) in his schools:

> Never explain : act
> Never make a speech : ask questions
> Never imitate mistakes : correct
> Never speak with single words : use sentences
> Never speak too much : make students speak much
> Never use the book : use your lesson-plan
> Never go too fast : keep the pace of the student
> Never speak too slowly : speak normally
> Never speak too quickly : speak naturally
> Never be impatient : take it easy

As Stern (1983) points out:

> Linguistically, language teaching was to be based on phonetics and on scientifically established coherent grammar. The learning of languages was viewed as analogous to first language acquisition .... It demanded inventiveness on the part of teachers and led to the development of new non-translational techniques of language instruction. The use of a text as a basis of language learning, demonstrations of pictures and objects, the emphasis on questions and answers, spoken narratives, dictation, imitation, and a host of new types of grammatical exercises have resulted from the direct method.

Harold E.Palmer and A.S.Hornby in the 1920s and 1930s and some British applied linguists adopted many of the techniques first developed by the users of the direct method. There were some major problems in the use of the direct method. If one has to totally avoid the use of the first language, there may be misunderstandings in trying to convey meaning; secondly, the large resources of the first language were left completely unexploited, thereby resulting in uneconomical ways of teaching like extensive use of pictures, demonstrations, etc. even to teach simple items; thirdly, beyond the elementary stages of teaching and learning, the direct method has very little application, for example, in teaching languages to adult learners, who may not need procedures advocated by the direct method.

IV. 'Sound linguistic principles' became the key phrase in language teaching methodology during the first half of the present century; a number of teachers, phoneticians and linguists appeared on the scene to evolve several new methods.

Daniel Jones published a number of source books: *The Pronunciation of English* (1909), the *English Pronouncing Dictionary* (1917), and *Outline of English Phonetics* (1918). Harold E. Palmer, who was a Direct Method teacher and materials writer published a number of books on methodology. *The Scientific Study and Teaching of Languages* (1917), *The Oral Method of Teaching Languages* (1921), *The Principles of Language-Study* (1921), and a number of course-books like *English Through Questions and Answers* (1930), etc. Michael West, who worked in Bengal in India, published *The New Method Grammar* (1938), *The New Method English Practice Books* (3 vols.) (1939), and a number of New Method Readers. Lawrence Faucett's *The Oxford English Course* (1933) is a course 'package' that established a pattern. Michael West's *General Service List of English Words* appeared in 1953. A.S.Hornby's *An Advanced Learner's Dictionary of Current English* (1952), *A Guide to Patterns and Usage in English* (1954), and *The Teaching of Structural Words and Sentence Patterns* (a set of four manuals that appeared during 1959-1966) and a number of books by others like Pit Corder and others established language teaching as a profession. The British approach was mainly built up by phoneticians and experienced language teachers.

On the other side of the Atlantic, quite a few developments took place about the same time. The first English Language Institute at Michigan University was started in 1939 with Charles Fries as its director. American structuralism, derived from

Bloomfield's *Language* (1933), had a marked influence on language teaching theory; a number of linguists in the Bloomfieldian tradition used Bloomfield's concepts for developing language pedagogy. As a result of the writings of Charles Fries, Robert Lado, Kenneth Pike, Eugene Nida, Zellig Harris, H.A. Gleason and Charles Hockett in the fifties, several methods with emphasis on audiolingualism originated in America. Fries showed how the sound system, the structures, and the lexical material could be derived from available lingusitic knowledge and organized for language teaching purposes; he further demanded 'an adequate descriptive analysis of both the language to be studied and the native language of the student.' In accordance with the contrastive linguistic principle, the English Language Institute produced some language courses for Latin-American students and Chinese students. Lado, who succeeded Fries as the director of the Institute, was a great believer in contrastive linguistics; his *Linguistics Across Cultures* (1957) applied the contrastive principle systematically to make it applicable to curriculum development, the preparation and evaluation of teaching materials, to the diagnosis of learning problems, and to testing.

The 'Army Method' of American wartime language programmes in World War II, the writings of Fries, Lado and others inspired by Bloomfieldian thinking, the new technology of the language laboratory, the influence of behaviouristic psychology based on B.F. Skinner's *Verbal Behaviour* (1957), and the grants made available for language research and development were responsible for the development of the audiolingual theory in the USA. Audiolingualism openly claimed that it was derived from linguistics and influenced by behaviourists such as Skinner and Osgood.

The audiolingual method was based on some of the characteristic features of Bloomfieldian lingusistics and the Skinnerian model of learning, the basic tenets of which are:

i. Language is speech, not writing.
ii. A language is what its native speakers say, not what someone thinks they ought to say.
iii. Languages are different; they have similarities and differences which can be systematically studied.
iv. Language is behaviour and behaviour is a matter of habit.

Language learning is a mechanical skill and no intellectual process is involved in it. Because it is mechanical, the linguistic behaviour can be conditioned. So, in teaching a language the teacher should follow the stimulus-response-reinforcement pattern; in language teaching there should be controlled, spaced, repetition.

v. Teach language, not about language.

Linguists described langauge in terms of certain levels: phonology, morphology and syntax. Audiolingualism believed in the separation of the skills—listening, speaking, reading and writing (LSRW); the audiolingual method used certain practical techniques like mimicry, memorization, pattern practice and the language laboratory; it encouraged the use of dialogues and substitution tables. The underlying theoretical assumptions like a scientific approach to the study and teaching of languages, preparing materials based on frequency counts of words and structures, emphasis on *selection, gradation,* and *presentation* in a systematic manner, belief in behaviourism, etc. constitute the *approach.* Within an approach there can be several methods like the audiolingual and the audiovisual developed in France based on visual presentations of scenario etc. that emphasized the social use of language, or even the 'bilingual method' advocated by Dodson (1967) which allowed the controlled and judicious use of the first language, the reading method, etc. They can all be brought under what has come to be known as the *Structural Approach.* Presentation, establishment, and classroom cultivation are matters of *technique.* Thus, within the broad frame of the Structural Approach, which emphasized the teaching of vocabulary and structures in a graded sequence that has been arrived at on the basis of an objective description of the language to be learnt, several methods and techniques were advocated. The audiolingual method is in part a reflection of the availability of audiotechnology during the 1950s and the structural views on language. This makes it an improved version of the direct method.

The most important aspects of the audiolingual method are summarized by Richards and Rodgers (1986):

i. Language teaching begins with the spoken language; the material is taught orally before it is presented in written form.

ii. The target language is the language of the classroom.
iii. New language points are introduced and practised situationally.
iv. Vocabulary selection procedures are followed to ensure that an essential service vocabulary is covered.
v. Items of grammar are graded following the principle that simple forms should be taught before complex ones.
vi. Reading and writing are introduced once a sufficient lexical and grammatical basis is established.

The period between 1958 and 1964 is called by Stern (1974) the Golden Age of audiolingualism. By the end of the decade its theoretical basis was found to be weak, particularly after the attack on structural linguistics and behaviouristic psychology by Chomsky (1959: 'A Review of *Verbal Behaviour* by B.F. Skinner'); empirical research showed that the audiolingual method was not as sophisticated as it was thought to be and that in the long run the techniques used resulted in boredom among learners.

V. Chomsky argued that language acquisition could not take place through habit formation because language was far too complicated to be learned in such a manner. There must be, Chomsky reasoned, some innate capacity that humans possessed which predisposed them to look for basic structures in language. Furthermore, people could create and comprehend novel utterances—utterances they could not have possibly encountered in the language that was spoken to them; errors such as *eated* and *sleeped* were common in children's speech and such errors suggested that children were not repeating what was said to them; learners learning English as a second language make the same sort of over-generalization. Children learning their L_1 and second-language learners make errors in a systematic way.

Pit Corder (1967) in 'The Significance of Learners' Errors' suggested that learners might naturally adhere to a learner-generated or 'built-in' syllabus. The language the learners spoke was termed an 'interlanguage' by Selinker (1972) since it was intermediate between the first language and the second language; interlanguage was considered to be a language in its own right and any point along the interlanguage continuum was held to be fully describable by rules.

As a result of the serious challenge thrown to Bloomfieldian and Skinnerian assumptions, a new set of assumptions came up:

i. Language is not behaviour; the use of language is more like writing a play than performing in one; language learning is a process of creative construction that involves cognition and interaction.
ii. Any behaviour is controlled by cognitive processes; skills are actions which are originally voluntary and which later become automatic.
iii. Practice without understanding the basic principles will be meaningless just as the description of a language without meaning is meaningless; mere repetition tends to weaken understanding.
iv. Teaching is not conditioning but creating conditions for learning; to learn is to learn the valid generalizations, discriminations and relationships because language is a related system of categories and classes. And learning of any sort is largely a matter of drawing out what is innate in mind; it is a matter of growth and maturation of relatively fixed capacities, under appropriate external conditions.
v. Languages do differ, but they also have a great deal in common; and learning a second language is always in some measure repeating an old experience.
vi. Errors are not something to be avoided, but welcome signs that show learners are actively testing hypotheses; the first language is not a source of interference, but a source of hypothesis-formation about how the other language functioned.

Thus, language learning was seen as a cognitive, mentalistic process with learners ultimately responsible for their own learning. With this shift in focus to the active role of the learner many factors that affected language learning were studied: social, motivational, affective, experiential, instrumental, biological, and cognitive and factors related to their aptitude and personality. Since Chomsky first proposed how language learning, which is solely a process of rule formation, takes place, even second-language researchers working within the framework of Universal Grammar (proposed by Chomsky in 1981 as part of Government and Binding theory) have shitted to exploring the idea that rule learning involves setting or fixing the parameters of principles of the Universal Grammar in a manner consistent with the data of a particular language. Some other researchers like Schmidt (1983) feel that the role of imitation has been seriously overlooked and that a great deal of language acquisition is really brought about by learners having memorized sentences and pharses like *How do you do?*, *How are you?*, *I beg your pardon,* etc. There are others who argue that nonlinguistic processes are more important than linguistic ones.

The Chomskyan revolution had a profound effect in bringing about a change in the directions in linguistics as well as psychology more at the theoretical and research level; but it contributed little to alter the way language was actually taught in classrooms. Like the structural linguists, transformational-generative grammarians (TG) focussed on sentence-level syntax and mechanical transformations.

VI. It was only when Dell Hymes (1966) introduced the concept of communicative competence in the USA and British applied linguists such as D.A. Wilkins, Christopher Candlin, Henry Widdowson, Christopher Brumfit, Keith Johnson, and others (drawing on the work of British functional linguists like J.R. Firth and M.A.K. Halliday) recognized the functional and communicative aspects of language that a real shift took place in the approach, methods and techniques in language pedagogy. The goal of language instruction shifted to building up learners' communicative competence. It was declared that there are 'rules of use, without which rules of grammar would be useless'; a distinction was made between grammatical rules of *usage* that enable users to construct correct sentences and the *use* of language to accomplish some kind of communicative purpose (Widdowson 1978). 'Sound socio-linguistic principles' became the key phrase in language teaching.

The European Common Market played an important role in getting the applied linguists to prepare syllabuses and teaching materials. With increased need for teaching adults the major languages of the European Common Market for increased interaction, the Council of Europe started playing a key role in language education. Wilkins' advocacy of a notional-functional syllabus in his book *Notional Syllabus* (1976) was one manifestation of the shift from the Structural Approach to a more functional approach. This meant building a course around the uses or functions to which language is put; for example, one lesson can be planned on requesting information, another on apologizing, and a third one on expressing gratitude, etc. The familiar structural patterns remained, but they were ordered differently, and organized around fuctional headings. van Ek and Alexander (1975) formulated concrete objectives, including inventories of language functions, notions and structures; but they made no proposals for gradation of the material to be used since grading according to functional complexity did not make much sense for the simple reason that syntactic complexity and functions are two different parameters. Wilkins proposed that the functions be recycled and that successive cycles be used to reintroduce more complicated structures. Thus, the first time learners can be taught how to introduce one person to another ('This is...'); sometime later, they can learn to say 'I'd like you to meet....' and yet another, they can learn 'Allow me to introduce you to....', etc.

Widdowson recognizes that the functional-notional approach has shifted the focal point in foreign language teaching to the communicative aspects of language, but does not recognize Wilkins' claim that it 'takes communicative facts of the language into account'. According to Widdowson:

> Communication does not take place through the linguistic exponence of concepts and functions on self-contained units of meaning. It takes place as discourse, whereby meanings are negotiated through interaction (Widdowson 1979).

The interactional view treats language as a vehicle for the realization of interpersonal relations—for transaction among invididuals; the 'process' of arriving at a response is emphasized.

Applied linguists like Krashen and Terrell (1983) advocated basing courses on topics (e.g., family, weather, clothing) and situations (e.g., a job interview, a visit to a doctor, etc.). Krashen's Monitor Model of second language development (1981) is an example where both 'processes' and 'conditions' meet because the focus is on the semantic dimension of language.

In fact, there is an interesting problem regarding the dialectical relationship between the system and its use; we cannot *use* a language unless we *learn* the *rules* (the system) and we can learn the rules only through using the language. Krashen's Monitor Model of second language development (1981) presents an over-simplified framework of this paradox through the setting up of a dichotomy—an 'acquired system' which is 'sub-conscious' and a 'learned system' which is conscious—thereby rejecting the interaction between the two. According to Krashen, the adult learner has 'two independent systems for developing ability' in a second language—'sub-conscious acquisition' and 'conscious learning'. Here 'acquisition' means 'picking up' the language in a natural way; that is why Krashen calls his method the 'Natural Method'; 'learning', on the contrary, refers to 'conscious' grammar learning, which is 'knowing about' a language, rather than learning to perform. He further adds that 'conscious learning is available to the performer only as a Monitor' (hence, the name 'Monitor Model') and the Monitor works sometimes before and sometimes after the utterance is produced. In Krashen's formulation, there are three conditions for the Monitor to operate.

> a) the availability to sufficient *time*, (b) *focus* of attention on language form or correctness as against meaning, and (c) knowledge or relevant grammatical *rules*. The '*time*' condition is a necessary one, not sufficient without '*focus*' which is an all important necessary condition. The 'comprehensible input' of Krashen implies that sufficient *quantity of exposure* is the condition for the process of acquisition to take place.

Krashen totally rejects memorization through conscious effort from the domain of language acquisition and he does not explain how pauses for mid-course correction take place wherein the speaker uses 'conscious grammar' to repair his/her speech. But, Krashen's model makes use of 'processes' (like habit formation, induction, inferencing, hypothesis-testing, generalization, etc.) and 'conditions' (the human and physical conditions that are conducive for language learning to take place).

Another interesting approach is the *procedural syllabus* (Prabhu and Carrol 1980), which does not take language as its basic at all; learners learn language through the performance of certain tasks and activities.

As a result of the shift from linguistic competence to communicative competence, several communicative syllabuses have been proposed. The following are some of the important ones:

Syllabus type	*Name associated with it*
functional	Jupp and Hodlin (1975)
structures plus functions	Wilkins (1976)
notional	Wilkins (1976)
learner-generated	Candlin (1976)
interactional	Widdowson (1979)
functional-spiral around a structural core	Brumfit (1980)
structural, functional, instrumental	Alen (1980)
competency-based	Grognet and Crandall (1982)
task-based	Prabhu (1983)

The emphasis in all these is on 'language for communication' and hence their approach is called 'communicative'. All these approaches differ in several ways from the structural approach and the audiolingual method.

The following table (from Finocchiaro and Brumfit 1983:91-93) gives the major differences between the Audio-lingual Method and the Communicative Approach.

	Audio-lingual	*Communicative Language Teaching*
1.	Attends to structure and form more than meaning.	Meaning is paramount.
2.	Demands memorization of structure-based dialogues	Dialogues, if used, centre around corrective functions and are not normally memorized.
3.	Language items are not necessarily contextualized.	Contextualization is a basic premise.
4.	Language learning is learning structures, sounds, or words.	Language learning is learning to communicate.
5.	Mastery, or 'over-learning', is sought.	Effective communication is sought.
6.	Drilling is a central technique.	Drilling may occur, but peripherally.
7.	Native-speaker like pronunciation is sought.	Comprehensible pronunciation is sought.
8.	Grammatical explanation is avoided.	Any device which helps the learners is accepted varying according to their age, interest, etc.

9. Communicative activities only come after a long process of rigid drills and exercises.	Attempts to communicate may be encouraged from the very beginning.
10. The use of the student's native language is forbidden.	Judicious use of native language is accepted where feasible.
11. Translation is forbidden at early levels.	Translation may be used where students need or benefit from it.
12. Reading and writing are deferred till speech is mastered.	Reading and writing can start from the very first day, if desired.
13. The target linguistic system will be learned through the overt teaching of the patterns of the system.	The target linguistic system will be learned best through the process of struggling to communicate.
14. Linguistic competence is the desired goal.	Communicative competence is the desired goal (i.e., the ability to use the linguistic system effectively and appropriately).
15. Varieties of language are recognized but not emphasized.	Linguistic variation is a central concept in materials and methodology.
16. The sequence of units is determined solely by principles of linguistic complexity.	Sequencing is determined by any consideration of content, function, or meaning which maintains interest.
17. The teacher controls the learners and prevents them from doing anything that conflicts with the theory.	Teachers help learners in any way that motivates them to work with the language.
18. Language is habit;—so errors must be prevented at all costs.	Language is created by the individual often through trial and error.
19. Accuracy, in terms of formal correctness, is the primary goal.	Fluency and acceptable language is the primary goal: accuracy is judged not in the abstract but in context.
20. Students are expected to interact with the language system, embodied in machines or controlled materials.	Students are expected to interact with other people, either in the flesh, through pair and groupwork, or in their workings.
21. The teacher is expected to specify the language that students are to use.	The teacher cannot know exactly what language the students will use.
22. Intrinsic motivation will spring from an interest in the structure of the language.	Intrinsic motivation will spring from an interest in what is being communicated by the language.

In essence, advocates of the communicative approach claim that learners' motivation will be increased if they feel that they are working on communicative skills; they assert that a language is learnt effectively when the focus is not on language and that learners learn how to communicate by communicating, by interacting with their teachers and fellow students. Most language teachers do not talk about structures, phonemes and allophones; they talk about communication, communicative competence, language varieties and norms, discourse, learner needs and attitudes and negotiation of meaning.

VII. It must be pointed out that language testing has not kept pace with all the developments in language teaching and applied linguists have done very little in this area. It is true that any language teaching technique can also be used for language testing—a traditional dictation, a translation task, any reading assignment, any question-answer technique, a writing chore, a piece of conversation, a dramatization, an oral interview, a cloze test that uses the fill-in-the-blank technique; any use of language when used for evaluation becomes a language test. From this primitive point of view, tests are used only for assigning or justifying marks and grades, which can be justified as a necessary evil.

A better view of tests will place tests in language instruction as an integral part of classroom management. Testing can be viewed as essential to instruction and learning in the same way as accounting is to business and something more than that in terms of accountability. Good language tests are instructional, managerial, motivational, diagnostic (focussing attention on specific teaching-learning problems), curricular (defining curriculum as a whole) in function.

Most of the language tests that are used now are surface tests, meaning they test only surface problems in language; the learners are asked to 'supply' the correct forms as in fill-in-the-blank type, spelling, etc. Often, even the surface tests are used only to supply what is given in the text. Text-based, surface-oriented language tests test only learners' ability to recall what they memorize; they are reproductive.

Outside the text people speak, listen, read, write, think, compose, describe, promise, lie, pray, curse, etc. and do meaning processing in order to achieve certain life-oriented goals and negotiate meaning as realized in pain, pleasure and the like. Language testing in the communicative approach can open up a number of possibilities that are literally unlimited. Testing the learner's knowledge of the text is not the goal; testing the learner's ability to use the language and the way (s)he negotiates meaning to realize certain goals and harmonizing language teaching and testing so that the two can go together as almost indistinguishable are to be the areas of research in language testing. A variety of testing procedures reflecting the wide-ranging uses of language can be thought of but this is yet to take place. For example, given some episode, either in the text or outside it—say, a story, a piece of conversation, a poem, etc. can be converted into several different narrative modes; a dialogue can be converted into reporting which can also be in the form of a letter. Even in a cat and rat story, the 'rat' can be asked to write a letter to someone, may be the creator or the grandma, and they, in turn, can reply. The episodic expansion can become part of the language teaching-testing activity; instead of testing skills (LSRW), applied linguists must evolve integrated tests that test the learner's communicative competence if testing is to be in tune with language teaching.

VIII. Most language teachers argue that each of the methods and techniques has something interesting to offer; they adopt a point of view of eclecticism but there is no agreement as to how the different approaches and methods could be combined. Way back in 1965, Mackey in *Language Teaching Analysis* pointed out:

> Such terms as the 'Direct Method', 'the Simplification Method', 'the Situation Method', 'the Natural Method', 'the Film Method', 'the Conversational Method', 'the Oral Method', 'the Linguistic Method', can only be vague and inadequate because they limit themselves to a single aspect of a complex subject, inferring that that aspect alone is all that matters.

The same is true of even the later methods.

Michael Swan taking 'A Critical look at the Communicative Approach' twenty years later (ELT Journal 1985) says:

> During the last few years, under the influence of the 'Communicative Approach', language teaching seems to have made great progress. Syllabus design has become a good deal more sophisticated, and we are able to give our students a better and more complete picture than before of how language is used. In methodology, the change has been dramatic. The boring and mechanical exercise types which were so common ten or fifteen years ago have virtually disappeared, to be replaced by a splendid variety of exciting and engaging practice activities. All this is very positive... And yet... a dogma remains a dogma, and in this respect the 'communicative revolution' is little different from its predecessors in the language teaching field... Along with its many virtues, the Communicative Approach has most of the typical vices of an intellectual revolution; it over-generalizes valid but limited insights until they become virtually meaningless; it makes exaggerated claims for the power and novelty of its doctrines; it misrepresents the currents of thoughts it has replaced; it is often characterized by serious intellectual confusion; it is choked with jargon.

Post-structuralist thinkers too (whose seminal ideas were outlined in the unit 'After Structuralism'), have taken a critical look at the distinctions maintained in language teaching; they have subverted all the binary distinctions and dichotomies that are found in the field—language and literature, speech and writing, reading and writing, context and text. Phonocentrism and logocentrism have been under attack; Derrida has argued that speech is a form of writing and that the text is a gas. In post-structuralist thinking there is no question of reading the text objectively; since meaning slips beneath the circularity of signifiers, there is no determinate comprehension of a text. According to Barthes (1987): 'Reading is the projection and fulfilment of individual desire in the interpretation of the text.' Reader Response theorists have argued that we are meaning-breathing animals and that we breathe meaning into the text. It is also argued that 'reading and writing join hands, change places, and finally become distinguishable only as two names for the same activity.' (Atkins and Johnson 1985); in other words, language teaching/testing must take place as an integrated process and not in terms of segregated skills like LSRW. Several such radical notions tend to shake up many of the well-established perceptions and practices, and raise issues regarding 'real communication'.

Several humanistic approaches like Caleb Gattegno's *Silent Way* (1972) which helps learners develop their own 'inner criteria', Georgi Lozanov's *Suggestopedia* (1978) which advocates a childlike role for the learners to make them feel secure and less inhibited so that they can be more spontaneous, Asher's (1982) the Total Physical Response Approach and Krashen's (1983) the Natural Approach are some of the competing approaches that claim to be innovative and effective.

All these various 'approaches', 'methods' and 'techniques' have put the learner and the teacher in a buyer's market; they can pick and choose from a wide variety of ideas. Language teaching is no longer visualized in terms of a single undifferentiated methodological prescription. Language teaching can break away from the 'method concept'; teachers can become fully aware of the possibilities, build up their resources, and get educated and not just trained; learning has become interesting, challenging, and creative in every sense and the learner an explorer.

Questions and topics for discussion

1. Answers to questions like (a) what is language?, (b) what is meant by language proficiency? (c) what are the cognitive processes involved in language learning?, (d) what are the factors that contribute to interaction, and (e) what are the conditions that allow for the successful use of cognitive as well as interactive processes? can very well be found in the classroom. Instead of going to the class with preconceived notions, researchers should try to find answers to the questions listed above (and many more related problems) in the classroom interactions. Do you agree? What is your opinion? Give reasons for your answer.
2. "The best method is the method that works in a given setting." Do you agree with this statement? How will you explain it to teachers?
3. The grammar-translation method has come in for a lot of criticism. Can you explain why?
4. Outline the role of grammar and translation in second-language teaching.
5. "There is nothing so practical as a good theory." Explain the significance of this statement.

6. You must have by now come across three terms: 'teaching', 'learning', and 'acquisition'. Are they interrelated? If yes, how?
7. "A good teacher must be a good learner". Discuss this statement based on your own experience as a teacher.
8. "Our teachers can talk about the achievements and limitations of the Direct Method, Communicative Approach, Needs and Tasks-centred approaches but can't teach English as a second/foreign language because they have been exposed to only one variety of English." Is this so? If 'yes', why? If 'no', why is it that the standard of both written and spoken English in India has gone down to a very low level?
9. What approach will you advocate for the teaching of the mother tongue?
10. Is there a difference between teaching Hindi as a second language and teaching English as a second language in non-Hindi areas in India? If so, what are they? Illustrate your answer.
11. 'Testing can be objective, precise, reliable, scientific.' The structuralist, sentence-based, level-oriented view of language fitted in quite well with the psychometric samples of individual elements to be tested and they thought it could be objective, scientific, etc. Do you think that language testing should reexamine the goals of language testing? Give reasons for your answer.
12. It is very easy to say that integrative tests should be used but measuring the total communicative competence of the learner is very difficult. — Comment. Illustrate your answer.
13. Sociolinguistic and psycholinguistic insights can be used in language testing. Can you suggest some ways of doing this? Illustrate your answer.
14. 'A standard cloze test is a text in which every n^{th} word (5th word or 10th word) has been deleted and the testee has to restore the text by filling in the deleted items. In doing so, it is claimed, that the learner will use 'linguistic knowledge, textual knowledge and knowledge of the world.' This is too general a statement; not all cloze tests can do it, it depends on the nature and difficulty of the text in question.' Do you agree? Give your opinion on cloze tests. Illustrate your answer.
15. In a cloze test one can expect the exact word used in the original text or any other acceptable word in the context of the text. The first method is, obviously, more objective. But do you think it is fair? Give your opinion.
16. A cloze test can be combined with the multiple-choice type which can make it more open-ended. How can we do this? Illustrate your answer.

17. What do you think of dictation as a test of not only spelling but also of reading, writing and listening?
18. Communicative testing needs further research; it is in its infancy. — Explain and illustrate.
19. Performance tests are necessarily integrative tests and the usual quantitative assessment procedures are unsuitable. So we must think of new quantitative assessment procedures. How can we do this? Illustrate your answer.
20. 'Not all tests can be used in all situations' — Explain and illustrate.

23 AN INDIAN EXPERIMENT

'Languages are made not by learned people, but by people, and not only reasoning ones, but by all sorts of people.'

— A.P. Sumarokov

Focal points

I. India, it is said, is a linguist's paradise; in addition, it is the applied linguists' laboratory where any number of experiments can be conducted; experiments in any of the following or related areas—bilingualism / biculturalism, multilingualism / multiculturalism, language planning, language in contact, pidginization, emergence of Indian English, the linguistic phenomenon called *Urdu*; problems of translation, teaching languages in trying circumstances (may be the mother tongue or the other tongue), etc. can be visualized since there are a number of interesting problems.

Even collecting the basic data is a problem; the 1961 Census of India registered about 170 'languages' 'used' by only one person! If only one person 'uses' a language, can we call it a language? For what purpose is it used? Some estimates say that there are about 300 languages and dialects; quite often the official data reflect the attitude of the speakers to their language (in the 1971 census 23,222 people named Bihari their mother tongue) and not any survey based on some linguistic criteria.

Even Jawaharlal Nehru (1946) in his *Discovery of India* writes:

> The oft-repeated story of India's having five hundred or more languages is a fiction of the philologist's and the census commissioner's mind, who note down every variation in dialect and every petty hill-tongue on the Assam-Bengal frontier with Burma as a separate language, although it is sometimes spoken only by a few hundred or a few thousand persons.

But these 'petty hill tongues' and 'every variation in dialects' play very crucial roles in the lives of people, these being their 'home dialect'. For example, no applied linguist can take into account only the major languages like Hindi, Assamese, Bengali, Gujarati, Marathi, Tamil, Telugu, Malayalam, Kannada, Sindhi, and the like, and ignore Garhwali, Kui, Meithei, Mundari, or Tulu.

There are emotional problems that go with the classification and naming of languages. The Rajasthanis in Madhya Pradesh, who speak Malavi, consider it a dialect of Rajasthani and not of Hindi, which it is according to scholars. Dogri, which was considered a dialect of Punjabi, has now been recognized as a regional language by the government and academies because Dogri uses the Devanagari script and not the Gurmukhi script in which Punjabi is written; demands are made to include Dogri in the VIII Schedule of the Constitution of India. Sindhi and Nepali are 'languages without States' because they are not confined to any geographical area or state; Nepali is an 'additional official language' in Darjeeling. Konkani, which was considered a dialect of Marathi, has been recognized as an independent literary language by the Central Sahitya Akademi. It is said that there are about 24 different names for different forms of Oriya; Sambalpuri of Western Oriya is a language according to some. Is Bihari a language or a term that is used to cover basically Maithili, Magadhi (Magahi), and Bhojpuri? Bihari languages (Maithili, Magahi and Bhojpuri) are dialects of Hindi, according to some; but S.K. Chatterji and U.N. Tiwari, following G. Grierson, separate them into a group distinct from Hindi; some regard Maithili and Magahi as individual languages. There are others who believe that 'Bihari languages' along with Bengali, Assamese and Oriya, hail from Magadhi Prakrit which is believed to have been the court language of the Magadha kingdom in the times of Maurya Empire. Maithili champions have demanded a state of Mithila; the Sahitya Akademi has accepted Maithili as an independent literary language. Rajasthani is regarded as a language by some but there are about 75 different form of Rajasthani, the 'important' ones being Marwari, Mevari, and Haraoti, Bagri, and Dhundhari; 'Marwari' and 'Rajasthani' are used interchangeably by some. There is a demand for the inclusion of Rajasthani in the VIII Schedule. These are all interesting areas for the sociolinguist; India is a sociolinguist's paradise indeed!

II. Hindi is a complicated phenomenon; it not only represents a complex language system but is also mixed up with politics, patriotism, national sentiments and the like. Alfred Pietrzyk jointly with John Gumperz and Charles Ferguson (1964) divided the Hindi area into three strata; the first stratum is a spectrum of mutually intelligible 'local' folk dialects which vary from village to village, from caste group to caste group. A superimposed, second stratum comprises 'sub-regional' dialects used in wider areas, in small bazaar towns, and in certain urban and rural situations requiring a common medium. Superimposed above the local and sub-regional dialects is the urban stratum of 'standard' varieties collectively referred to as Hindi-Urdu. It is the native speech of a part of the urban population and is widely used as a second or third idiom because of its considerable communicational and prestige advantages (Baidya, N.V. (ed.) *Contemporary India)*.

The words 'Hindustani' and 'Hindi' are associated with Hindustan (i.e., India) and it should mean 'a resident of Hindustan'; if we ask a Hindi speaker about his/her nationality, we always get the information about his/her state, or region, or town, or the caste or community. The term 'Hindi' includes several speech forms like Awadhi, Braj Bhasha, Khari Boli, Bundelkhandi, Bangaru (also called Haryanvi), Kannauji, etc. Kari Boli (which is a boli = a dialect) is considered the standard language; Braj and Awadhi have the richest and oldest written tradition; Tulsi Das' *Ramayana* is in Awadhi. There is a lot of vagueness about the boundaries of Hindi dialect areas which make it more of a continuum. 'Apart from differences resulting from geographical factors,' says Dhirendra Varma (1954) in his *Braj Bhasha*, 'popular vernaculars have also peculiarities brought about by religious, caste, and class affiliations. The speech of some Muslim peasants differs from that of their Hindu neighbours. The speech of the former has borrowed from Khari Boli and Iranian. To stress the high standing of their caste, Brahmin peasants deliberately use in their speech numerous 'tatsama' words from Sanskrit.

The Constitution of India has given Hindi in Devanagari script the status of the official language of the country but Urdu is included as a separate language in the VIII Schedule; Urdu is the official language of Pakistan. Mohandas Karamchand Gandhi ragarded Hindustani as the common language of Hindus and Muslims and he was in favour of using two scripts — Devanagari and Urdu. 'What is Hindustani? Vaguely we may say that this word includes both Hindi and Urdu, as spoken and as written in two scripts, and we endeavour to strike a golden mean between the two, and call this idea of ours Hindustani' (Nehru 1948). Premchand, a noted writer, wrote in Hindustani and proved that the synthesis of Hindi and Urdu is possible; it is possible because of the common basis of the two languages; the differences are minimal. There are also other varieties of Hindi-Urdu—non-native or acquired varieties spoken in the southern parts of India, the contact varieties like the Hyderabadi variety (also called 'Dakhini Urdu/Hindi' used in the erstwhile Nizam's state), Bazaar Hindi as used in Bombay or in temple cities/trade centres.

All major Indian languages, whether it is Bengali, Oriya, Marathi, Tamil, or Telugu, have regional as well as social variations; in the border areas between any two languages there is always a continuum, and as a result, a continuous conflict between the linguistic groups. In some areas, there is an overwhelming majority of one language residing in a compact area within another linguistic area, a state. For example, Telugus in Tamil Nadu have for several generations resided chiefly in Madras, its capital; when the state of Andhra Pradesh was being formed, some Andhra people demanded that Madras be included in Andhra; some Tamilians demanded that some border areas be included in Tamil Nadu. Within Andhra Pradesh there are three major dialects—Coastal Andhra, Rayalaseema and Telengana; people living in the Telengana region feel that their region is neglected and their speech is looked down upon by the Coastal Andhra speakers of the 'standard' dialect; the Rayalaseema region has similar grievances. Similarly, in Maharashtra there is a feeling that the Vidharbha region is dominated by the western Maharashtrians; whether it is Assam or Punjab or Kerala, there is always a feeling that some linguistic group is exploited. Quite often religious, political, caste, and other interests get mixed up with language issues in India and language conflicts take diverse forms—demand for linguistic states, recognition of the languages of the minority groups, language-based inter-state disputes, and so on.

III. The problem of a compulsory official language in India is equally complex. The formation of linguistic states in 1956 contributed to a revival of national life and accelerated national consolidation; favourable conditions were created for the speedy development of national cultures, of languages and their literature, the regional press, theatre, the cinema, etc. At the same time, regionalism was just growing into an alarming state; every linguistic region tried to develop its own regional sentiments; 'Maharashtra for Maharashtrians', 'Assam for Assamese', 'We Tamils', etc., on the one hand, and 'national integration' on the other; ideally these movements should not end up in a conflict. But the source of conflict lies in socio-economic factors. The dispute between Bengal and Assam or Orissa and Andhra or Maharashtra and Karnataka or Punjab and Haryana and several other inter-state disputes represent the conflicts among regions. People in Tamil Nadu look at Hindi as the language of a region and there is a fear that one region will dominate over the other.

The question of national-language is not socially neutral; in fact, in the process of taking decisions about a 'common' national language, three important factors are to be taken into account—language, society, and communication. Without communication no social relationship is possible; if one social group feels it cannot communicate with the other in a particular language, that group feels insecure. It is necessary to analyse the movements and sociolinguistic aspects behind language slogans; unequal economic development, specific economic conditions, the idealized history of a region, memories of which are activated by the regional political forces as part of the political struggle in a given region and supported by the elite, the zealously guarded regional traditions, the revival of the regional culture, and several other factors are to be considered.

Jawaharlal Nehru said in 1956, during the parliamentary discussion on the Report of the States Reorganization Commission:

> I recognize that the language of the people is a vital matter for their develoment, whether it is education, administration or any other matter. But there is a distinction between developing the language to the fullest extent, and this passion for building up a wall around a linguistic area and calling it a border. I completely accept the statement that people cannot really grow except through their language, but it does not follow that in order to make them and their language grow, a barrier must be erected between them and others (Jawaharlal Nehru's Speeches, March 1953-August 1957)

Different groups exploited the people in every region and built walls around their languages; what ought to have emerged as nationalism has been turned into chauvinism; as a result, the awakening of national life after independence has taken complex and controversial forms at the expense of even economic life. Language, which performs a uniting function, also detaches members of a given community or group or entity from other groups, especially when there are conflicting perceptions.

IV. In the context of all the complex factors and forces pointed out so far, naturally, any educational enterprise will have to be extensive and complex; it must be pluralistic in planning and implementation; mono-methodological approaches must be abandoned since the one-system-for-one-nation-or-community principle will not work in a pluralistic set-up like the Indian one.

Educational planners and educational linguists will have to take into account, in addition to the pluralistic conditions, the problem of numbers, and the changing perceptions of the people of India. It must be remembered that language teaching in India is the world's largest language teaching operation in a democratic manner. Very few can visualize the magnitude of the problem. In 1986-87 (only tentative figures are available), the student enrolment at the *primary* level (about 90 million) was almost double the total population of the U.K and at the middle school level (about 28 million) it was almost equal to the total population of Canada; the students and teachers at the secondary school level (about 17 million) constitute the total population of Australia, and the learners at the college and university level alone represent almost double the total population of Singapore. The *student* enrolment at all levels taken together equals half the total population of the USA and the *teachers* to be trained at all levels equal nearly the total population of Hong Kong. Such is the magnitude of the problem (J.C. Aggarwal and Sarita Aggarwal 1990).

Each one of these learners, at the language education level, will have to be taught at least one of the fourteen major Indian languages as the primary language, and two other languages under the three-languages formula if that is taken seriusly. With all kinds of variations in each language, with each language performing certain roles in society, with all kinds of exposures inside and outside the classrooms, the learners somehow manage to learn at least two or three languages in most parts of the country.

According to the 1971 census, there were at least 25 million users of English with varying degrees of competence; some call this *Indian English* and some others *Indians' English*. There is a wide spectrum of views on the status of English in India; at one extreme, one finds Kachru (1976), who feels that English has replaced Sanskrit or Indian Persian as an '*Indianized* link language' and, at the other extreme, there are people who feel that English should be thrown out and that the alien language is not needed for unity; in between the two positions, we have Pandit Nehru's oft-quoted statement, the assurance he gave to non-Hindi speakers:

> ....for an indefinite period—I do not know how long—I should have, I would have English as an associate, additional language which can be used, not because of facilities and all that, but because I do not wish the people of non-Hindi areas to feel that certain doors of advance are closed to them because they are forced to correspond—the government, I mean—in the Hindi language. They can correspond in English. So, I would have it as an alternate language as long as people require it and the decision for that, I would leave

not to Hindi-knowing people, but to non-Hindi knowing people (from the speech delivered on August 7, 1959).

Even assuming that English will remain in some form, either British or Indian, we are not clear whether it will be the medium of instruction or not. Should English be studied like any other foreign language like French, German, Russian, or Spanish? There are all kinds of English medium schools in the country and even those who publicly declare that English must be thrown out send their children and grandchildren to 'good' English medium schools. After all, even Lord Macaulay said this in his famous *Minute on Education* (1835) and later in his letters:

> We have to educate a people who cannot at present be educated by means of their mother tongue. We must teach them some foreign language. The claim of our own language it is hardly necessary to recapitulate (*The Life and Letters of Lord Macaulay* Vol.1, 1876).

It is interesting to note that the Woods Despatch of 1854 recommended that education could be imparted in both English and Indian languages and English could be taught whenever there was demand for it; but there has always been a demand for it! By 1870s, children of all classes had entered the race for the western type of education through English and the race still continues. The Government of India Act of 1919 recommended that the Indian languages should be the medium of instruction at the school level and at the college level it should be English; after forty years in 1950, the University Education Commission presents arguments for and against the continuation of English and concludes in favour of using the English language as a 'language of comprehension'. It sees English as '...one of the potent factors in the development of unity in the country.... In fact, the concept of nationality and the sentiment of nationalism are largely the gift of the English language and literature in India' and as '...an instrument for the continuance and fostering of the unity which it has helped to create' (1950:316). On the question of English as the medium of instruction, however, the report says, 'it is educationally unsound to make a foreign tongue the means of acquiring knowledge.... Both the individual and the nation develop a split consciousness...' The Commission says English has 'become so much a part of our national habit' and, in the same breath points out '...use of English divides the people into two nations, the few who govern and the many who are governed, the one unable to talk the language of the other, and mutually uncomprehending, which is a negation of democracy' (1950:316).

English has been variously described as the 'window on the world', the 'language of development', the 'language of science and technology', the 'language of modernization', the 'language of research', etc. People perceive it as the 'language of opportunity' because any person seeking socio-economic advancement finds ability in English an asset; the people are more practical than the policy-makers; people will have to survive in the modern competitive world. If Hindi is made a language of opportunity, people will learn it; students in Tamil Nadu increasingly take to Hindi in the hope of better opportunities; but Hindi is yet to become like English a language of modernization, science and technology, which restricts Hindi as a language of opportunity.

V. All these factors—pluralism, population, and perceptions—make any language teaching activity highly complex.

The problem of training teachers of English in India is a case in point. There are thousands and thousands of teachers to be trained at various levels and there are millions of learners eager to learn English; the resources are limited and the area is vast—India is almost like Europe in its complexity; there are all kinds of varieties of English used in the country—from a near native variety to a bazaar variety.

India too, like many other parts of the world, used what has been called the 'grammar-translation method', almost up to 1915. It was no method but a kind of bilingual work with focus on grammar and literature. Since there was no 'method', there was no question of teacher training. The period between 1915 and 1955 saw the growth of the Direct Method, under the influence of Henry Sweet, M. West, Palmer, P.C. Wren, Jespersen, and others like Champion; pre-service training for school level teaching was given importance, with changing labels like L.T., B.T., amd B.Ed. (only the label was changed but not the content); there was no in-service training and, usually, the school inspectors were the interpretors of the Direct Method—actually, it was the Direct Method of the School Directorate. College level teaching was not thought to require any training. Anyway, there was no specialized training to the teaching of English.

The first English Language Teaching Institute was established in Allahabad in 1954 with the collaboration of the British Council. Between 1955 and 1985, there was a lot of emphasis of in-service training for teachers of English. Pre-service training in the colleges of education did not keep pace with the growth of knowledge in the field and got neglected during this period; the structural syllabus prepared at the London School was brought to Madras by the British Council and the All India Seminar on the teaching of English held at Nagpur in December, 1957 was the first move on an all India basis to adopt a structural syllabus for the teaching of English in secondary schools; this weakened the teaching of grammar in a big way. The Central Institute of English was established in 1958 by an Act of Parliament for improving the standards of the teaching of English in the country; a study group appointed by the Ministry of Education in 1964 submitted its report *The Study of English in India* in 1967; another report was prepared in 1971. As part of the in-service training, Summer Institutes were started and this gave birth to all kinds of crash courses.

But the absence of any kind of language planning and political will in implementation, and lack of coordination among various agencies—central, state, universities, etc.—resulted in an aimless drift; most of the Boards of Education and universities in the country do not have a clearly defined set of aims. In fact, the aims and objectives are decided only by the 'examination system'. The ideal of 'delinking of degrees from jobs' made by the Government of India in 1985 (*Challenge of Education—A Policy Perspective* also known as NEP) reflects the quality of education imparted in the schools and colleges; degrees have very little value in the job market since they have been devalued.

The English teaching situation in India needs a new thrust; there has to be serious rethinking on several issues like making use of the resources of the first language, the positive use of translation in the teaching of the second language, evolving a pluralistic poly-methodological plan of action that leaves the choice to the learner according to his/her style of learning so that any learner at any level who wishes to learn any language for any purpose for any length of time using any medium (s)he likes will be able to do so at his/her own pace in school or out of school, using a method (or methods) that is best suited to him/her. The theorizers are busy trying to theorize; teachers are busy trying to 'cover' the 'portion' and in trying to 'cover the portion' they stand exposed! If we do not act with a sense of urgency, the great drift will continue in the sea of confusion and all of us will become anachronisms in the field—may be there won't be any field at all.

The Indian experiment requires a careful study; there have been so many Commissions—from the Radhakrishnan Commission (1948-49), the Mudaliar Commission (1952-53) and the Kothari Commission (1964-66) to the Ramamurty Commission (1990) — but the basic problems have not been solved; in fact, there are more serious problems now. As Boris. I. Kluyev (1981), a Russian Indologist, in his *India - National and Language Problem* points out,

> ...specific studies of national processes in developing countries, in particular in India, are also necessary to avoid a possibly unproductive approach to these processes, considering them to be exclusive phenomena with unique specificity inherent only in certain regions of the world, or to be some sort of transitional conditions whose nature and trend of development have not been revealed with sufficient certainty, and, therefore, regarding them as peripheral phenomena in the general theory of nation.

The analysis of the complex problems concerning society, language, and the teaching of languages in a multicultural and multilingual country like India has great theoretical importance in addition to its practical applications.

Questions and topics for discussion

1. "The three-language formula has been interpreted to mean a two-language formula in one state and as a one-language formula in a couple of states." Why is this so? Give suggestions for making it a workable formula.
2. "Multilingualism is a distinctive feature of the linguistic scene in every state in India." Explain this statement and show how multilingualism can be used as a resource.

3. "Any language teaching operation takes place in a context of highly variable external features, and must be adjusted to suit them." Explain this with reference to the teaching of English as a second language in India.
4. Evaluate the textbooks meant for the teaching of L_1 in your area/state in terms of the following dichotomies:
   a) Standard variety—non-standard variety.
   b) Literary variety—non-literary variety.
   c) Written variety—spoken variety.

   Evaluate textbooks from the primary school level to the college level.
5. 'Since L_1 is taught from the primary school level it need not be included in the undergraduate curriculum' — Give arguments for and against this statement.
6. 'The Hindi Prachar Sabhas can try out the communicative approach in teaching Hindi as the L_2 in the South. People will be more interested in learning Hindi for communication,'
   a) Comment on this statement.
   b) Evaluate the textbooks produced by the *Hindi Prachar Sabhas* in terms of their communicative value.
7. 'The national network T.V. in India is teaching Hindi in a communicative way.' — Discuss.
8. 'When we have not been able to evolve an acceptable communicative approach for the teaching of L_1, any attempt to introduce it for the teaching of a second language, say English, will only be tantamount to taking a trip to a no-man's land.'
   a) Do you agree? Explain your answer.
   b) Should one's mother tongue be taught in a communicative way at all?
   c) Do you agree with the view that one learns the communicative values of one's mother tongue/L_1 in day-to-day life outside the classroom and in a much better way? Explain your answer.
9. 'There is a dialectical relationship between L_1 and L_2; the gravitational pull of L_1 is so strong that L_2 can never be mastered to perfection but it is only with the help of L_2 any meaningful mastery of L_1 can take place.'

   Do you agree with this view? If so, why?
   If not, why not? Explain your answer.
10. 'To teach a second language in the communicative approach one has to use 'authentic texts'; only texts that are used in typically British situations by native speakers of standard British English have to be used in the Indian class rooms.'
    a) Do you agree with this view? Explain your answer.

b) What is the functional relevance of such an approach in the Indian situation?

11. 'An R.K. Narayan or a Kamala Das uses a fictitious language that has no norm or referent, for no rickshaw puller in a south-Indian town like Malgudi will ever speak English as he does in the fiction of R.K. Narayan. So there is no question of authenticity in such texts.' Would you reject all the writings of Indians from the ESL curriculum on the score that they lack authenticity? Explain.

12. 'Emphasis on 'fluency' will only demolish the already weakening 'accuracy' in the use of English.'—Do you agree with this view? - Explain.

13. 'It is certainly not new methods we need, but a new attitude — an attitude which allows the students to learn, that waits for the student to learn, that allows the student choices in what he/she shall learn.' — Explain.

Suggested reading

Aggarwal, J.C. 1984, *Landmarks in the History of Modern Indian Education.* Delhi : Vikas.

This book presents all the vital documents related to education in India, from 'Macaulay's Minute of Education (1835)' to 'Sixth Five-Year Plan (1980-1985)'.

Brumfit, C.J., and K. Johnson (eds.) 1979. *The Communicative Approach to Language Teaching.* Oxford : OUP.

This is one of the important books in the area of study. It has seminal papers by Wilkins, Widdowson and Candlin.

Cazden, C., V. John, and D. Hymes. (eds.) 1972. *Functions of Language in the Classroom.* Columbia : Teachers' College Press.

This book has many good papers on the wider relations between classroom language and social attidues to language. The studies are mainly American.

Howatt, A.P.R. 1984. *A History of English Language Teaching. Oxford : OUP.*

This book presents a highly readable historical account of the teaching of English from the Renaissance to the present day. The issues in the teaching of English as a second language from Elizabethan London to Prabhu's Bangalore experiment have been summed up. There is a very good bibliography covering all the issues touched on in this chapter.

Richards, Jack, C., and Theodore S. Rodgers. 1986. *Approaches and Methods in Language Teaching. A Description and Analysis.* Cambridge : Cambridge University Press.

This is a very good text book for an introduction to second language teaching courses. It presents an overview and analysis of major approaches and methods used in second and foreign language teaching.

Stern, H.H. 1983. *Fundamental Concepts of Language Teaching.* Oxford : Oxford University Press.

Various aspects of applied linguistic research are presented in historical and inter-disciplinary perspectives. A very useful book for a clear understanding of the issues involved as well as research in the area.

Stubbs, Michael. 1976. *Language, Schools and Classrooms.* London : Methuen.

This book presents an introductory discussion of studies of language in education, including a critical discussion of Bernstein and Labov.

Stubbs, Michael, and Sara Delamont. (eds.). 1976. *Explorations in Classroom Observations.* Wiley.

This book has a collection of studies of classroom behaviour, all based on direct observation and recording in real classrooms. Several of the papers concentrate on aspects of communication in classrooms.

Trudgill, Peter. 1975. *Accent, Dialect and the School.* London : Edward Arnold.

This book presents a useful introductory discussion of the relation between standard and non-standard accent and dialect, and educational problems, proposing a 'bidialectalism' approach.

Walker, R., and Clem Adelman. 1975. *A Guide to Classroom Observation.* Methuen.

This book is the best introduction to doing classroom research, intended mainly for student teachers. It is full of transcripts of teacher-pupil dialogue, photographic sequences of classroom incidents and very practical advice on what and how to observe in classrooms.

Widdowson, H.G. 1983. *Learning Purpose and Language Use.* Oxford : OUP.

This book presents a highly readable theoretical probe into the concept of English for Specific Purposes. The book proposes an ethnomethdological approach to the issues raised and presents a good discussion on various issues of linguistics from the perspective of language users.

CHAPTER SIX

Language to Language

"All the arts are brothers; each one is a light to the others."
— *Voltaire*

24 ON TRANSLATION

'Translation is like a woman; if beautiful, it cannot be faithful and if faithful, it cannot be beautiful.' — *Anon*

Foca points

I. Perhaps no other activity involving language has cost so many human lives as Bible translation has done. In the age of Reformation, a translator was executed because he translated a particular sentence or a phrase in a certain controversial manner.

The translation battle raged throughout Dolet's age. The Reformation, after all, was primarily a dispute between translators. Translation became an affair of the state and a matter of Religion (Edmond Carry, 1963, in Bassnett McGuire, 1980).

The problem of making a delicate distinction between what constituted a faithful rendering and what was a stylistic variation was a major issue for centuries; the 'correct' interpretation of the original and its 'loyal' recreation in the other language have always been the central issues in all translation activities. Today translation may not cost human lives but it has become the most important unifying force in our tower of Babel. Whether in organizations like the U.N.O or in multilingual settings like in India, translation assumes a crucial role in promoting human understanding. In his preface to ***Better Translation for Better Communication — A survey of the translation market, present, and future,*** *prepared for the European Communities* Marcel van Dijk points out:

> Translation constitues an essential tool for better communication. The world written translation market is around 150 million pages per annum and probably occupies 175,000 persons full time, for a turnover of about 3,000 million dollars. This market is expanding by 9 to 10% per annum. ... It is thus necessary not only to translate better, but also to be in a position to translate more in order to create an increased demand, and thus to improve communication.

He further declares,

> The tower of Babel never will be built, because we now know that the sky has no limits : the strategem of the confusion of languages is thus no longer necessary. All languages are worthy of respect, and translation permits men to communicate better and thus to understand each other better.

Translation is not the only means by which the language barrier can be crossed. We may try to reduce the number of languages used in the world; we may attempt to increase the linguistic ability of the speakers in the world, so as to make them multilinguals and thereby obviating the need for translation; we may evolve a simplified artificial or natural language like Esperanto or Basic English to make it an international language. All the three have been tried out but the results have remained limited. Consequently, translation is to a large extent the most efficient way of breaking the language barrier and promoting better communication.

II. *Collins Cobuild English Language Dictionary* (1987) defines the terms 'translate' and 'translation' as follows:

translate	1. If you *translate* something that someone has said or written 1.1. you say it or write it in a different language. 1.2. you express it in a different way, using a different system, alphabet, etc. e.g, The temperature is sixteen degrees Centigrade or, if you translate into Fahrenheit, sixty degrees.

2. If you *translate* something such as an idea you express it in a different way, for example by putting the idea into practice.
3. If you *translate* a remark, gesture, action, etc. in a particular way, you decide this is what it means. e.g. I gave him what I hoped would be translated as a thoughtful look.

translation

1. A *translation* is a piece of writing or speech that has been translated from a different language.
2. *Translation* is the translating of speech or writing from one language to another.
3. *Translation* is also the expressing of something in a different way. e.g., The novel cannot survive translation into film.

The dictionary also says that *trans-* is added to other words to make words with the meaning 'across', 'moving from one to another', as in 'transcontinental', 'transnational', etc. Etymologically, it is related to 'transfer'. *Transliteration* is writing a word, passage, etc. in the characters of a different language or system (e.g. the Tamil word can be written using the Roman alphabet as *sambar*). Transcription is writing something in full form, shorthand notes or in a special form of writing, for example, using the phonetic alphabet.

Another commonly used word is *interpretation*; if you interpret what someone is saying, you translate it immediately into another language, so that speakers of that language can understand. The *interpretation* of a particular situation, law, statement, etc. is the explanation of what it means. Different people may have different interpretations of the same thing. (*Collins Cobuild Dictionary*).

E. Tanke, the head of translation at Siemens, defines translation as follows:

> Transfer of a text from a source language into a text in the target language, the objective being a perfect equivalence of meaning between the two texts.

The International Association of Conference Interpreters defines interpretation as follows:

> To interpret is not simply to translate a speech word for word; it is to transpose it with its entire semantic, emotional and aesthetic baggage into a language using completely different means of expression. To interpret is intially to comprehend perfectly the message so as to be able to detach it from its verbal support and to reconstitute it subsequently with all its nuances in another language. This is a constant exchange and interchange of mentalities, of one cultural universe with another.

Translation and interpretation involve, directly or indirectly, explanation, explication, paraphrase, synonyıny, adaption, etc.; in short, they involve *the search for equivalence*—formal, semantic, stylistic, rhetorical, pragmatic, associative as well as equivalence in tone and cadence (rhythm). This is no easy task since what is involved in translation is the maximal preservation of what the original exemplified as well as what it says and means because the search for equivalence will take the transcreator/translator below the surface where there may be currents, strong, obscure and deep. That is why Dryden says that translating is 'much like dancing on ropes with fettered legs; a man shuns fall by using caution; but the gracefulness of motion is not to be expected.' This, in a way, rules out the search for 'complete equivalence.'

III. People have been translating for ages but now there is a realization that there is no adequate theory of translation; scholars have talked about specific problems in translating a work from one language to another but there has been no systematic thinking about the problems in the area of translation.

Is it possible to construct a theory of translation? Is it a subject for theory construction? If translation is possible and even desirable, then its methods and criteria need to be investigated. If properly investigated, it might turn out that a theory of translation is, in fact, a theory about comparing languages. Translation theory, as an area in applied linguistics, might help us to construct a theory of language. George Steiner (1975) in his *After Babel* points out that the study of language is now a science but translation is an art. Maybe, in applied linguistics, we can investigate how scientific the art of translation can be or how artistic the science of the study of language can be!

In a broad sense, one can say that the use of language itself involves translation. Following Vygotsky's four-way classification (thought without language, inner speech, social speech, and language without thought), one can say that our thoughts are translated into inner sppech and our inner speech is translated into social/outer speech; but this sort of translation happens within one language.

It may be useful at this point to consider Roman Jakobson's (1959) three-way classification of translation which captures the shades of meaning with respect to some aspects of translation:

a) *Intralingual translation*, or rewording (i.e., paraphrasing) — an interpretation of verbal signs by means of other signs in the same language.
b) *Interlingual translation* or translation — an interpretation of the verbal signs of one language by means of the signs of another language.
c) *Intersemiotic translation* — an interpretation of verbal signs by means of signs of non-verbal signs systems.

IV. The transfer or interpretation of signs (within a language or from one language to another) involves the transfer of messages too. Can messages be equivalent when codes are different? Does it involve 'creative transposition'? Way back in 1540, Dolet pointed out that in the act of translation the translator must (a) grasp the sense and spirit of the author of the original text, (b) have an in-depth knowledge of the language of the original, (c) be faithful to the meaning of the sentence, (d) produce a version in plain speech, and (e) use sweet, even style so as to ravish the reader's ear and intellect. In order to achieve these effects, the translator must become a transcreator with a lot of latitude; such a translation may be called *transcreation* since the original is recreated; this kind of *liberalism* means giving the translator a translator's licence like the poetic licence in the case of the author of the original; is the translator free to take out and add whatever (s)he pleases? *Strict literalism* will not allow this kind of licence since the matching (word-by-word, unit-by-unit, sense-by-sense) will be lost. Can the translated version be faithful and at the same time be 'beautiful' and autonomous in the other tongue?—is the crucial question.

V. There are theoreticians who claim that translation is a Roman invention. Any historical survey of the activity of translation should start from the views of both Cicero and Horace on translation, views which had great influence on successive generations. For a better understanding of the theoretical aspects of translation, an analysis of translation studied down the ages may be helpful. Nevertheless, a mere chronological study of locating the different lines of approach in a temporal context is not being done here, because the same line of approach is seen to emerge again and again with differing degrees of language or communicative or functional needs of translation.

George Steiner (1975) has classified translation studies into four periods, thus:

1) From the statements of Cicero and Horace on translation upto the publication of Alexander Fraser Tytler's *Essay on the Principle of Translation* in 1791. During this period there is an 'immediate empirical focus', for the statements and theories of translation stem directly from the practical work of translating.
2) The period from 1791 to 1946 is a period characterized by theory and hermeneutic enquiry with the development of a vocabulary and methodology to approach translation.
3) The third period begins with the publication of the first papers on machine translation in the 1940s, and characterized by the introduction of structural linguistics and communication theory into the study of translation. It goes into the 1960s.
4) In the early 1960s the fourth period (of Steiner) has its origins in and co-exists with the third period. This period shows 'a reversion to hermeneutic, almost metaphysical inquiries into translation and interpretation.'

The kind of periodization or compartmentalization may not help us understand the theory, for some of the views expressed in the first period (in Steiner's classification) are valid even today.

Different 'lines of approach' co-exist during any period. The major 'lines of approach' to translation have been (a) the sense-to-sense approach, and (b) the word-to-word approach. Even in the early history these approaches can be seen. (a) In the ninth century King Alfred (reign 871-99), who had translated a number of Latin texts, claimed that he was translating 'sometimes word by word, sometimes sense by sense'. (b) The Lindisfarne Gospels (copied out 700 AD) had a literal rendering of the Latin original inserted between the lines in the tenth century in Northumbrian dialect. These glosses subordinated notions of stylistic excellence to the word-for-word method. (c) In his *Circular Letter on Translation of 1530* Martin Luther lays emphasis on the significance of an 'accessible and aesthetically satisfying vernacular style'. This is close to the theoretical position of the late twentieth century, too.

Text linguists regard this longstanding controversy over 'literal' versus 'free' translation approaches as reflective of the inaccurate views that there can be an equivalence of language elements independently of their setting of occurrence, and that such equivalence is somehow relevant to actual usage.

> The 'literal' translator decomposes the text into single elements (or small groups of elements) and replaces each into a corresponding element (or group) in the goal language. the 'free' translator judges the function of the whole text in discourse and searches for elements that could fulfil that function in a goal—language situation. The success or failure of either approach is uncertain; an unduly 'literal' translation may be awkward or even unintelligible, while an unduly 'free' one may cause the original text to disintegrate and disappear altogether.
>
> (de Beaugrande and Dressler 1981:216)

Effective translation, then, has to strike a balance between the two approaches outlined above.

VI. The dynamic processes involved in the act of translation and the static models that have been proposed by various scholars to account for the process and the product can be understood if we look at the various components of the activity called translation. Chart 8 shows the actors and aspects in the 'drama'.

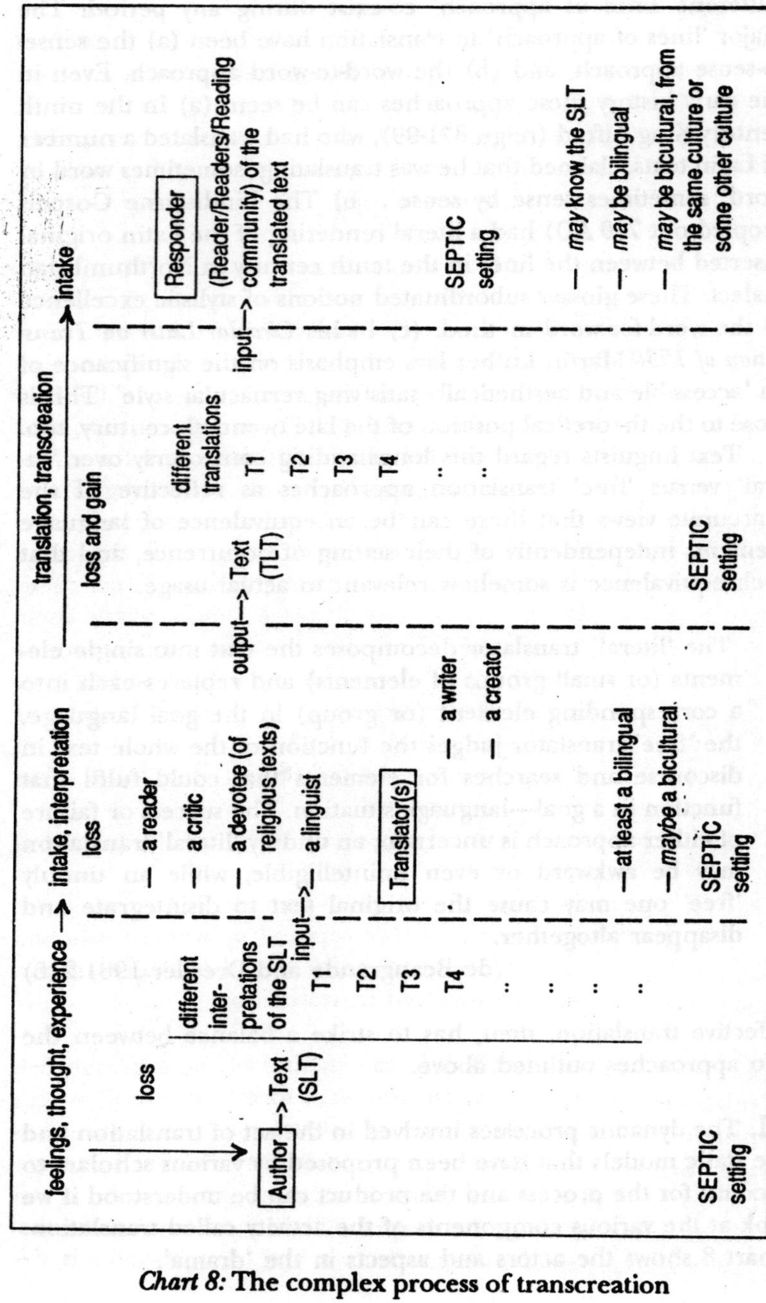

Chart 8: **The complex process of transcreation**

Explanations to terms in the Chart:

i. SLT = Source Language Text; TLT = Target Language Text

ii. SEPTIC setting = socio-economic-political-temporal-ideological-cultural setting

iii. When the author 'translates' his/her feelings into a human language, in the process of expression there will be a 'loss'. The creation is done in a setting.

iv. The SLT must be perceived in its setting.

v. The translator is a reader as well as an author.

vi. Different translators may understand the same SLT in different ways; they may succeed in transferring the 'essence' of the text, but depending on the perception, interpretation, ability, ideology, etc. of each translator there will be variations in the translated text (TLT); variations may also depend on the purpose for which it is done and for whom it is done. A translator does his/her work in a setting. There may be loss or gain depending on the transcreation.

vii. Different readers (responders) may understand the same TLT in different ways; there will be variations in their readings of the SLT if they know the Source Language and their concept of equivalence. There may be different perceptions of the SLT and the TLT depending upon the setting too. There may be differences between a translator's reading of the SLT and a reader's reading of the TLT.

viii. No human product can be perfect (Steiner); so there is no question of perfect equivalence.

ix. These notions are further explained in the models proposed by others too.

The three important models proposed by western scholars arc outlined below in order to point out the nature of the processes and problems involved in translation.

VII. i. J.C. Catford (1965) defines meaning as 'the total network of relations entered into by any linguistic form'; according to him translation is 'the replacement of textual material in one language (SL) by equivalent textual materal in another language (TL). After pointing out that translation equivalence is an empirical phenomenon, he makes a distinction between *textual equivalence* and *formal correspondence*; a textual equivalent is defined as 'any TL form (text or portion of text) which is observed to be the equivalent of a given SL form (text or portion of text)' and formal correspondence as 'any TL category which may be said to occupy, as nearly as possible, the 'same' place in the economy of the TL as the given SL category occupies in the SL'. Catford claims that the concept of formal correspondence is useful though not justifiable.

Examples: Textual Equivalence:-

SL (Hindi)		*TL (English)*
yah (ek) kitaab hai	—>	This is a book.

Formal Correspondence:

SL (Hindi)		*TL (English)*
SOV (Simple Sentence)	—>	SVO (Simple Sentence)

Catford has tried to give translation a technical status by defining it rigorously and precisely; he has introduced different types of translation such as phonological, graphological, grammatical and lexical translations based on a theory of language as developed by M.A.K. Halliday. Catford is very much influenced by the Hallidayan notions of Rank, Exponence, and Delicacy (Halliday 1961) and the theory-based model of Catford becomes its limitation. Since Catford's theory is based on the Hallidayan systemic model, which excludes units above the sentence from its hierarchy of exponence, some vital aspects of the phenomenon of translation are ignored in Catford's model. Some of the vital aspects of translation that have not received attention are: the aim of the translator, the translator's attitude toward the SL text and its writer, the intended audience and function of translation, and the discoursal features of SL & TL texts.

But Catford's distinction between substitution and transference (an implantation of SL meanings in TL text) initiated a debate on semantic equivalence. For example, Levy (1963, in Holmes, 1970) pointed out that translation should not be considered a 'monistic composition' but an interpretation and conglomerate of two structures. In the terminology of Text Linguistics, translation is the interaction between an *actualized system* (SL) and a *virtual system* (TL). In this *process* there will be *loss* as well as *gain* where the concept of loss and gain are to be viewed in a broader perspective. In the production of the SL text there will be loss when the author moves from experience and thought to immediate expression and in translating a text there will be further loss; but a resourceful translator may compensate for the loss through gains in the process of reproduction through 'shifts'.

Catford's distinction between *linguistic* and *cultural untranslatability* is quite useful. Popovic (1976) provides a detailed explanation of *untranslatability*. While Catford starts from within linguistics, Popovic starts from a theory of literary communication. Popovic distinguishes several types of shifts that take place during translation:

a) *Constitutive shift*: This takes place as a result of difference between SL and TL.
b) *Generic shift*: The constitutive features of the text as a literary genre may change from one language to another.
c) *Individual shift*: This may take place owing to the translator's own style and idiolect.
d) *Negative shift*: This may take place as a result of incorrect translation, due to 'misinterpretation'.
e) *Topic shift*: This happens in changing the topical facts in the original.

After discussing the shifts involved in translation, Popovic gives four types of equivalence: *linguistic* (where there is equivalence at the lexical level—e.g., word for word), *paradigmatic* (where there is equivalence at the grammatical level), *stylistic* (where there is semantic and expressive equivalence), and *textual* (where there is equivalence at the level of the syntagmatic structuring of the text). Popovic then proposes two types of *untranslatability*: (a) where the TL system lacks denotation or connotation the SL text cannot be replaced adquately; and (b) where the relation between the creative subject (the author) and its linguistic expression in the SL text itself does not find an adequate expression, it becomes untranslatable in the TL text.

Example: A young Indian woman's remarks on her husband:

aap baRe *vo* hãi (*You are naughty* is a poor translation equivalent of the culture-bound Hindi sentence)

Popovic's goal of 'expressive identity' between the SL and TL texts presents a contrast with Catford's linguistic model.

ii. Eugene Nida (1975) bases his theory of translation on insights taken from transformational-generative grammar, Hymes' notion of communicative competence, the theory of case grammar, information theory, and a number of other disciplines to make his model more pragmatic and communicative. Nida defines translation as a process which 'consists in producing in the receptor language (RL) the closest natural equivalent to the message of the source language, first in meaning and secondly in style'. Nida uses the term 'receptor language' to focus on the receptor, the receiver of the message. Nida rejects the view that translating consists of matching one set of surface structures with another.According to the tripartite scheme of translation proposed by Nida, the process of finding the formal and dynamic equivalents in translation involves *analysis, transfer,* and *restructuring.*

Analysis consists of three steps:

a) grammatical analysis to see if the formation of a grammatical category in the RL can be non-existent/ambiguous/obscure/implicit/explicit/optional/obligatory/etc.;
b) analysis of referential meaning; and
c) analysis of connotative meaning.

During the stage of transfer, the results of the grammatical analysis are transferred from the SL to the RL and this typically happens in the translator's brain; Nida points out that there are problems of semantic adjustments, structural adjustments, etc. In the third stage, the translator has to become more creative in order to handle the problems in restructuring that may arise from the varieties of language or of styles that may be considered effective and appropriate.

Nida's model moves from a purely syntax-oriented semantic theory of translation to a pragmatic one; this is the main contribution of Nida to the theory of translation. His theory is discourse-based and receptor-oriented; but Nida is concerned exclusively with the problem of Bible translation. Nida's concept of *dynamic equivalence* brings in the notion of *equivalent effect* - the relationship between the reader and the text in the SL and the reader and the text in the receptor language. Reader response theories too give a lot of importance to this in literary criticism and the concept of dynamic equivalence explains why a dozen translators translating the 'same' text bring out a dozen versions in the TL; each translator responds to the SL text in a different way because the SL text is not static; the process of finding an equivalence in the receptor language is also dynamic.

At the same time, among the variations there is an *invariant core,* according to Popovic; he argues that the invariant core consists of the stable, basic and constant semantic elements in the text, the existence of which can be proved by experimental semantic condensation. There is something that exists in common among the variations in the translation of any particular text. For example, the 'essence' of the *Ramayana* or the *Mahabharatha* that has been retold in several languages can be considered the *invariant core.* That commonality may be considered the semiotic category according to Albrecht Neubert (1967, in Bassnett-McGuire, 1980). Equivalence over all results from the relation between the signs themselves, the relationship between the signs and what they stand for, and the relationship between the signs and what they stand for and those who use them.

iii. Peter Newmark's (1981) theory of translation is an attempt at proposing a model which is discourse- and receptor-oriented. By stating that semantic (in isolation) as well as pragmatic (in context) meaning should be taken into consideration, Newmark, like Nida, asserts that translation theory has moved from the sentence to the discourse level.

A major contribution made by Newmark is his classification of different kinds of translation. Nida's theory was oriented towards Bible translation, but in Newmark we find different kinds of equivalences that are necessary for different kinds of translation, whether they are literal or liberal. Newmark has based this theory on Buhler's and Jakobson's concept of the function of language. Looking at the text and the functions of language from the translator's point of view, Newmark presents *Text Functions* and *Translation Levels.* This can be shown as follows:

Text Function

A	B	C
Expressive	Informational	Communicative

Translation Level

X	Referential
Y	Textual
Z	Subjective

Newmark visualizes the translator as possessing an instrument consisting of three levels, X,Y,Z and with that he observes a text which exhibits the three functions of language A,B,C in varying degrees. The translator's instrument may be focussed mainly at A for a poem, or B for a technical report, or C for an advertisement. In non-literary translation, the information function B, which matches with the translator's referential level, becomes more prominent thereby making Level X influential; similarly, in the case of a literary text, the expressive function is the dominant one, and inevitably the translator's Z becomes more influential.

Newmark proposes different methods of translation processes for different kinds of texts. Grouping varied texts together, he points out that there are two main methods of translation—*semantic translation* (that remains as faithful as possible to the semantic and syntactic structures of the SL as allowed by the TL), and *communicative translation* (that attempts to produce the same effect on the TL readers as was produced by the original on the SL readers). This classification can be shown as follows:

Source Language Bias — Target Language Bias

Literal ↘ Faithful ↘ Semantic / Communicative ↙ Idiomatic ↙ Free

At the same time, he points out that the two kinds of translation cannot be put into water-tight compartments; 'all translations must be in some degree, both communicative and semantic, social and individual. It is a matter of difference of emphasis.' (Newmark 1981:62).

VIII. Apart from the three important linguists whose ideas were outlined above, there are others who have pointed out the problems in the area of translation. The question of defining *equivalence*, the central issue in the theory of translation, has been discussed by literary critics from the point of view of artistic procedures. These procedures, according to them, are not to be treated in isolation as an abstract notion, but have to be located within the specific socio-cultural-political-economic-temporal setting or context within which they are utilized. This makes the notion of equivalence socio-cultural and not just linguistic; the notion of equivalence will involve among other things social psychology, cultural anthropology, and ethnomethodology. In other words, equivalence in translation is not to be visualized as a search for sameness since nothing can be the same (You don't step into the same river again because you cannot; everytime you are different and the river is different.)

Georges Mounin, the French theorist, who perceives translation as a series of operations focussed on *significations* and *functions* within a given culture, emphasizes the *dialectic* character of the translation *process*. The most important postulates that contribute to this formulation of Mounin are:

i) idiosyncratic personal experience is untranslatable;
ii) comparison between the base units of any two languages is not theoretically sustainable; and
iii) communication is possible only when account is taken of the respective situations of author and translator.

IX. The concept of equivalence must also take into account, in addition to socio-cultural factors, 'environmental factors' that contribute to what might be called 'associative meaning'.

The expression 'a *warm* reception', within the milieu of native speakers in the USA and the UK, suggests 'pleasantness, hospitality, friendliness, etc.'; but the same expression in tropical areas like Saudi Arabia or the Indian sub-continent in summer may not evoke such feelings. Similarly, 'a *cold* reception' may be more welcome in tropical areas on account of the climatic conditions. Such ecological features are reflected even in prayers; the English pray 'for the *sunshine* of thy glory', whereas people in tropical areas pray for 'the *shadow* of thy feet'. These factors pose problems in interpretation, appreciation, and translation. Shakespeare's lines, 'Shall I compare thee to a summer's day' (comparing one's beloved to a warm, pleasant summer day) or 'Thy eternal summer shall not fade' (longing for the continuation of warmth) may pose problems in finding equivalences.

Even common words like 'father, mother, wife' etc. have deeper associative meanings that go beyond surface equivalences. For instance, 'wife' is not 'paṯni' (which has more religious connotations in some Indian communities) and 'maaṯa' is not equivalent to 'mother' (particularly in an orthodox Indian set up where there are associations with 'goddess' and 'Shakti'). 'Maaṯaa' has a core meaning which goes beyond the meaning of 'mother'. Hence its collocation with the Ganges, the cow, and Bharaṯ. Ganga maaṯaa, Gau maaṯaa and Bharaṯ maaṯaa when translated into English lose their significance.

There are expressions like 'aṯman', 'shanṯi', 'dheerga sumangali bhava', 'sukhi bhava', 'saubhagyavati ho', 'chiranjivii ho', 'chauknaa and baghaarnaa' (in the context of cooking in India) which do not have equivalences outside the culture in which they are used; but these are specific problems and not problems in the theory of translation. They are very important like idioms in a language which are idiosyncratic and peculiar to a system. They have to be handled differently and cannot be incorporated in a general theory. At the same time, they bring to focus the untranslatable nature of certain aspects of human experience as expressed in a given langauge.

X. The focus on reader in some recent theories of literature, literary criticism and text processing and the concept of *intertextuality* that exists among texts (both intralingual and interlingual) introduce some important parameters in the study of translation. If a translated text must have the same *relevance* as it has in the context of other SL texts, the concept of intertextuality becomes part of the notion of equivalence; how to capture effectively the relevance of intertextuality in the target language is another important problem in the theory of translation. This problem can be represented as follows:

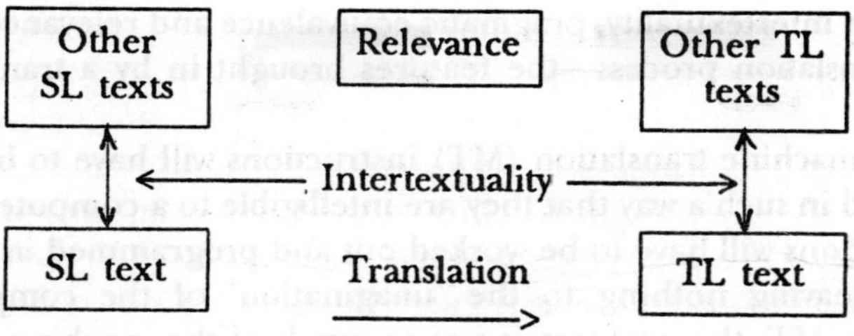

If a theory of translation is to make explicit and systematic what happens in the black box (mind) of a translator, who is a transcreator, it must take into account the following factors:

a) Translation is a dynamic, dialectic, semiotic actualization process with specific differences of approach between 'inter' and 'intra' lingual processes.
b) These processes subsume the search for equivalences via semiotic categories and have their culmination in the reader's search for intertextuality.

These are challenging tasks for the translation theorist.

XI. Some of the answers to the problems mentioned so far may be found in machine translation. Translation theory, particularly in the modern technological age, is influenced as much by linguistic theories as by advances in science and technology. Sophisticated computers, word processors, and Artificial Intelligence (AI) have contributed a lot to the actual translation of texts. When the concept of machine translation was first introduced, it was felt that translation was only a matter of transfer of a sign (in the SL) to another sign (in the TL). Each word or phrase in the SL was looked up in a dictionary and the equivalent word or phrase in the TL was selected; at the end, the equivalents were rearranged in the conventional word order in the TL. Very soon, it was discovered that this kind of transfer was not effective and that the Fully Automatic High Quality-Translation (FAHQT) did not reflect the complexity of human languages.

As translation theory moved from sentence to discourse level, it was found that machines could not cope with a high degree of complexity. A machine, however complex and marvellous, is still a machine, without intuition, imagination and creativity. Can it bring in intertextuality, pragmatic equivalence and relevance into the translation process—the features brought in by a transcreator?

In machine translation (MT) instructions will have to be formulated in such a way that they are intelligible to a computer; the instructions will have to be worked out and programmed in great detail leaving nothing to the 'imagination' of the computer. Thus, in MT, the problem is not so much of the machine, as of the explicit and systematic formulation of the process of translation. In other words, there is an urgent need for formulating a detailed theory of translation. All issues like equivalence and relevance, polysemy and ambiguity, meaning—literal, metaphorical, cultural, intertextual, etc., and all things expressed and suppressed in a text will have to be worked out before a machine is asked to translate a text. The most important advantage of the machine over a human translator is speed and cost; in addition, the machine's vast storage capacity and its retrieval speed can be exploited. These advantages make CATS (Computer Aided Translation Systems) very popular. In CATS texts are pre-edited before being fed into the computer as machine-readable texts for equivalence retrieval; after being processed, texts are post-edited to check for possible discrepancies. It is thus hoped that translators can use computers as effective aids to enhance and speed up human translation skills so that in the technological era MT can become the translator's best companion.

Questions and topics for discussion

1. Translate the following advertisements in English into your first language and point out the problems if any in capturing the same effect:
   a) Neighbour's Envy - Owner's Pride

      — a TV ad.
   b) Don't cry, my child. I know the world seems strange and new; but you are safe in my arms. No harm will ever come to you.

      — an ad. for baby products.
   c) The no lift; no spill; just press Airpot from Eagle.
   d) Make your money work for you.
   e) Dubai Duty Free's Finest Surprise Continues.
2. Try to translate the following statements into your first language and see how far you can establish equivalence. Point out the nature of the problems in translating each statement.

a) Society is composed of beautiful idiots and brilliant lunatics.
b) Every wife understands everything except her husband and every husband everything except his wife.
c) Forbidden fruit is always tempting.
d) The only conquests which are permanent are our conquests over ourselves.
e) Everyone is a rebel and usually in wild revolt against one's own self.
f) Lovers never get tired of each other, because they are always talking about themselves.

3. Yeats' poem *A Coat* is given in unit 18.
Try to translate it into your first language. Ask three or four persons whose first language is the same as yours to translate it and then compare the variations in the translated texts. Account for the variations.
4. Distinguish between the following pairs of terms:
a) translation and transcreation
b) translation and interpretation
c) translation and transfer of information
d) transcription and transliteration
e) equivalence and relevance.
5. Of the three models presented in this unit—Catford's, Nida's, and Newmark's—which one do you prefer? Give reasons for your answer.
6. 'Loss of information is a part of any communication process, and hence the fact that some loss occurs in translation should not be surprising, nor should it constitute a basis for questioning the legitimacy of translation.' — Eugene A. Nida. What is your opinion? Illustrate your answer.
7. '"Is translating an art, a skill, or a science?" is a question wrongly phrased. The issue is not one of alternatives but of supplementary factors.' - Nida. Explain and Illustrate.
8. 'A translator who cannot properly anticipate the reactions of his/ her prospective audience is doomed to be less than successful.' — Explain the statement given above. Illustrate your answer.
9. Machine translation has provided the immediate motivation for translation theory. Can you justify this statement by giving arguments.
10. 'All human languages follow rules. Any precisely formulated rule can be programmed. An entire set of programmed rules comprises a computer translation system. The feasibility of computer translation is determined by the extent to which the rules of human language can be defined.' — Explain. Illustrate your answer with reference to some category of your first language and English.

11. Have you heard of SYSTRAN used in NASA? Find out what it is.
12. Tomorrow, even machines will obey the spoken voice and will speak. But in what langauge? Can you speculate on this with reference to translation?
13. In the past, the role of the literary critic was regarded as determinative with respect to the adequacy of a translation. In recent years, however, the role of the average receptor has become far more important in judging the validity of various translations.- Comment. Illustrate your answer.
14. Do you think discourse analysis and stylistics are closely related to translation theory? Give arguments in support of your answer.
15. Psycholinguistics and sociolinguistics are two of the major background areas for translation theory. Do you agree? Give reasons for your answer.

25 LEXICOLOGY

> *'Tongues, like governments, have a natural tendency to degeneration; we have long preserved our constitution, let us make some struggles for our languages.'*
>
> — *Samuel Johnson (1755)*

Focal points

I. Zgusta, Ladislav (1988:vi) in his *Lexicography Today* says:

'Lexicography is one of the few areas in which linguistic activity has an immediate impact on many people, is very expensive (relative to the scale of measurement usual in the humanities) in terms of both time and money, and can be rather lucrative. In spite of this, it is only recently that lexicographers have become aware of the fact that lexicography, while tending to be compartmentalized by the languages dealt with, can be conceived of in a more cohesive way as a body of theory, methods, and procedures applied and adapted to data from languages.'

Though dictionary-making is essentially a practical activity, much of the recent work in lexicography has explicitly related itself to linguistic theories in general and the theories of lexical semantics in particular.

II. In the present-day world, with all the developments in machine translation systems, computer-based dictionaries and standardized computer languages, lexicography can no longer be an obscure pastime of some word collectors. Dictionary-making is fast developing into a professional activity demanding a lot of research into lexicographical method.

Different lexicographers have described their work as 'dull' (Samuel Johnson), 'exciting' (Eric Partridge), 'enjoyable' and 'tedious'; it is dull and tedious because it is basically compilation and it is exciting and enjoyable since a lexicographer deals among other things with the ever-changing meanings of words.

The term *lexicography* is glossed as 'the process of compiling dictionaries', a 'process related to a range of observable phenomena (i.e., the *vocabulary,* or lexis, or *lexicon*) and a set of theoretical principles (lexicology) with which to tackle them' (Hartmann 1983:3). According to Zgusta (1973:14), 'lexicology concentrates more on general properties and features', lexicography on individual units as the focus of interest.

The result is the dictionary, which is defined as a reference book or list of words (usually in alphabetical order) together with a guide to their meanings, pronunciation, spelling, or equivalents in other languages.

> Lexicography (and its practitioner, the lexicographer) is thus concerned with the job of describing all or some of the words of one or more languages in terms of their characteristic features, notably of their meaning.
>
> (Hartmann op.cit:4)

Hartmann includes two other factors that are equally important—the users of the dictionary and the various purposes for which a dictionary is used. The following chart given in Hartmann (ibid:11) summarizes the factors of dictionary use:

Information	*Operations*
meaning/synonyms/ pronunciation/syntax/ spelling/etymology/ names/facts etc.	finding meanings, finding words, translating, etc.
Situations of dictionary use	
Users	*Purposes*
child/ pupil/trainee teacher/critic/ scientist/secretary, etc.	extending knowledge of the mother tongue, learning a foreign language, playing word games, composing a report, reading/decoding foreign language texts, etc.

III. There are various kinds of dictionaries, monolingual, bilingual and multilingual dictionaries, pedagogical dictionaries, etymological dictionaries, translation/interlingual dictionaries, data-based dictionaries, pronouncing dictionaries, pictorial dictionaries, pocket dictionaries, dictionaries of scientific terms, idioms, phrasal verbs, proverbs, quotations, lexicons, thesauruses, etc. and even combinations of some of the types mentioned above.

Tom McArthur points this out in his introduction to *Longman Lexicon of Contemporary English* (1981):

> Lexicography has traditionally used the alphabet as its principal means of organizing information about words.... There has, however, been an alternative tradition, in which compilers have used groups of topics instead of the alphabet as their basic for organization.... The alphabetical dictionary has a logic, but it is not the logic of everyday life. In principle, one feels, words should be defined in the company they usually keep.

In the reverse-dictionary, called a lexicon/a thesaurus, the idea is given 'to find the word or words by which the idea may be most fitly and aptly expressed.' Comenius in 1631 and Roget in 1852 (*Roget's Thesaurus*) classified words according to semantic fields, the former with a religious bias and the latter with a scheme of universal concepts. *Longman Lexicon* is limited in scope with 'only fourteen semantic fields of a pragmatic, everyday nature'.

IV. The question 'what are dictionaries for?' has been asked many times. Samuel Johnson asked it in 1747, and gave the answer:

> The value of a work must be estimated by its use: It is not enough that a dictionary delights the critic, unless at the same time it instructs the learner.

The need for an 'authority', an 'academy', the need for guidance on matters linguistic since toleration in language had gone far enough (Lord Chesterfield 1754 in Hartmann op.cit.19) and a 'seal of approval for users, in short, the very idea of having a dictionary at all arose out of the need for standardization and a source of reference that will give the learned words, their meanings, and equivalents in other language'. These were the primary motivations for dictionary-making.

In the history of dictionary-making, bilingual and multilingual dictionaries precede monolingual works. In the Western tradition, there are manuscripts dating back to the eighth century A.D. with collected glosses of Latin words with their English equivalents but they could not be called dictionaries. When the collections grew in size, the need for arranging them in some order arose; one way was to arrange them systematically according to the areas of interest—names of birds, animals, plants, etc. The publication of *Nomenclator omnium rerum* (1567) by Hadrianus Junius, a huge polyglot compilation in Latin, Greek, French, and English, was a great achievement. The other technique, alphabetisation, is found in manuscripts even in the 15th century; *The Dictionary of Syr Thomas Eliot Knyght* (1538) and the *Abcedarium Anglico Latinum* (1552), after the introduction of printing, are laudable attempts in this direction.

The first English-English dictionary was compiled by Robert Cawdrey (1604); this happened at the time of Shakespeare.

Cawdrey's dictionary has 2500 entries of mostly 'hard words' or learned words (and very few common words); it was meant for the common man as a reference book to enable him to understand and to use the learned words. For a long time dictionaries tended to maintain this tradition of listing only the learned words. Dr. Johnson's great *Dictionary of the English Language* in two volumes which was published in 1755 was accepted as 'the limit of perfection'; Dr. Johnson defined his corpus (examples taken are from 1560-1660), gave reasons for excluding certain types of words (such as highly specialized technical terms and 'four-letter' words, which were put into dictionaries only in the 20th century), and left out dialectal forms, proverbs, and proper nouns; his emphasis was on literary usage; it is more like a dictionary of quotations because Johnson felt that the best writers are the most worth reading and recording. We can find the Johnsonian fashion in OED (Oxford English Dictionary) even today. Moreover, the recording of the best gave a privileged status to the dictionary and the dictionary assumed a normative role which it has even today. Johnson is well known for his personal views on certain words; for example, he defines the word *oats* as 'a grain which is generally given to horses, but in Scotland supports the people'.

During the 19th century, there was a new perception of lexicography. Trench (1857:3-4) expressed it as follows.

> A Dictionary...is an inventory of the language... It is not the task of the maker of it to select the good words of the language. If he fancies that it is so, and begins to pick and choose, to leave this and take that, he will quickly go astray. The business which he has undertaken is to collect and arrange all the words, whether good or bad.... He is an historian of it, not a critic.

This was a corrective to the earlier Johnsonian tradition and a pointer to the coming generation of dictionary-makers. Darwin's dictum 'if we know not how a thing became, we know it not' became a guiding principle and the great OED proclaimed on its title page, that it was based 'on historical principles'. The 19th century philological tradition greatly influenced lexicography.

Since Ferdinand de Saussure, the objective record of the synchronic system became the guiding principle of dictionary-makers; the choice of words that go into a dictionary is to be determined by sophisticated assessments of frequency and of users' needs, rather than the literary bias or the author's whims and fancies or historical facts. Etymological dictionaries recorded historical facts and etymology is not to be given in a dictionary for the people; it was considered an 'extra', just as it was in the 17th century.

But a well-known dictionary like *Webster's New International Dictionary* (1934-second edition) justifies etymology because it is 'a record of the origin and development that is of value and interest for its own sake as well as necessary to a full understanding of the word itself'. Webster believed that God spoke to Adam and thus gave Adam 'language as well as the faculty of speech'; he accepted the belief that after the great flood several language families developed differently as a result of the great changes incident to the increase of knowledge and to people's social circumstances. This led Noah Webster to include Etymology as part of his dictionaries. New technologies, the spread of English and its interaction with all the major languages of the world, new perceptions like feminist vocabulary, Indian English, discipline-based dictionaries, etc. have created lots of potentialities for specialized and general, all-purpose dictionaries. This expansion has also given birth to a number of theoretical issues in formulating lexicology regarding the nature and function of dictionaries.

V. The compilation and editing of even conventional dictionaries have many practical as well as theoretical problems. First of all, a dictionary-maker has to take a decision about what a *word* is since dictionaries are essentially lists of, what might be called, lexical entries. For example, the item *bank* (whose written forms are *bank, banks, bank's, banks', banked, banking,* etc.) has several different meanings; a lexicographer must decide how many lexical entries (all indexed by the head-word *bank*) are to be put in the dictionary; decisions must be taken about the extensions and derivations like *banker, banker's order, banking hours, blood-bank,* etc. How to list irregular forms is another problem; for instance, the entry for *rode* must tell the user that it is the past-tense form of 'ride' and the entry under *ride* must also include the same information viewed from the other end. In other words, the same information must be given twice; this will increase the number of entries and the volume of the dictionary. Similarly, a decision must be taken about complex and compound words — items like *man, manly, sure, unsure, friend, befriend, friendlier, friendliest, boy-friend,* etc. — are they to be shown as separate entires or under related heads? Several such decisions are to be taken regarding the morphology of words and how they are to be shown in the dictionary.

In addition, a dictionary must also give information of three other kinds: phonological, syntactic and semantic; the user must get some information about the pronunciation of a particular item, how it is used in a sentence and to what grammatical class it belongs, and its meaning or meanings. It may be useful to have registral and stylistic guidance; for example, *formal, taboo word* etc. A dictionary or lexicon has always been regarded as an appendix to the grammar of the language. Gleason (1973) holds that the distinction between grammar and lexicon is not clear cut; therefore, a dictionary 'must take cognizance of various grammatical features' (p.31) and argues that 'the ordinary speaker/listener's processing of language' (processing paradigmatically and syntagmatically) 'should figure prominently in normal use of the dictionary' (p.29). In other words, the list of words must also contain the grammar that governs the words. In some dictionaries, as in A.S. Hornby's *Oxford Advanced Learner's Dictionary of Current English,* in addition to the information about word-classes (whether a noun is countable or uncountable or whether a verb is transitive or intransitive in a particular meaning), verb patterns are given as a guide to show the learner/user how to use verbs to form correct sentences. A set of tables in which various verb patterns are set out with examples and a link between the tables and the verb entries in the Dictionary is provided with code numbers.

Garvin (1973:22-3) suggests that the following grammatical details should be included in a machine (translation) dictionary (This holds good for a general dictionary, too):

i. *Word-class information,* which not only includes indication of conventional parts of speech but distinction in terms of syntactic functioning of words. For example,

table (n) butter n (u)
table (v) butter v (T)
(n = noun; v = verb; u = uncountable; T = transitive)

ii. *Agreement information,* which must include information on modifier-head agreement as well as whether the agreement is of the ordinary or exceptional type, meaning whether ordinary or special morphological rules apply.
In the above entries the information (U) for 'butter' is on the character of agreement of the lexeme.

iii. *Modifiability information,* which must state what dependent words a given word may be modified by, that is, what adjectives may modify a given noun, what adverbs can modify a given adjective, etc.

iv. *Complementation information* concerning types of complements which might be associated with any word that may have a complement in association with it; for example, verbs and nouns of location may have certain types of complements of place accompanying them as in *put it in some place, keep them there, sneak into the room,* etc.

v. *Governor class information* for words which may be governed by other words and information in regard to the particular kinds of words which may govern them; for adjectives the kinds of nouns they qualify, and for adverbs, the kinds of adjectives they modify, etc.

vi. *Government information* for those words which govern dependent structures, the kind of dependent structures which they may govern; for instance, the kind of case a verb or noun may govern.

vii. *Subject class information* which specifies, say for verbs, the class of subjects which a given verb may take such as animate, inanimate, human, etc.

viii. *Object class information* which is similar to the subject class information.

Many 'words' (like *a, an, the, of, on,* etc.) that perform grammatical functions strictly speaking do not belong to the lexicon since they are structural words; but it is reasonable to include them in the dictionary since they form part of the link between grammar and lexicon.

VI. A lexicographer will have to take decisions about how to handle *homonymy, polysemy, idioms, metaphors,* etc. in handling the semantic component of the lexicon. The word 'mouth', for example, is a simple polysemous lexeme—i.e., one lexeme with several meanings ('organ of the body', 'entrance of a cave', 'mouth of a river', etc.); but, 'bank$_1$' ('side of a river') and 'bank$_2$' ('financial institution') or 'port$_1$' ('harbour') and 'port$_2$' ('kind of fortified wine') or 'can$_1$' ('be able to'), 'can$_2$' ('a kind of receptacle' as in 'It's can'), 'can$_3$' (a transitive verb as in 'can the fish' to mean 'put in a can/tin' that goes with other forms like *cans, canned,* etc.) are homonyms. All these differences are to be shown in terms of the part-of-speech to which they belong, etymological grounds for the distinctions maintained, word-formation (as in *bank - banker - banking* in one sense of the word). There are also idiomatic and metaphorical uses like 'Don't put words into my mouth', 'This newspaper is the mouthpiece of the socialists', 'He mouthed his words slowly', etc. In some cases, semantic relatedness is important as in 'kill' and 'die' or 'give' and 'receive' or 'reach' and 'arrive'.

In addition, stylistic information that assigns values that are socially, culturally, and situationally determined must find a place in a dictionary; information concerning the use of items in formal/informal situations, whether they are used in only one variety (like British English/American English) or all varieties, whether they are used in the standard variety or only in the dialects, and other kinds of information like slang/taboo, etc. are to be shown in a general dictionary. Eric Partridge says: 'A good dictionary will, wherever necessary, show you how the word is used.'

These variations may have something to do with pronunciation, in which case that has to be indicated. As A.C. Gimson (1973) points out that a general dictionary cannot afford to give all the variant forms as a pronouncing dictionary can. The most important variations (dialectal like British/American) have to be, however, included. A broad phonemic transcription, supported by a key in the appendices, would be helpful.

While proper understanding of phonological. grammatical and semantic information is essential if a lexicographer is to have a clear grasp of the material (s)he is trying to put across to the users (s)he must make the dictionary serviceable and communicative.

VII. To many people a dictionary means a bilingual dictionary since bilingual dictionaries are often used in foreign language learning and translation (human as well as machine). As Zgusta (1971 in Hartmann 1983:41) points out:

> The basic purpose of a bilingual dictionary is to coordinate with the lexical units of one language those lexical units of another language which are equivalent in their lexical meaning. This means that the problems of a bilingual lexicographer get doubled and a multilingual's multiplied!

The problems connected with the search for equivalence were discussed in detail in the previous unit 'On Translation'. Depending on the purpose for which a bilingual dictionary is compiled, one has to find answers to a number of questions; if a bilingual dictionary moves from L_1 to L_2 (like Hindi —> English, Telugu —> English), there are a set of problems whereas, if it proceeds from L_2 to L_1 (English —> Hindi, English —> Telugu), the problems are different.

> ...the L_2/L_1 lexicographer can always resort to definition, description, paraphrase, etc., and comprehension is thus ensured. But all such items are lost in L_1/L_2 dictionary; since they are not part of the L_1 lexicon, there is no way of entering them in the dictionary. Consequently, my Polish-English dictionary gives a more or less full account of the Polish lexicon, but its coverage of the English lexicn is reduced by what was left in the Polish sieve or filter through which it has been passed. This applied both to the structural information and to the cultural information. (Tomazevsky, 'On bilingual dictionaries' in Hartmann op.cit.:49).

Bilingual/multilingual dictionaries must give full coverage of culture-specific vocabulary, and, at the same time, pay more attention to syntax, pronunciation and spelling, meaning and idiomatic phrases. This involves decisions involving what to put in the dictionary and what to exclude, how and where to enter them, how to make the users aware of their availability, how to convey a given idea in the other language (equivalence and relevance), etc.

VIII. The pedagogical/learner's dictionary (monolingual or bilingual) like the *Advanced Learner's Dictionary of Current English* tries to harmonize the theoretical and linguistic factors with pedagogical considerations like (a) learners' difficulties (high-frequency words, multiple meanings, derivatives, compounds and idioms in the language to be learnt), (b) the level for which the dictionary is meant (advanced learners, beginners, etc.), (c) the purpose for which it is written (literary, technical, scientific, etc.), and (d) the users' needs (usage oriented, word-meaning oriented, reference needs, etc.). In other words, the lexicographer of a pedagogical dictionary must be fully aware of dictionary teaching and learning principles and the applied linguistic nature of a learner's dictionary; (s)he must keep abreast of relevant developments in applied linguistics in order to make the dictionary useful. For example, a lexicographer compiling a dictionary for 'languages for special purposes' can benefit a lot from the recent literature of ESP (English for Special Purposes); a lot of work has been done in ESP taking into account occupational requirements (like the requirements of telephone operators, airline pilots, etc.), vocational training programmes (technical trades), and academic or professional study (law, medicine, etc.). The purpose for which a dictionary is compiled will decide the nature of the headword, its spelling, pronunciation, definition, examples, illustration, equivalents in other languages (if it is bi-/multi-lingual), etc. A list of technical terms alone will not be a specialist learner's dictionary.

All this involves a lot of research, wide-ranging user surveys, data-banks, etc. without which satisfactory results cannot be achieved. These things may involve teamwork.

IX. As F.R. Abate (1985) points out: 'The dictionary conceived as a book...has outlived its usefulness.' In future, the main tool of reference will be the data base. There was a time when people thought that 'men have become the tools of their tools'; but, today machines act as assistants to human beings, in several areas like translation, dictionary-making, text-processing, testing, and, maybe, very soon even in talking and thinking. We are close to the possibility for the user to ask questions and get answers from a computerized data base in natural languages; indications of pronunciation will be available orally. Computers can function as bilingual dictionaries, responding to requests for translation of words and idioms by searching its memory for the appropriate item and giving the print out in a jiffy. Problems of information retrieval—that is, how to get the required information without wasting time—can be solved easily. The power of the computer can be used to analyse textual material with respect to such properties as the frequency of words, sounds, sentence patterns, and so on so that learner's dictionaries can be compiled on the basis of frequency studies. A word list with over 350,000 entries can be put on computer tape and any item can be recalled in no time. Dictionaries can be put on computer tape and constantly updated.

Dr. Johnson, the great lexicographer, said in 1786:

> 'Dictionaries are like watches; the worst is better than none, and the best cannot be expected to go quite true.'

Very soon we can expect dictionaries that will be quite true, with the precision of quartz watches.

Questions and topics for discussion

1. Comment on the following dictionary entries:
   extravagant: iks-trav'e-gent, adj. wandering beyond bounds: irregular: unrestrained: excessive: profuse in expenses: wasteful—ns. *extrav'agance*, excess : lavish expenditure : (Milt.) digression; *extrav'agancy* (Shak.) vagrancy: extravagance. - adv. extrav'agantly. - v.i. extrav'agate, to wander: to exceed proper bounds. [L. extra, beyond, vagans, - antis, pr.p. of vagari; to wander.]
   - *Chambers' Twentieth Century Dictionary* (1960:378).
2. Given below is an entry from *Rogets' Thesaurus*, for the same word, *extravagant*. Compare the two entries in terms of their functions in language use:
   Adj. *dear*, high-priced, expensive, ritzy; costly, multi-million; *extravagant*, dear-bought, Pyrrhic; dear at the price, overpriced, overpaid; exhorbitant, excessive, extortionate; beyond one's means, not affordable, prohibitive.
   of price, adj. *valuable;* priceless, beyond price, above p.; unpayable; inestimable, precious. - *Roget's Thesaurus* (1966:318)

3. Comment on the following extracts from a bilingual (English-Hindi) dictionary:

   i) religion (dharma)
   (English) (Hindi)

   Can we say that 'dharma' is 'religion'? Is the semantic range of 'dharma' much wider than that of 'religion'? What would you as a lexicographer like to do in such cases?

   ii) yesterday (kal)
   tomorrow (kal)

   Do you think that it will be useful to add (the day after today) in the case of 'tomorrow' and (the day before today) in the case of 'yesterday'? Give reasons for your answer.

   iii) Culture-bound items do not have exact equivalents across languages. How should a maker of bilingual dictionaries handle these problems?

4. 'We should expect these five kinds of information about words from the ideal dictionary. They are in ascending order of complexity: the phonemic structure of the word, its morphemic structure, the grammatical modifications it undergoes, its syntactic habits, and its meanings.' — A.A. Hill.
   Do you agree? Give reasons for your answers.

5. 'Modern dictionaries do their utmost to *record* usage, not to *prescribe* it.' — Mitford M. Mattews.
   Is this possible? Do you think it is against the very function of a dictionary? Justify your answer.

6. Lying behind every dictionary is a philosophy of dictionary that determines a great many decisions. Comment. Illustrate your answer.

7. Here is a news item:
   Starner was arrested on the complaint of a young woman who charged that he had accosted her with: 'Hello, chicken.'
   'Your Honor,' said Starner, 'Just look in Webster's dictionary and you will find that I have transgressed no laws'. Magistrate Moore got a copy of Webster's and turning to the word in dispute found: 'chicken - the young of birds, a child, a young woman.'
   Magistrate Moore discharged the prisoner.
   Do you agree with Magistrate Moore? Look up other dictionaries and see what they say. Then give your judgement.

8. 'What's the word? It's on the tip of my tongue.' But the word, hovering just out of reach, continues to elude you. What will you do to find such words?

9. How do dictionaries define very common words like 'man', 'woman', 'dog', 'pig', etc.? It will be very amusing to see how miserably they fail to define what is known to everybody. Collect six or

seven 'definitions' of the words given above and point out why they fail to define such words.

Suggested reading (Translation)

Bassnett-McGuire, Susan. 1980. *Translation Studies.* London : Methuen. This is a very useful introduction to the theory of translation. It discusses the central issues of the theory of translation, the historical development of the translation theory and the specific problems of literary translation.

Catford, J.C. 1965. *A Linguistic Theory of Translation: An Essay in Applied Linguistics.* London : OUP.
This short study contains some insights into the translation process viewed from a particular angle. Its chief defect is that its author approaches the subject of translation as a way of exemplifying his linguistic theory.

Newmark, P. 1981. *Approaches to Translation.* Oxford : Pergamon Press. The major contribution of this book is the detailed treatment of the difference between semantic and communicative translations. In the latter the comprehension and response of the receptors is brought in.

Nida, E. 1975. *Language Structure and Translation : Essays by Eugene A. Nida.* (ed.). Anwar S.Dil. Stanford : Stanford University Press.
This is a selected anthology of Nida's papers (1958-1974) covering the areas of semantic structure, translational equivalence, language and communication and Bible translation.

Papovic, Anton. 1976. *A Dictionary for the Analysis of Literary Translation.* Edmonton, Alberta : Department of Comparative Literature, University of Alberta.
This is a very useful reference book.

Suggested reading (Lexicology)

Advance in Lexicology : Second Annual Conference of the UW Centre for the New Oxford English Dictionary. Proceedings of the Conference, November 9-11, 1986. Canada : University of Waterloo, 1986.
The current thinking on issues like lexicon, English word formation and the like are presented. There is also a report about a programme of automatic parsing of the definitions in a machine-readable English monolingual dictionary with the purpose of building a lexical data base with both syntactic and semantic data.

Bailey, Richard N. (ed.). 1987. *Dictionaries of English : Prospects for the Record of Our Language.* Ann Arbor, Michigan : The University of Michigan Press.
This volume contains papers on English Lexicography, historical

and contemporary. There is a comparison of a representative sample of English vocabulary as presented in various English monolingual dictionaries.

Bartholomew, Doris A., and Louise C. Schoenhals. 1983. *Bilingual Dictionaries for Indigenous Languages*. Mexico : Summer Institute of/Linguistics.

This is a well-founded and practical guide to methods and procedures to be applied, particularly in the compilation of dictionaries of richly morphological languages. Spanish and the Indian languages of Mexico are in the focus of attention.

Hartmann, Reinhard R.K. (ed.) 1983. *Lexicography : Principles and Practice*. London : Academic Press.

There is a lucid clarification of some basic notions such as 'lexeme', all-inclusive versus segmental dictionaries, 'meta language' etc. Dictionaries for machine translation, for terminological data banks, and for the human users are differentiated.

McDavid, Raven I., Jr., and Audrey R. Duckert (eds.). 1973. *Lexicography in English*. Annals of the New York Academy of Sciences, 211. New York: New York Academy of Sciences.

This book contains many useful and fairly introductory papers. Each group of papers is followed by a report on the discussion. It contains, among others, papers by Gleason, Garvin, Gimson and Zgusta, all 1973.

Zgusta, Ladislav. 1971. *Manual of Lexicography*. The Hague/Paris : Mouton.

This is a survey of the theory of lexicography and its methods and procedures.

CHAPTER SEVEN

And Many More ...

'It is only in language that the ideology inscribed in the language can be challenged.'

26 LANGUAGE AND SEX

'One is not born a woman; one becomes one.'

— Simone de Beauvoir

Focal points

I. The rubric, *sociolinguistcs,* encompasses a continuum of approaches to language and society, ranging from those whose aims are almost purely linguistic to those whose aims are entirely social (Trudgill, 1978). At the social end, the aim is to study social knowledge and social pressures through talk, 'to use the linguistic data to get at the social knowledge that lies behind it, not to further our understanding about language' (Trudgill, 1978). In the work of sociolinguists such as Labov and Trudgill, sometimes called 'secular linguistics', social phenomena like race, social class, set, situation, etc. are used as independent variables in terms of which linguistic variations and change are interpreted; this is only part of the story since there are many other facets to be considered in the study of language and society like language attitudes, etc. Some of the important areas are: language and religion, language and race, language and sex. The focus in this Unit is on language and sex.

Goffman (1977) points out:

> Every society seems to develop its own conception of what is essential' to, and characteristic of, the two sex classes, this conception embracing both praised and dispraised attributes. Here are the ideals of masculinity and femininity, under-

> standings about ultimate human nature which provide grounds (at least in Western society) for identifying the whole of the person, and provide also a source of accounts that can be drawn in a million ways to excuse, justify, explain, or disapprove the behaviour of an individual or the arrangement under which he lives, these accounts being given both by the individual who was accounted for and by such others as have found reason to account for him. Norms of masculinity and femininity also bear on the objective (albeit mainly socially acquired) differences between sex-classes, but, as suggested, do not coincide with these differences, failing to cover some, misattributing others, and, of course, accounting for a considerable number by means of a questionable doctrine—in our society, a doctrine of biological influences.

This is justification enough for including the study of language and relations between the sexes in what we have called applied linguistics.

Whether it is the popular saying that ten measures of speech descended on the earth and men took only one and women nine, or the common belief that a baby girl starts speaking earlier than a boy, or the notion that boys are good at mathematics and girls at language, there are all kinds of conceptions and misconceptions about the language of the sexes expressed through language. There is so much to be read in human language itself about man's attitude towards women than in anything written in it.

Whether it is a Haryanvi 'poet', who, in the name of humour says things such as "Let's compare a TV and a *biwi* (wife); on the TV you get a five year guarantee but there is no such guarantee on the *biwi*," or a Pagan like Aristotle (384-322) B.C.), who said that 'we should look upon the female state as being, as it were, a deformity, one which occurs in the ordinary course of nature....on account of its weakness it quickly approaches its maturity and old age since inferior things all reach their end more quickly' (*Generation of Animals*, trans. by Peck), or a Roman Catholic like Thomas Aquinas (13th cent. A.D.) who said that the female is a 'misbegotten' male, or a Jew like Freud (20th cent. A.D.), who made women envy the private parts of man, or a mythical Markandeya, who said, 'By serving their husbands only can women win heaven', or the Saint Vyasa through Draupadi advising another woman, Satyabhama, 'keeping aside vanity and controlling desire and wrath, I always serve with devotion the sons of Pandu with their wives' (*Mahabharata,* trans. by P.C Roy)—one can see, irrespective of religion, country, race, the period in which they lived, more or less the same perceptions about women in language.

II. Otto Jespersen, the well-known Danish grammarian, in his book *Language, Its Nature, Development and Origin* (1922, p.27) says:

> It is the use of intensifiers which is responsible for the lack of precision in women's speech... women by virtue of their sex shrank from coarse and gross expressions and had a preference for veiled and indirect expressions which precluded them from being as effective as men. Women had a debilitating effect upon language and it was reasonable for men certainly with great justice to object... there is a danger of the language becoming languid and insipid if we were to content ourselves with women's expressions.

Many have stated that men's speech is forceful, efficient, blunt, authoritative, serious, effective and masterful while women's speech is weak, trivial, ineffective, tentative, hesitant, euphemistic, hyperpolite, and is often marked by gossip and meaningless expressions. Several studies regarding the masculinity-femininity (MF) measurement that reveal the sex-stereotypicality are available (Smith 1985).

It is generally believed that women use words that are related to their special interests like sewing, cooking, dressing, colour, etc. and that a man does not know them since he doesn't use them. Robin Lakoff's book *Language and Women's Place* (175) confirms this; she says that 'shit' is more commonly found in male vocabulary and 'oh dear' in female vocabulary; she further adds that women use more question tags (like 'you went there, didn't you?') and hedges like 'well', 'you know', etc., since they are unclear and uncertain about what they say. Women often use words like 'so' (as in 'so cute') and 'very' (as in 'very pretty'). Several others have said that women's grammar is hyper-correct;

for example, they don't use 'ain't'; there is no humour in the language of women and they 'speak in italics', meaning the pitch is high.

III. The asymmetry in the representation of *men* and *women* in language is reflected in the order of precedence given to *males* and *females* when they are referred to together; the more expected order will be: husband and wife, son and daughter, brother and sister, king and queen, Adam and Eve, etc.

Eakins and Eakins (1976) suggest that women more often than men are referred to in terms of their partners: 'John's wife', 'Harry's daughter', and so on; a woman whose husband is dead is 'Ed's widow', but the man whose wife is deceased is not referred to as 'Vera's widower'.

If we compare the following pairs of words, we can see that the masculine gender has been not only stable in the English language but also dominant: mister-mistress (an illegal one); sir-madam (a brothel keeper); governor-governess (a tutor in a private house); courtier-courtesan (a woman who takes payment for 'services' rendered); king-queen (sexual connotations); wizard-witch (derogatory); Lord-Lady (a doll-like decorative object); dog-bitch (derogatory), etc. In other words, words that denote the feminine gender have a lesser value. Words like 'whore' and 'harlot' which were used to refer to both the sexes are now used to refer only to women. When we say 'He is a professional', it is respectable; but 'She is a professional' has a bad odour about it. This process of 'semantic degeneration' shows the evaluation of women as a group.

Expressions like 'The proper study of mankind is Man' (Pope), 'The child is father of the man' (Wordsworth), 'Man is a noble animal', 'Man is the measure of all things' (Pythagoras), etc. show that 'man' is generic; the pronoun 'he'is also generic: 'A bicyclist can bet that he is not safe from dogs.' (Note that in Goffman's quotation given at the beginning of this unit 'he' and 'him' are used in the generic sense.) In semantic studies 'man' is taken as 'unmarked' because he is everywhere, but 'woman' is marked.

IV. Goffman's (1976) analysis of more than 500 pictorial advertisements depicting women, men and children leads him to the conclusion that 'Advertisers conventionalize our conventions, stylize what is already a stylization...' His analysis concludes that 'women frequently, men very infrequently, are posed in a display of the 'bashful knee-bend' and 'the resulting configurations can be read as an acceptance of subordination, an expression of ingratiation, submissiveness, and appeasement.' 'Drivers : Belt the wife and kids - and keep them safe', advises a road safety poster in London. A billboard ad. for a fiat car says, 'If it were a lady it would get its bottom pinched.'

Courtney and Whipple (1974) reviewed the results of four studies that analyse the roles of women in television commercials; females were often portrayed in domestic roles, while males dominate the media; women were often seen performing domestic tasks involving the advertised product, while males were most often seen demonstrating novel features of the product. More recent studies (Maracek et al., 1978) support the major observations of the earlier work and show that not much change has taken place. In India too, the situation is not different in television commercials and newspaper and magazine advertisements.

V. Language reflects the deep-rooted attitudes enshrined in our minds; the male is the norm in the world of language and, therefore, in the world outside. 'Those who have the power to name the world are in a position to shape it' — this started with Adam when he was asked by the Lord God to name every beast of the field, and every fowl of the air; the Lord God also took one of Adam's ribs and out of the one 'taken from man, made he a woman,' 'Adam called his wife's name Eve.'

The philosopher Nietzsche says that all of us, women and men, live in the famous 'prison-house of language;' according to him, 'We have to cease to think if we refuse to do it in the prison-house of language.' If language is a prison-house, the question is: Who made it? It is obvious that language is man-made; the tragedy of the human situation is that over a period of time man (the male) made the famous prison and now both men and women are caught in it; women as well as men carry the burden of the symbolic order called language and even for those who wish to shed it, it is difficult if not impossible.

The sexual principle, the man-woman biological difference, has become an organizing principle of the most common and important symbolic order—language; the most elementary function of the sexual 'subculture' is to ensure that people are equipped with concepts of masculinity and femininity that enable them to distinguish between men and women but the secondary characteristics that interpret the biological information in terms of a sociocultural point of view to make us think and feel 'as a man' or 'as a woman' become more important. 'Beliefs about sex differences are very pervasive features of our society and can be documented in literature for children and adults (Kramarae 1981), in television (Howitt 1982), in educational resources (Gershuny 1977; Nilsen 1977, and in commercial advertisements (Courtney and Whipple 1974; Goffman 1976), to name but a few. These beliefs are called *sex stereotypes* and they include, in addition to beliefs about very basic quintessential differences such as beliefs about important but non-essential differences and even trivial ones (for instance, beliefs about sex differences in colour vocabulary)' (Smith 1985:26-27). Bruse Feirstein's satire of contemporary masculinity in North America, subtitled *A Guide Book to All that is Truly Masculine* proclaims in its title: *Real Men Don't Eat Quiche.* 'The book includes sections on: 'The Real Man's Library' (e.g., Ian Fleming's *Goldfinger*); 'The Real Man's Nutritional Guide' (e.g., as a general rule, Real Men won't eat anything that is poached, sauteed, minced, blended, braised, curried, flambed, stirfried, or on brochette), and 'Two Colours That Do Not Appear in a Real Man's Wardrobe ('Puce And Mauve')...Feirstein has succeeded in capturing the gist and scope of some important (American) masculine values' (Smith ibid:27).

Like the pre-Copernican geo-centric world, the word and the world have become andocentric. According to Freud notions like Oedipus complex and Electra complex ('father fixation') are culturally made, but Jacques Lacan, the famous French psychoanalyst in the post-Freudian era, says that these complexes are made by the symbolic system (since culture is made by language). It is the authority and law of the father that makes the symbolic order and all that it implies. The rules of seeing (whether it is Oedipus or Electra complex) are made by the rules of saying; the tunnel vision is controlled by the blinkers that we put on, and for a new vision, we need not only 'fish eyes' but also a different kind of expression, a different kind of language. At the ssame time, we cannot reject the entire symbolic order that exists today since a total rejection will leave all of us psychotic; we cannot throw out the old order and live in a vacuum.

What then is the solution? We may have to find some 'viewing points' in the prison house of language from where we can 'discover' a new-speak; every system has the seeds of change in itself; the symbolic order has to be desedimented so that the hidden 'textual powers' in language are released for changing the metaphysical fixations about 'sexual power' and 'sex roles'. We use language as individuals and there is no such thing as man's language or woman's language. This will mean, firstly, that we cannot make generalizations about use of language on the basis of biological distinctions; all human beings express their feelings and emotions in language; professional areas of interest may determine language (called 'register') but not sex or the colour of the skin. A qualitative change in our outlook towards what is called 'women's language' will change our 'deterministic' attitude to language and enable all of us to discover new ways of living in the prison-house itself.

There is a lot of scope for research in this sector of applied linguistics.

Questions and topics for discussion

1. Collect some proverbs about women in your first language and see what attitudes they reveal.
2. 'Woman was God's *second* mistake.'

   — Nietzsche

   What was the first one? How do we 'correct' these mistakes, particularly as teachers.
3. 'For the female of the species is more deadly than the male.' - Kipling.

   How does language reinforce this concept? Give examples from your first language.
4. In Indian languages, generally, the order of precedence is: Sita Ram, Radha Krishna, Lakshmi Narayan, Parvati Parameshwar, etc. because of the Goddess worship tradition unlike in the Hebrew tradition. Does it reveal any difference between the two sexes and show that Indians treat women differently? Illustrate your answer.
5. 'What is at issue is not the female subject's biological 'inferiority', but her symbolic exclusion or 'lack'.' Explain this statement by giving examples from your first language.
6. 'The word 'father' represents the state, the church, power, the

system, and the word along with its values gets internalized.' How would you react to this as a teacher who uses teaching materials that perpetuate this system? What suggestions can you offer to change this order of things?

7. 'Women have no super-ego.' - What does it mean?
8. So far feminism has developed along these lines:
   a. Women reject the symbolic order in the name of difference; this is *radical feminism*.
   b. Women demand equal access to the symbolic order; this is *liberal feminism*.
   c. Women reject the dichotomy between masculinity and femininity as metaphysical and challenge the notion of identity; this can be called *rational feminism*.

   Give your view on these and relate it to language. Illustrate your answer.
9. Examine any of the secondary level textbooks in English or in any of the Indian languages in terms of the framework outlined in this section. Give your comments.

27 LANGUAGE AND MACHINE

'Wouldst thou' - so the helmsman answered —
'Learn the secret of the sea?
Only those who brave its dangers
Comprehend its mystery.'

— *H.W. Longfellow*

Focal points

I. 1901—Marconi sent radio signals across the Atlantic; we thus began this century with a big bang and have never looked back. The phenomenal expansion of the electronics industry, including computers, is pushing us to a new epoch in the history of human beings. If the characteristic feature of the *First Industrial Revolution* was substitution of mechanical power for the muscle power of men, women, and animals, the *Second Industrial Revolution* (also known as Cybernetic Revolution) has created implements which are extensions of the human mind. As of today, there is every basis to believe that before the end of this century machine systems will be available to perform complex tasks in multiple ways; computers handle banking business; they prepare diets, diagnose illnesses, and even prescribe medicines; they evaluate the performance of employees, and, in some cases, even hire them, archaeologists have used machines to decipher ancient hieroglyphics; language translation is being done by computers. In short, the electronic computer is a 'talented teenager'; machines that think have become a factor in our lives, and they will become increasingly important. The history of the evolution of the present-day computer from the mechanical adding machine constructed by Blaise Pascal in 1642 shows the growing awareness about the capabilities of the system called human/natural intelligence; modern cybernetics actually makes us feel like the 'rustics rang'd around' gaping at the master's head:

> 'And still they gaz'd, and still the wonder grew
> That one small head could carry all he knew.'
>
> — Goldsmith

II. The search for artificial/synthetic intelligence must begin with a study of the nature of natural intelligence and the study of human language may well be a window on the cerebral life. As Ambose Bierce says in *The Devil's Dictionary,* the brain is 'an apparatus with which we think that we think'. Thinking involves language and, in order to understand the process of thinking, we must understand the brain mechanism underlying human linguistic ability. A great deal of work has been done by neurophysiologists like Penfield, Roberts, and others, and, as a result, one can consider constructing machines capable of performing functions previously reserved for humans, such as learning, abstract thought, creativity and generalizing, reading and writing poetry, developing sufficient vocabulary and grammar to talk about love, God, universal Mind and such other things.

There are a number of similarities and differences between the human brain and the electronic computer: both systems have a capacity to receive, store and deliver 'information'; for example, doing arithmetic, making decisions, performing deductive logic, solving problems, etc. Rose (1974) in his *The Cybernetic Revolution* classifies the differences between the brain and the computer as follows:

i) *Memory:* The human brain has an estimated capacity of about 10^{15} (about one million billion) 'bits of information' carried in directly accessible storage, in addition to auxiliary 'files' stored in far recesses of the memory. The high speed random access computer memory at present involves 10^8 bits which may be expanded to perhaps 10^{12} bits by auxiliary storage. (Recently, space shuttle programmes and Star Wars programmes have expanded this to a great extent).

ii) *Memory Access:* The brain retrieves information by ***associating*** certain facts with others, while the computer does this by saving the *address* of the information in the programme itself or in a table to which the programme has access.

iii) *Reliability:* The brain is capable of reorganizing its network in order to deal with damage to its 'neurons' or the living cells. The computer too has great reliability but is ***incapable of repairing itself.***

iv) *Deterministic Structure:* The brain is a self-organizing system, for much of the brain's structure is composed of randomly connected elements capable of developing a required organization; on the other hand, a computer is wired to a given diagram and has basically a pre-determined structure, though machines capable of simulating a self-organizing system ***in a limited way*** are also available.

v) *Learning:* Natural intelligence is capable of learning and can be trained to learn enormous things upto making a computer. This quality is still in its infancy as regards computers; natural intelligence can create artificial intelligence but artificial intelligence cannot create the natural one.

iv) *Communication:* Humans can communicate with each other using natural languages; computers that can communicate with each other are being attempted but the difficulties are enormous.

vii) *Creative thought:* Since we do not know how human beings create ideas, etc. there has not been much progress in this area.

In order to be more precise, one has to define what is meant by 'information' since all the factors mentioned above are about information storage and its processing. The question is: Does it include the 'semantic' content of messages? In the case of a computer, 'information' can only mean 'a selection from a set of the available set'; natural intelligence uses the term 'information' for news, knowledge, intelligence, feelings, experiences, and a whole lot of other things. All these diverse meanings cannot be included in the term 'information' when used in the context of artificial intelligence; here, 'information' has to be reduced to its quantitative aspect, the physical aspect, like in the case of the transmission of electrical energy. In other words, it is bound to be a metrical theory of information; if there are *n* messages to select from and if each message is on a par with every other in that it is as likely to be chosen as any other, then the *n* number of messages will constitute the amount of information available. This view of 'information' is very essential for constructing artificial intelligence and thinking computers.

Discussing Jakobson's communication model, Sebeok (1963) maintains:

> ...of the six communicative functions, two—the emotive and the phatic—certainly occur in subhuman species as well; two others—the cognitive and the conative...probably occur; but the remaining two—the poetic and the metalingual—seem to be exclusively human.

Whether the emotive and poetic functions can be reduced to a quantitative and physical level without distorting the concept of 'information' is the crucial question in the area of 'artificial intelligence'.

III. The approach to language processing and communication (i.e., 'information') management is, at one level, more or less like standardized *approaches to games*, though it is more complicated at another level.

There are many methods for playing games. Broadly, they fall into six classes:

i) *Algorithm:* This is a programme in which every step is precisely described and which leads to a specified goal. It is even possible to guarantee a winning game.
ii) *Exhaustion:* In simple games, one can consider all the possibilities arising out of every move and all the resulting conse-

quences. A computer enables one to extend this procedure to more complex games but it breaks down for games such as draughts (checkers) or chess. The number of possibilities before *each move* swells to a million and such an exploration is beyond the memory capacities of most modern computers.

iii) *Dictionary:* It is, however, possible to reduce this number by using the experience gained in past games so that a few of the most plausible alternatives could be considered. For example, chess players 'learn' many standard openings and end games, and apply this in given situations regardless of how that situation has been reached.

iv) *Rote learning:* If a game is lost, the losing moves are eliminated by working backwards and the information is stored. There is also a *positive rote learning* method wherein information about games won is stored in regard to good plays, as well as a *negative rote learning* method wherein all possible 'plays' at each position are stored with provision for random selection; the computer 'learns' to make winning moves. The NOPE (nim one-pile educator) programme, for example, is a 'fast learner' and never makes the same mistake twice.

v) *Known principle:* By applying the theory of probability, probabilities are calculated on the basis of 'long runs'; fairly accurate predictions can be made, but certainty cannot be guaranteed.

vi) *Minimax:* This procedure is based on finding the optimum direction in which to proceed by setting up intermediate goals or look-ahead objectives.

A.L. Samuel programmed a computer that plays an excellent game of checkers; his computer looks ahead a few moves by evaluating the resulting positions and 'learns' something after each move. It is trained to defeat some of the foremost players in the USA and is considered a landmark in the construction of synthetic intelligence. The 'grandmaster' achievement is still beyond imagination. However, these chess-playing-machines are only a step towards what is called the General Problem Solver (GPS); GPS is a heuristic way for programming computers to solve a wide variety of problems like pattern recognition, various kinds of learning (by trial and error, by generalization, by rote), automatic problem solving, theorem proving, linguistic skills, 'conversational' programming language, etc.

As an illustration of problem solving, consider, for instance, a travelling salesperson's problem, i.e., the linking together of a number of towns and cities by as short a route as possible. A Graph Traverser Programme, based on a simple search algorithm, first estimates the distance of a given state from the objective and then selects an operator that transforms the state into a procedure.

The idea of a machine which acts intelligently should ultimately lead us to a machine that will perform a number of tasks and solve a number of problems and not just one problem alone like playing a game of chess. It is true that a computer can store 'information' much more quickly and accurately and it can 'erase' from its memory any useless or damaging information; human beings cannot voluntarily forget information stored in long-term memory. But the human brain is capable of performing several tasks because the brain has specialized centres dealing with various inputs and tasks; it is not clear how the brain controls the sequences of parallel operations. The brain has a built-in redundancy such that a failure of many neurons will not disrupt its normal operation; it can reduce the effects of a 'local failure' by reorganizing its connections. Above all, it has built-in goals, e.g., hunger, avoidance of pain, etc. as a result of the evolutionary process. In other words, the brain is a multi-dimensional machine, a mobile automata.

Attempts are being made, in addition to constructing playing machines, to construct 'reading machines' with the help of computer eyes so that they can, at least, recognize patterns; the concept of 'emotional' machines is still in its infancy. Work is continuing in a number of universities in the USA and Japan in robot technology—a mobile automata that can perform complex functions like feeling the environment in order to 'navigate' in and manipulate it.

IV. A detailed study of natural language processing that involves a highly complicated code can go a long way in the construction of mobile automata. Garvin (1963) says:

> Linguistic analysis is not deterministic in the practical sense; there are no known algorithms which will guarantee success

> in linguistic analysis, and the complete exploitation of every possible combinatory criterion might involve an equally astronomical number of steps as the number of moves to be explored.

For instance, 'Life is but a walking shadow' has a combination of 23 letters using the 26 letters of the English alphabet; if we ask a computer to produce $(26)^{23}$, the combination given above from Shakespeare's *Macbeth* will be found in the deep debris of the possible combinations; including several thousand nonsensical combinations. A 'scanning or filtering' device will have to be 'intelligent', and as creative as Shakespeare, in order to 'recognize' this particular combination. If this is the state for one line of poetry, writing a poem, a play, a book on philosophy or politics is a formidable task.

As Garvin (1963) says,

> The program must ideally be capable of doing two things: it must first recognize an individual content element in the natural language text (a single word or a relevant combination of words); second, it must be able to decide on some comparability criterion, for each of the content elements it has formed.

The logical relationships that are explicit and implicit in a body of text are to be explicitly captured.

V. Despite the great challenges, a lot of good work has been done in the area of language-processing.

Science Today 2001, January 1989 reports that India too has active groups in Machine Translation. The research group in Tamil University, Tanjavur (Tamil Nadu) has attempted Russian to Tamil translation at the sentence level. The National Centre for Software Technology (NCST), Bombay, has started work on English to Hindi translation. The IIT (Indian Institute of Technology) Kanpur group is trying to apply Sanskrit *vyakarna* and artificial intelligence to modern Indian languages. In the organization of the lexicon, for example, there have been many successful efforts. The following are a few schemes that are effectively used:

i) *Sequential organization:* The simplest way to organize is to store the entries in consecutive blocks. Here inserting a new entry can be done very efficiently but searching is not so easy. One will have to examine all the elements (potentially) before one can come up with an answer.

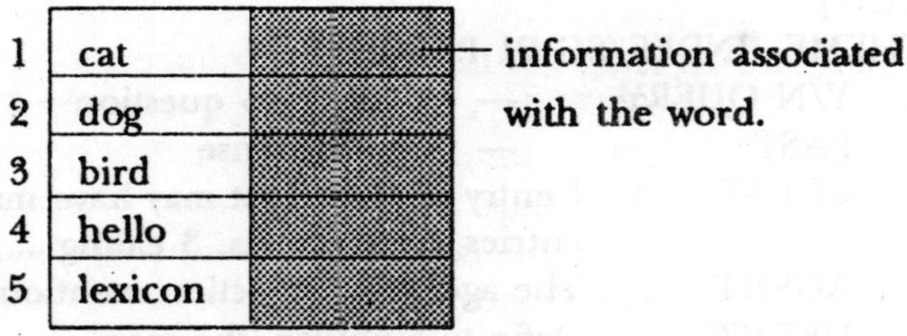

ii) *Sorted organization:* This is lexicographically organized data. Here search becomes extremely fast, though insertions is a time-consuming process. To make space for the new entry one may end up moving a lot of entries (potentially all of them) down the memory.

iii) *Trees:* Organizing the data in trees makes it easier to insert a new item. The organization is in terms of 'binary search' trees. The trees may become grossly unbalanced for all the leaf nodes may not be at the same distance from the roots. An 'unbalanced' tree is not very efficient to search. One will have to do periodic 're-balancing'.

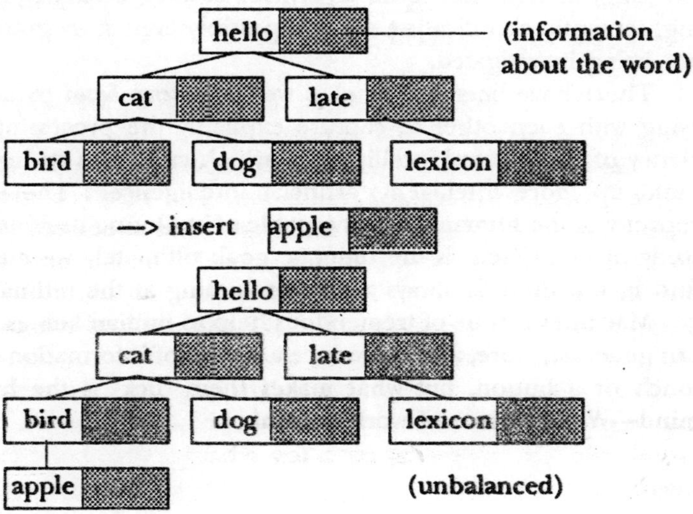

The representation of a Yes/No question is given below, as a sample (a simplified version):

Yes/No question: *Did the man eat a peach?*
(Y/N QUERY (PAST e1 EAT [AGENT (DEF/SGml MAN)]
[THEME (INDEF/SG P1 PEACH)]

Notes:

Y/N QUERY	—	Yes/No question
PAST	—	Past tense
el EAT	-	I entry of 'eat'. [eat may have many entries 1 eat; 2 eats, 3 eating.....]
AGENT	-	The agent of the action mentioned.
DEF/SG	-	Definite Singular 'the man'
ml MAN	-	I entry of 'man'.
THEME	-	The theme of the sentence.
INDEF/SG	-	indefinite singular 'a peach'
Pl PEACH	-	I Entry of 'peach'.

It is really a remarkable feat that the human intelligence is doing—managing with all these complicated systems efficiently in communications. (All examples from *Natural Language Processing for Linguists*, 1990).

In *Computational linguistics* such areas as automatic syntactic analysis, sentence generation, grammar testing, automatic abstracting, information retrieval, stylistic studies, content processing, semantic classification studies, possibly even story grammars are being investigated.

There have been *text based* as well as *schema based* paradigms vying with each other to capture explicitly the processing efficiency of the 'natural intelligences' which can go as an input to build up more intelligent 'artificial intelligences'. The innate capacity of the human mind is capable of exploring itself and the study of one's 'self' is the ultimate goal; ultimately we may not find it, but there is always a thrill in aiming at the ultimate.

Machines can be of tremendous help to human beings. They can generate, store, and reproduce a variety of information at the touch of a button, but what makes them 'tick' is the human mind—What a piece of work is man!

Questions and topics for discussion

1. We often talk about I.Q. What is I.Q.?
   In what way is it related to language?
2. Can we differentiate among 'information', 'knowledge' and 'wisdom'? Can 'wisdom' become part of 'artificial intelligence'? Explain your answer.
3. It has been said that intelligence is not one 'monolithic block'. What are the various components of what is called intelligence? Try to collect as many definitions of intelligence as possible.

28 YET MANY MORE ...

'The more you know, the less you think you know.'

Focal points

I. At a scientific meeting in Paris in April 1961, Dr. Paul Broca stated that we speak with the left hemisphere. Since then, the extensive work done in the area of *neurolinguistics* shows that for most normal right-handed people the left side of the brain is the language side.

Generally, the nervous system is symmetrical; what exists on the left exists on the right. But the two sides of the brain are asymmetrical; as the child develops, the two sides of the brain become specialised for different functions; one-sidedness or *lateralization* takes place. At the same time, the two cerebral hemispheres are connected by a membrane called corpus callusum; this 'freeway' between the two halves consists of millions of nerve fibres connecting the cells of the left and right hemispheres. The asymmetry of the human brain is one of the unique characteristics of human beings; there is division of labour built in.

Dr. Penfield, the well-known neuro-surgeon, says in *Speech and Brain Mechanisms* (1959):

> The brain of the dog resembles the human brain in general organization. The brain of the chimpanzee is even more like ours. All the lobes are present. The pathways of muscular

> control are similar. Chimpanzee and dog have larger areas of cerebral cortex, like our own, used for seeing, hearing, feeling. They have even larger areas for smelling. More than that, animals have in their brains a mysterious store of useful instincts that I like to consider racial memories. These racial memories guide them at crucial times in life—teach them how to build a home and what to hunt. Man's brain is curiously lacking in these patterns of instinctive guidance for his behaviour. But to balance all that man has the ability to learn... The infant possesses a speech mechanism... The brain of man is not so very different from that of a dog or monkey in outward form, but there is within it an altered organization that makes speech possible. Thanks to this endowment, man can communicate...

During normal speech, two mechanisms are employed and both are present only in the human brain. There is an *ideational mechanism* and a *motor mechanism;* these are located in the left hemisphere. In the ideational speech mechanism there are four sets of neuron patterns—the sound units of words employed when listening to speech, the verbal units followed for speaking, the visual units for reading and the manual units for writing. According to Dr. Penfield 'articulation depends upon the employment of *special* motor areas in the cortex.' When listening to speech a connection is established between the sound units employed and the verbal units; with the help of the special motor mechanism we speak and reply. In the beginning, this involves conscious selection and decision, but in time it becomes automatic. Similarly, writing is controlled by the motor mechanism in the cortex. This motor mechanism is quite separate from the primary motor mechanism. When a dog barks, the primary motor mechanism is employed. Human beings alone can talk about barking.

Accidents, disease, and surgical operations provide a great deal of information about the specific functions of different areas of the cortex. Dr. Penfield and his associates stimulated different parts of the cortex of patients who required brain surgery and 'mapped' the parts. A study of language disorders called *aphasia* shows that there are different kinds of aphasia; some patients can speak perfectly well but cannot understand what is said to them;

some find it difficult to find the right word or grammatical patterns; some aphasiacs substitute words in the same semantic class. 'Split-brain' patients provide some useful evidence. If the right hemisphere is removed, language remains intact; but, if the left hemisphere is removed, language ability is removed.

Any attempt towards constructing 'talking machines' and 'thinking machines' must study human language carefully. Although acoustic theory and electronic technology are very advanced, we have a long way to go in overcoming the 'machine quality' in speech production; but attempts towards artificial intelligence construction reveal a lot about the properties of natural language and its use and our understanding of the complexities of language and its use, in turn, will help us to construct 'thinking machines'. As an ancient epigram says: 'Though many a thing is unfathomable for mankind, nothing looms more ineffable than the mind of man' (and woman too!). Some day we might stumble on something that might reveal to us the secrets of the human brain's wisdom.

II. Effective communication does not depend only on the use of verbal signals; between expression and impression, there is a lot of suppression, and, often, we read between the lines. We also communicate through the way we speak, through facial expressions, through laughter (which is also peculiarly human), between speech events, through the distance that is maintained between a speaker and hearer. We use gestures—winking, blinking, looks, movement of the hands. *Kinesics,* the study of the visual aspects of non-verbal interpersonal communication, also called the 'body language', and *proxemics,* the study of the ways in which space is handled in human communication, are interesting areas in communicology.

Lastly, it must be said that occasional flashes of silence 'speak'; silence communicates. As Oscar Wilde points out one must know the precise psychological moment when to say nothing.

'There is a time of speaking and a
time of being still.'

— William Caxton (1485)

Suggested reading

(Language and Sex)

Showalter, Elaine. (ed.). 1982. *The New Feminist Criticism: Essays on Women, Literature, and Theory*. New York: Pantheon.

This work presents a short history of feminist literary criticism. The essays are divided into three sections: 'What do Feminist Critics Want? The Academy and the Canon', 'Feminist Criticisms and Women's Cultures' and 'Women's Writing and Feminist Critical Theories'. The volume also contains an extremely helpful 21-page bibliography,

Smith, P.M. 1985. *Language, the Sexes and Society*. Oxford: Basil Blackwell.

This is a highly readable book bringing in the issues of language and sex into a single social psychological framework.

(Language and Machine)

de Beaugrande, R. 1981. 'Linguistic Theory and Metatheory for a Science of Texts'. *TEXT*, 1(2) : 113-61.

An abstract but important paper. It discusses the important aspects of a computer grammar. The discussion on systems models, process models, procedural models and simulation models of linguistic description is important for an understanding of the nature of computer grammars.

Schank, R. and R. Abelson. 1977. *Scripts, Plans, Goals and Understanding*. Hillsdale, N.J. : Erlbaum.

A very influential book in the area of artificial intelligence. The discussion is on the representation of knowledge in the processing of narratives.

(Neurolinguistics)

Newmeyer, Frederick J. 1988C. *Linguistics : The Cambridge Survey - Vol.III. Language : Psychological and Biological Aspects*. Cambridge : Cambridge University Press.

This book has papers on both the psychological and neurological aspects of language. Apart from the paper, 'Neurolinguistics : An Overview of Language-brain Relations in Aphasia,' there are papers on the biological basis for language and speech-language pathology, too.

Penfield, W., and L. Roberts. 1959. *Speech and Brain Mechanism*. Princeton : Princeton Univeristy Press.

This is a good introduction to neurolinguistics.

REFERENCES

Abate, Frank R. 1985. 'Dictionaries Past and Future : Issues and Prospects.' *Dictionaries : Journal of the Dictionary Society of North America*, 7, 1985 : 270-83

Abrams, M.H. 1972. 'What's the Use of Theorizing About the Art?' In M.W. Bloomfield (ed.). 1972. *The Search of Literary Theory*. Ithaca and London; Cornell University Press.

Advances in Lexicology : Second Annual Conference of the U.W. Centre for the New Oxford English Dictionary. Proceedings of the Conference, Nov 9-11, 1986. Canada : University of Waterloo, 1986.

Aggarwal, J.C. 1984. *Landmarks in the History of Modern Indian Education.* Delhi : Vikas.

Aggarwal, J.C., and Sarita Aggarwal. 1990. *Education in India (A Comparative Study of States and Union Territories)*. New Delhi : Concept Publishing Co.

Allen, J.P.B., and S. Pit Corder (eds.). 1973. *The Edinburgh Course in Applied Linguistics. Volume 1. Readings for Applied Linguistics.* London : OUP.

Allen, J.P.B., and S. Pit Corder (eds.). 1974. *The Edinburgh Course in Applied linguistics.* Volume 3. *Techniques in Applied Linguistics.* London : OUP.

Allen, J.P.B., and S. Pit Corder (eds.). 1975. *The Edinburgh Course in Applied Linguistics. Volume 2. Papers in Applied Linguistics.* London : OUP.

Allen, J.P.B., and A. Davies.(eds.). 1977. *The Edinburgh Course in Applied Linguistics. Volume 4. Testing and Experimental Methods.* London : OUP.

Anderson, R.C., R.E. Reynolds, D.L.Schallert, and E.T. Goetz. 1977 'Frameworks for Comprehending Discourse.' *American Educational Research Journal*, 14(4) : 367-381.

Asher, James. 1982. *Learning Another Language through Actions : The Complete Teacher's guidebook.* 2nd ed. Los Gatos, Calif. : Sky Oaks.

Atkins, G. Douglas, and M.L. Johnson. (eds.). 1985. *Writing and Reading Differently. Deconstruction and the Teaching of Composition and Literature.* University Press of Kansas.

Austin, J.J.L. 1962. *How to Do Things With Words.* Oxford : Clarendon Press.

Bailey, Richard W. (ed.). 1987. *Dictionaries of English : Prospects for the Record of Our Language.* Ann Arbor, Michigan : The University of Michigan Press.

Bal, Miekie 1985. *Narratology : Introduction to the Theory of Narrative.* Trans. Christine van Boheemen. Toronto : University of Toronto Press.

Barthalomew, Doris A., and Louise C. Schoenhels. 1983. *Bilingual Dictionaries for Indigenous Languages.* Mexico : Summer Institute of Linguistics.

Barthes, Roland. 1966. In English 1977. 'Introduction to the Structural Analysis of Narratives.' In *Image - Music Text.* London : Fontana.

—— 1970. In English 1974. *S/Z.* New York : Hill and Wang.

—— 1971. 'From Work to Text.' In *Image - Music Text.* trans. S. Heath. 1977. London : Fontana.

—— In French 1966. *Critique et vérité.* Trans. Kartine Pilcher Keuneman. (ed.). 1987. *Criticism and Truth.* Minneapolis : University of Minnesota Press.

Bassnett-McGuire, Susan. 1980. *Translation Studies.* London : Methuen.

de Beaugrande, R. 1980. *Text, Discourse and Process : Toward a Multidisciplinary Science of Texts.* Norwood : Ablex.

—— 1981. 'Linguistic Theory and Metatheory for a Science of Texts.' *Text,* 1(2) : 113-61.

—— 1982. 'The Story of Grammars and the Grammar of Stories.' *Journal of Pragmatics,* 6 : 383-422.

—— and W. Dressler. 1981. 2nd Imp. 1983. *Introduction to Text Linguistics.* London : Longman.

Bell, R. 1976. *Sociolinguistics : Goals, Approaches and Problems.* London : Batsford.

Bernstein, Basil. 1958. 'Some Sociological Determinants of Perception.' *British Journal of Sociology.* 9 : 159-74.

—— 1959. 'A Public Language : Some Sociological Implications of a Linguistic Form.' *British Journal of Sociology,* 10 : 311-26.

—— 1971. *Class, Codes and Control, Vol.1: Theoretical Studies towards a Sociology of Language.* London : Routledge and Kegan Paul.

Blakemore, D.L. 1988. 'The Organization of Discourse.' In F.J. Newmeyer. (ed.). 1988.d.

Bloom, H., P.de Man, J. Derrida, G. Hartman, and J. Hillis Miller (eds.). 1979. *Deconstruction and Criticism.* New York : Continuum.

Bolinger, D. 1975. *Aspects of Language.* 2nd ed. New York : Harcourt Brace Jovanovich.

Booth, Wayne C. 1961. 'Distance and Point of View.' *Essays in Criticism,* 11 : 60-79.

—— 1963. *The Rhetoric of Fiction.* 2nd ed. Chicago : University of Chicago Press.

Brower, Reuben (ed.). 1959. *On Translation.* Cambridge, Mass.: Harvard University Press.

Brown, G., and G. Yule. 1983. *Discourse Analysis.* Cambridge : Cambridge University Press.

Brown, R. 1958. 'How shall a thing be called?' *Psychological Review,* 65 : 14-21.

Brown, R., and C. Hanlon. 1970. 'Derivational Complexity and Order of Acquisition in Child Speech.' In J.R. Hayes (ed.). *Cognition and the Development of Language*. New York : John Wiley and Sons.

Brumfit, C.J. 1980. 'From Defining to Designing : Communicative Specifications versus Communicative Methodology in Foreign Language Teaching.' In Muller 1980.

—— and K. Johnson (eds.). 1979. *The Communicative Approach to Language Teaching*. Oxford : OUP.

Bullock Report. 1975. *A Language for Life*. Report of a Committee of Inquiry appointed by the Secretary of State for Education and Science under the Chairmanship of Lord Bullock. London : H.M. S.O.

Candlin, C.N. 1976. 'Communicative Language Teaching and the Debt to Pragmatics.' In C. Ramesh (ed.). *Georgetown University Round Table 1976*. Washington, D.C. : Georgetown University Press.

Carrell, P.L. 1988. 'Introduction : Interactive Approaches to Second Language Reading.' In Carrell et al. (eds.). 1988.

——, Joanne Devine, and David Eskey (eds.). 1988. *Interactive Approaches to Second Language Reading*. Cambridge : Cambridge University Press.

—— and J.C. Eisterhold. 1983/1988. 'Schema Theory and ESL Reading Pedagogy.' In Carrell et al. (eds.). 1988.

Catford, J.C. 1965. *A Linguistic Theory of Transltion : An Essay in Applied Linguistics*. London : OUP.

Cazden, C., V. John, and D. Hymes. (eds.). 1972. *Functions of Language in the Classroom*. Columbia : Teachers' College Press.

Chatman, Seymour. 1978. *Story and Discourse*. Ithaca, New York : Cornell University Press.

Chomsky, N. 1957. *Syntactic Structures*. The Hague : Mouton.

—— 1968. *Language and Mind*. New York: Harcourt Brace Jovanovich.

—— 1980. *Rules and Representations*. Oxford: Blackwell.

—— 1981. *Lectures in Government and Binding*. Dordrecht: Foris

Christie, F. et al. 1984. *Children's Writing: Reader*. Victoria: Deakin University Press.

Clark, H.H., and E.V.Clark. 1977. *Psychology and Language*. New York: Harcourt Brace Jovanovich, Inc.

Cobarrubias, Juan, and Joshua A.Fishman. (eds.). 1983. *Progress in Language Planning: International Perspectives*. Berlin/New York/Amsterdam: Mouton.

Cole, P., and J.Morgan (eds.). 1975. *Syntax and Semantics III: Speech Acts*. New York : Academic Press.

Corder, S.P. 1967. 'The Significance of Learners' Errors.' *IRAL*, 5 : 161-70; also in Richards (ed.) 1974.

—— 1971.' Idiosyncratic Dialects and Error Analysis.' *IRAL* 9 : 147-59.

—— *Introducing Applied Linguistics.* London : Penguin.

—— "Problems and Solutions in Applied Linguistics.' In Qvistgaard et al. (eds.) 1974.

Courtney, A.E., and T.W. Whipple, 1974. 'Women in TV Commercials.' *Journal of Communication,* 24 : 110-17.

Culler, Jonathan. 1975. *Structuralist Poetics.* London : Routledge and Kegan Paul.

—— 1975a. 'Defining Narrative Units.' In R.Fowler (ed.). 1975.

Derrida, J. 1967. In English 1977. *Of Grammatology.* Trans. Gayatri Chakravorty Spivak. Baltimore : Johns Hopkins University Press.

—— 1974. [French] *Glas.* Paris : Galilee. Cited in Norris, 1982.

—— 1979. 'Living On'. In H.Bloom et al.(eds.). 1979.

—— 1981. In French 1972. *Positions.* Trans. Alan Bass. London : Athlone Press.

Devine, J. 1988.'The Relationship between General Language Competence and Second Language Reading Proficiency : Implications for Teaching.' In P.L.Carrell et al. (eds.). 1988.

van Dijk, Marcel. 1983. *Better Translation for Better Communication.* A survey of the translation market, present and future, prepared for the Commission of the European Communities, Directorate-General Information Market and Innovation. Oxford, etc. : Pergamon.

van Dijk, T. 1977. *Text and Context.* London : Longman.

Dodson, C.J. 1967. *Language Teaching and the Bilingual Method.* London : Pitman.

Dornic, S. (ed.). 1977. *Attention and Performance-VI.* Hillsdale, N.J. : Erlbaum.

Eakins, B., and G. Eakins, 1976. 'Verbal Turn-taking and Exchanges in Faculty Dialogue.' In B.L.Dubois, and I.Crouch (eds.) *The Sociology of the Languages of American Women.* San Antonio, Texas : Trinity University Press.

—— 1978. *Sex Differences in Human Communication.* Boston : Houghton Hifflin.

Eco, Umberto. 1979. *The Role of the Reader.* Bloomington : Indiana University Press.

van Ek, J.A. 1975 *The Threshold Level in a European Unit/ Credit System for Moderr Language Learning by Adults.* Systems Development in Adult Language Learning. Strasbourg : Council of Europe.

—— and L.G.Alexander. 1975. *Threshold Level English.* Oxford : Pergamon.

Enkvist, N.E. 1973. *Linguistic Stylistics.* The Hague-Paris : Mouton.

Ferguson, C.A. 1959. 'Diglossia'. *Word* 15 : 325-40.

Fine, Jonathan (ed.). 1988. *Second Language Discourse : A Textbook of Current Research.* Vol.XXV in the series Advances in Discourse Process. Norwood : Ablex.

Finocchiaro, M., and C.Brumfit. 1983. *The Functional-Notional Approach : From Theory to Practice.* New York : Oxford University Press.

Fish, Stanley. 1980. *Is There a Text in This Class? : The Authority of Interpretive Communities.* Cambridge, Mass : Harvard University Press.

Fishman, J.A. 1972. 'Domains and the Relationship between Micro and Macrosociolinguistics.' In Gumperz and Hymes 1972.

Fodor, J.A. 1969. 'Current Approaches to Syntax Recognition.' *Perception of Language.* A symposium of the Learning Research and Development Centre, University of Pittsburgh.

Fowler, Roger (ed.). 1966. *Essays on Style and Language.* Routledge and Kegan Paul.

—— 'Style and the Concept of Deep Structure.' *Journal of Literary Semantics,* 1.

—— 1975. *Style and Structure in Literature.* Oxford : Blackwell.

Freeman, Donald C. (ed.). 1970. *Linguistics and Literary Style.* New York : Holt, Rinehart and Winston, Inc.

Garvin, Paul L. 1963. 'A Linguist's View of Language-data Processing.' In Paul L.Gravin. (ed.). 1963.

—— (ed.). 1963. *Natural Language and the Computer.* New York : McGraw-Hill, Inc.

—— 1973. 'Discussion Paper. Lexicon and Grammar : Theory and Practice.' In R.I.McDavid, Jr., and A.R.Duckert. (eds.). 1973.

Gass, S., and L.Selinker (eds.). 1983. *Language Transfer in Language Learning.* Rowley, Mass. : Newbury House.

Gattegno, Caleb. 1972. *Teaching Foreign Languages in Schools: The Silent Way.* 2nd ed. New York : Educational Solutions.

Genette, Gerard. 1972. In English 1980. *Narrative Discourse.* Ithaca, N.Y. : Cornell University Press.

Gershuny, H.L. 1977. 'Sexism in the Language of Literature.' In A.P.Nilsen, H.Bosmajian, H.L.Gershuny and J.P.Stanley (eds.). *Sexism and Language.* Urbana, Illinois : National Council of Teachers of English.

Giglioli, P.P. (ed.). 1972. *Language and Social Context.* Penguin.

Gimson, A.C. 1973. 'Phonology and the Lexicographer.' In R.I.McDavid, Jr., and A.R.Duckert (eds.). 1973.

Gleason, H.A., Jr. 1973. 'Grammatical Prerequisites.' In R.I. McDavid, Jr., and A.R. Duckert (eds.). 1973.

Goffman, E. 1957. 'Alienation from Interaction.' *Human Relations,* 19 : 47-60.

—— 1976. 'Gender Advertisements.' *Studies in the Anthropology of Visual Communication,* 4 : 65-154.

—— 1977. 'The Arrangement between the Sexes.' *Theory and Society,* 4 : 301-31.

Goodenough, W.H. 1957. 'Cultural Anthropology and Linguistics.' In

P.L. Gargvin (ed.). *Report of the 7th Annual Round Table Meeting on Linguistics and Language Study.* Washington : Georgetown University Press.

Goodman, K.S. 1973. 'On the Psycholinguistic Method of Teaching Reading.' In F. Smith (ed.). 1973.

Greene, Judith. 1972. *Psycholinguistics.* Penguin.

Grice, H.P. 1967. *Logic and Conversation : The William James Lectures.* Cambridge, M.A. : Harvard University Press.

—— 1975. 'Logic and Conversation.' In Cole and Morgan (eds.). 1975.

Grognet, Allene, and Joann Crandall. 1982. 'competency-based Curricula in Adult ESL.' *ERIC/CLL News Bulletin,* 6.1.

Gumperz, J.J. 1964. 'Hindi-Punjabi Code-Switching.' *Proceedings of the Ninth International Congress of Linguistics.* Mouton & Co.

—— 1982. *Language and Social Identity.* Cambridge : Cambridge University Press.

—— and D.H. Hymes. (eds.). 1972. *Directions in Sociolinguistcs: The Ethnography of Communication.* Ney York : Holt, Rinehart and Winston.

Hall, E.T. 1959, *The Silent Language.* Greenwich : Fawcett.

Halliday, M.A.K. 1961. 'Categories of the Theory of Grammar.' *Word,* 17 : 24-92.

—— 1966. 'Descriptive Linguistics in Literary Studies.' In M.A.K. Halliday and Angus McIntosh, *Patterns of Language, Papers in General, Descriptive and Applied Linguistics.* Longmans.

—— 1973. *Explorations in the Functions of Language.* London : Edward Arnold.

—— 1974. *Language and Social Man.* London : Longman.

—— 1978. *Language as a Social Semiotic : The Social Interpretation of Language and Meaning.* London : Edward Arnold.

—— 1982. 'Linguistics in Teacher Education.' In R. Carter (ed.). *Linguistics and the Teacher.* London : Routledge and Kegan Paul.

—— A. McIntosh, and P. Strevens. 1964. *The Linguistic Sciences and Language Teaching.* London : Longman.

Harris, Z.S. 1952. 'Discourse Analysis.' *Language,* 28:1-30 and 474-94.

Hartman, Geoffrey H. 1985. 'Understanding Criticism'. In Atkins and Johnson (eds.). 1985.

Hartmann, Reinhard R.K. (ed.). 1983. *Lexicography : Principles and Practice.* London : Academic Press.

Haugen, E. 1966. 'Dialect, Language and Nation.' In J.B. Pride and J. Holmes (eds.). 1972.

—— 1969. 'Language Planning, Theory and Practice.' Reprinted in A.Dil (ed.). *The Sociology of Language.* Stanford : Stanford University.

Henner-Stanchina, C., and P. Riley. 1978. 'Aspects of Autonomous Learning.' In *ELT Documents 103 : Individualization in Language Learning.* London : British Concil.

Holmes, J. (ed.). 1970. *The Nature of Translation.* The Hague : Mouton.

Howatt, A.P.R. 1984. *A History of English Language Teaching.* Oxford : OUP.

Howitt, D. 1982. *The Mass Media and Social Problems.* Oxford : Pergamon Press.

Hudson, R.A. 1980. *Sociolinguistics.* Cambridge : Cambridge University Press.

Hymes, D. 1966/72. 'On Communicative Competence.' Paper originally read at Research Planning Conference on Language Development among Disadvantaged Children, Yeshiva University, June 1966. Reprinted in part, in Pride and Holmes (eds.). 1972.

—— 1971. 'Competence and Performance in Linguistic Theory.' In R. Huxley and E. Ingram (eds.). *Language Acquisition : Models and Methods.* London : Academic Press.

—— 1973. 'On the Origins and Foundations of Inequality among Speakers.' *Language as a Human Problem.* Special issue of *Daedalus* 102(3) : 59-85.

—— 1977. *Foundations in Sociolinguistics.* London : Tavistock Publications Ltd.

Ingram, D.E. 1980. 'Applied Linguistics : A Search for Insight.' In R.B.Kaplan (ed.). 1980.

Iser, Wolfgang. 1974. *The Implied Reader : Patterns of Communication in Prose Fiction from Bunyan to Beckett.* Baltimore : Johns Hopkins University Press.

—— 1978. *The Act of Reading : A Theory of Aesthetic Response. Baltimore : Johns Hopkins University Press.*

Jackson, L.A. 1968. *Life in Classrooms.* New York : Holt, Rinehart and Winston.

Jakobson, Roman. 1959. 'On Linguistic Aspects of Translation.' In R. Brower (ed.). 1959.

—— and Jurij Tynjanov. 1928. 'Problemy izucenija literatury i jazyka' cited in T.G. Winner 1973. 'The Aesthetics and Poetics of the Prague Linguistic Circle.' *Poetics,* 8 : 77-96.

Johnson-Laird. 1983. *Mental Models.* Cambridge : Cambridge University Press.

Journal of Pragmatics, 6 : 1982. North-Holland.

Jupp, T.C., and S. Hodlin. 1975. *Industrial English : An Example of Theory and Practice in Functional Language Teaching.* London : Heinemann.

Kachru, Braj B. 1976. 'Models of English for the Third World: White Man's Linguistic Burden or Language Pragmatics?' *TESOL Quarterly,* 10,2 : 221-39.

Kaplan, R.B. 1978. 'Introduction'. In Kaplan, R.B. (ed.). 1980.

—— (ed.). 1980. *On the Scope of Applied Linguistics.* Rowley, Mass. : Newbury House, Inc.

Kelly, L.G. 1969. *25 Centuries of Language Teaching.* Rowley, Mass.: Newbury House.

Klima, E.S., and U. Bellugi. 1966. 'Syntactic Regularities in the Speech of Children.' In J. Lyons,. and R.J. Wales (eds.). *Psycholinguistics Papers.* Edinburgh : Edinburgh University Press.

Kluyev, Boris I. 1981. *India : National and Language Problem.* New Delhi/ Jullundur/Bangalore : Sterling.

Knapp, Karlfried, Werner Enninger, and Annelie Knapp-Pothhoff (eds.). 1987. *Analysing Intercultural Communication.* Berlin/New York/Amsterdam : Walter de Gruyter.

Krashen, S.D. 1981. *Second Language Acquisition and Second Language Learning.* Oxford, etc.: Pergamon.

—— 1983. "Newmarks' 'Ignorance Hypothesis' and Current Second Language Acquisition Theory." In S. Gass and L. Selinker (eds.). 1983.

—— and Tracy Terrell. 1983. *The Natural Approach : Language Acquisition in the Classroom.* Hayward, Calif.: The Alemany Press.

Krishnaswamy, N. 1983 'Understanding Values, TEIL, and the Third World.' In *Readings in English as an International Language.* Oxford : Pergamon Press. 1983.

—— 1984. 'Making Grammar Communicative.' In *Perspectives on Language Teaching.* Madras : Macmillan. 1985.

—— 1987. 'A Note on Literary Competence'. In *Critical Essays.* Madras : Macmillan. 1987.

—— 1988. 'The—ing trap', In *New Directions in English Language Teaching.* Jaipur: Point Publishers.

Kramarae, C. 1981. *Women and Men Speaking : Frameworks for Analysis.* Rowley, Mass.: Newbury House.

Labov, W. 1969/1972. 'The Logic of Non-standard English.' Extract in P.P. Giglioli (ed.). 1972.

—— 1972. *Sociolinguistic Patterns.* Philadelphia : University of Pennsylvania Press.

Lado, R. 1957. *Linguistics Across Cultures : Applied Linguistics for Language Teachers.* Ann Arbor : University of Michigan Press.

Lakoff, R. 1975. *Language and Woman's Place.* New York : Harper and Row.

Lawton, D. 1968. *Social Class, Language and Education.* London : Routledge and Kegan Paul.

—— 1981. *An Introduction to Teaching and Learning.* London : Hodder and Stoughton.

Leech, Geoffrey. N. 1965. "'This bread I break'—Language and Interpretation." *A Review of English Literature,* Vol.6, No.2, Reprinted in Donald C. Freeman (ed.). 1970.

—— 1969. *A Linguistic Guide to English Potery.* London : Longman.

—— 1983. *Principles of Pragmatics*. London: Longman.

Le Page, R.B. 1968. 'Problems of Description in Multilingual Communities.' *Transactions of the Philological Society*.

Levin, S.R. 1964. *Linguistic Structures in Poetry*. The Hague: Mouton.

Lozanov, Georgi. 1978. *Outlines of Suggestology and Suggestopedy*. London : Gordon and Breach.

Lyons, J. 1970. *New Horizons in Linguistics*. Harmondsworth : Penguin.

Mackey, W.F. 1965. *Language Teaching Analysis*. London : Longman.

de Man, P. 1979. 'Shelley Disfigured.' In Bloom et al. (eds.). 1979.

—— 1979a. *Allegories of Reading: Figural Language in Rousseau, Nietzsche, Rilke, and Proust*. New Haven, Conn.: Yale University Press.

Maracek, J., J.A. Piliavin, E. Fitzgimmons, E.C. Krogh, E. Leader, and B. Trudgill. 1978. 'Women, as TV Experts : The Voice of Authority?' *Journal of Communication*, 28 : 159-68.

McDavid, Raven I., Jr., and Audrey R. Duckert. (eds.). 1973. *Lexicography in English*. Annals of the New York Academy of Sciences, 211. New York: New York Academy of Sciences.

Milroy, Lesley. 1980. *Language and Social Networks*. Baltimore : University Park Press.

Muller, K.E. (ed.). 1980. *The Foreign Language Syllabus and Communicative Approaches to Teaching : Proceedings of a European-American Seminar*. Special issue of *Studies in Second Language Acquisition*, 3/1.

Natural Language Processing for Linguists. Course Notes for Intensive Course. 2-12 July1990. 2 volumes. Kanpur, India : IIT.

Nehru, Jawaharlal. *Selected works of Jawaharlal Nehru - 14 Volumes*. (ed.). S. Gopal. 1972-81. A Project of the Jawaharlal Nehru Memorial Fund, New Delhi : Orient Longman.

—— *Selected Works of Jawaharlal Nehru - II Series - 8 Volumes*. (ed.). S. Gopal 1984-89. New Delhi : Jawaharlal Nehru Memorial Fund.

Nemser, W. 1971. 'Approximative Systems of Foreign Language Learners.' *IRAL* 9 : 114-24

Newmark, P. 1981. *Approaches to Translation*. Oxford : Pergamon Press.

Newmeyer, Frederic J. (ed.). 1988c. *Linguistics : The Cambridge Survey Vol.III. Language : Psychological and Biological Aspects*. Cambridge : Cambridge University Press.

—— 1988d. *Linguistics : The Cambridge Survey - Vol.IV : Language - The Sociocultural Context*. Cambridge : Cambridge University Press.

Nida, E. 1975. *Language Structure and Translation : Essays by Eugene A. Nida* (ed.). Anwar S. Dil. Stanford : Stanford University Press.

Nilsen, A.P. 1977. 'Sexism as Shown through the English Vocabulary.' In A.P. Nilsen, H. Bosmajian, H.L. Gershuny and J.P. Stanley (eds.). *Sexism and Language*. Urbana, Illinois : National Council of Teachers of English.

Norris, Christopher. 1982. *Deconstruction : Theory and Practics.* London : Methuen.

Ohmann, Richard M. 1966. 'Literature as Sentences.' In S. Chatman and S.R. Levin (eds.). 1967. *Essays on the Language of Literature.* Boston : The Houghton Mifflin Company.

Palmer, J.D. 1980. 'Toward a Redefinition of Applied Linguistics.' In Kaplan (ed.). 1980.

—— 1980. 'Linguistics in *Medias Res.*' In R.B. Kaplan (ed.). 1980.

Paradis, Michel (ed.). 1978. *Aspects of Bilingualism.* Columbia : Horbeam Press, Inc.

Penfield, W., and L. Roberts. 1959. *Speech and Brain Mechanism.* Princeton: Princeton University Press.

Piattelli-Palmarini, M. (ed.). 1980. *Language and Learning. The Debate between Jean Piaget and Noam Chomsky.* London : Routledge and Kegan Paul.

Popovic, Anton. 1976. *A Dictionary for the Analysis of Literary Translation.* Edmonton, Alberta : Department of Comparative Literature, University of Alberta.

Prabhu, N.S. 1983. 'Procedural Syllabuses.' Paper presented at the RELC Seminar, Singapore. Cited in Richards and Rodgers 1986.

—— and D. Carrol. 1980. 'Teaching English as Communication—Proposals for Syllabus Design, Methodology, Evaluation'. *Regional Institute of English (South India) Newsletter.* Special Series 1,4.

Pride, J.B. and J. Holmes (eds.). 1972. *Sociolinguistics.* Penguin.

Prince Gerald. 1982. *Narratology : The Form and Functioning of Narrative.* Berlin : Mouton.

—— 1987. *A Dictionary of Narratology.* Lincoln & London : University of Nebraska Press.

Propp, Vladimir. 1928/1968. *Morphology of the Folktale.* 2nd ed. Trans. Laurence Scott. Austin : University of Texas Press.

Qvistgaard, J. et al. (eds.). 1974. *Applied Linguistics. Problems and Solutions.* Heidelberg.

Richards, J.C. (ed.). 1974. *Error Analysis : Perspectives on Second Language Acquisition.* London : Longman.

—— and Theodore S. Rodgers 1986. *Approaches and Methods in Language Teaching. A Description and Analysis.* Cambridge : Cambridge University Press.

Riffaterre, Michael. 1978. *Semiotics of Poetry.* Bloomington : Indiana University Press.

Rimmon-Kenan, Shlomith. 1983. *Narrative Fiction. Contemporary Poetics.* London/New York : Methuen.

Rivers, W.M. 1972. Expanded 2nd edn. 1976. *Speaking in Many Tongues: Essays in Foreign Language Teaching.* Rowley, Mass.: Newbury House.

Rose, J. 1974. *The Cybernetic Revolution.* London : Eleck Science.

Rumelhart, D. 1977. 'Toward an Interactive Model of Reading.' In S. Dornic (ed.). 1977.

de Saussure, Ferdinarnd. *Course in General Linguistics.* Trans. Wade Baskin. 1959. New York : McGraw Hill.

Saville-Trooke, Muriel. 1982. *The Ethnography of Communication. An Introduction.* Oxford : Basil Blackwell.

Schank, R., and R. Abelson. 1977. *Scripts, Plans, Goals and Understanding.* Hillsdale, N.J.:Erlbaum.

Schmidt, Richard. 1983. 'Interaction, Acculturation, and the Acquisition of Communicative Competence : A Case Study of an Adult,' In Nessa Wolfson and Elliot Judd. (eds.). 1983.

Searle, J.R. 1969. *Speech Acts : An Essay in the Philosophy of Language.* Cambridge : Cambridge University Press.

Sebeok, Thomas A. 1963. 'The Informational Model of Language : Analog and Digital Coding in Animal and Human Communication.' In Paul L. Garvin (ed.). 1963.

Selinker, L. 1969. 'Language Transfer.' *General Linguistics,* Vol.IX, No.2 : 671-92.

—— 1972. 'Interlanguage.' *IRAL* 10 : 209-31.

Showalter, Elaine. (ed.). 1982. *The New Feminist Criticism : Essays on Women, Literature, and Theory.* New York : Pantheon.

Silverman, Kaja. 1983. *The Subject of Semiotics.* New York : Oxford University Press.

Sinclair, J.McH. 1966. 'Taking a Poem to Pieces.' In Roger Fowler (ed.). 1966.

—— and R.M. Coulthard. 1974. *Towards an Analysis of Discourse. The English Used by Teachers and Pupils.* Oxford : OUP.

Skinner, B.F. 1957. *Verbal Behaviour.* Appleton-Century-Crofts.

Smith, F. (ed.). 1973. *Psycholinguistics and Reading.* New York : Holt, Rinehart and Winston. P.M.

Smith, P.M.. 1985. *Language, the Sexes and Society.* Oxford : Basil Blackwell.

Sperber, D., and D. Wilson. 1979. 'L' interpretation des énoncés'. *Communications,* 30 : 80-94. Cited in T. Pateman. 'How is understanding an advertisement possible?' In H. Davis and P. Walton. (eds.). 1983. *Language, Image, Media.* Oxford : Basil Blackwell.

—— 1986. *Relevance : Communication and Cognition.* Oxford : Blackwell.

Steiner, George. 1968./1972. *Extra-territorial: Papers on Literature and the Language Revolution.* London : Faber and Faber.

—— 1975. *After Babel: Aspects of Language and Translation.* London: OUP.

Stern, H.H. 1972. 'Preface' to Rivers. 1972 : vii-xi.

—— 1983. *Fundamental Concepts of Language Teaching.* Oxford : Oxford University Press.

Stubbs, Michael. 1976. *Language, Schools and Classrooms.* London : Methuen.

—— 1983. *Discourse Analysis. The Sociolinguistic Analysis of Natural Language.* Oxford : Basil Blackwell.

—— 1986. *Educational Linguistics.* Oxford : Basil Blackwell.

—— and, Sara Delamont (eds.). 1976. *Explorations in Classroom Observations.* Wiley.

Swan, Michael. 1985. 'A Critical Look at the Communicative Approach (1).' *ELT Journal,* Vol39/1. Jan. : 2-11.

—— 1985a. 'A Critical Look at the Communicative Approach (2).' *ELT Journal,* Vol.39/2 April : 76-87.

Thisted and Efron. 1987. Cited in C.R. Rao. 'Saying it with Statistics.' *SPAN.,* October 1990 : 15-17.

Thorne, J.P. 1965. 'Stylistics and Generative Grammar.' *Journal of Linguistics,* 1 : 49-59. Reprinted in Donald C. Freeman (ed.). 1970.

Throwbridge, Hoyt. 1952/1953. '"Leda and the Swan": A Longinian Analysis'. *Modern Philology,* Nov. 1953 : 118-29.

Titone, R. 1968. *Teaching Foreign Languages : A Historical Sketch.* Washington, D.C. : Georgetown University Press.

Todorov, Tzvetan. 1969. *Grammaire du Decameron.* The Hague : Mouton.

Trench, R.C. 1857. 'On some Deficiencies in our English Dictionaries.'. In *Transactions of the Philological Society,* 1857 : 1-60.

Trudgill, P. 1974. *Sociolinguistics : An Introduction.* Penguin.

Trudgill, Peter. 1975. *Accent, Dialect and the School.* London : Edward Arnold.

—— 1978. *Sociolinguistic Patterns in British English.* London : Edward Arnold.

Varma, Dhirendra. 1954. *Braj bhasha.* Illahabad. Cited in B.I. Kluyev 1981.

Varma, Dhirendra. 1964. *Gramin Hindi.* Illahabad. Cited in B.I. Kluyev 1981.

Verma, S.K. 1976. "Code-switching: Hindi-English", *Lingua* 38.

—— 1976. "Topicalization as a Stylistic Mechanism", *Poetics* Macb.

—— 1981. "Swadeshi English: Form & Function" in *New Englishes* (ed.) Pride (Newbury House).

—— 1991. "The Three Language Formula: Its Sociopolitical & Pedagogical Implications", *ITL,* 91-92, Belgium.

Verma, S.K., and N. Krishnaswamy. 1989. *Modern Linguistics: An Introduction.* Delhi : Oxford University Press.

Wales, Katie, 1989. *A Dictionary of Stylistics.* London and New York : Longman.

Walker, R., and Clem Adelman. 1975. *A Guide to Classroom Observation.* Methuen.

Widdowson, H.G. 1974. 'Stylistics'. In J.P.B. Allen, and S. Pit Corder (eds.). 1974.

—— 1975. *Stylistics and the Teaching of Literature.* London : Longman.

—— 1978. *Teaching Language as Communication.* Oxford : Oxford University Press.

—— 1979. 'Directions in the Teaching of Discourse.' In Brumfit and Johnson (eds.). 1979.

—— 1979a. 'The Communicative Approach and its Applications'. In Widdowson, *Explorations in Applied Linguistics.* Oxford : Oxford University Press.

—— 1983. *Learning Purpose and Language Use.* Oxford : Oxford University Press.

Wilkins, D.A. 1976. *Notional Syllabuses.* Oxford : Oxford University Press.

Wolf, Y., and J. Walters. 1988. 'Second Language Comprehension Processes : Theories and Methods.' In J. Fine (ed.). 1988.

Wolfson, Nessa, and Elliot Judd. (eds.). 1983. *Sociolinguistics and Language Acquisition.* Rowley, Mass.: Newbury House.

Yorio, C.A. 1971. 'Some Sources of Reading Problems in Foreign Language Learners.' *Language Learning,* 21(1) : 107-115.

Zgusta, Ladislav, 1971. *Manual of Lexicography.* The Hague/Paris : Mouton.

—— 1973. 'Lexicology : Generating Words.' In R.I. McDavid, Jr., and A.R. Duckert (eds.). 1973.

—— 1988. *Lexicography Today. An Annotated Bibliography of the Theory of Lexicography.* Tubingen : Niemeyer.

Index